THE CONTRACTUAL REALLOCATION OF PROCREATIVE RESOURCES AND PARENTAL RIGHTS

Titles in the Series:

All titles are provisional

The Contractual Reallocation of Procreative Resources and Parental Rights

The Natural Endowment Critique

WILLIAM JOSEPH WAGNER

Dartmouth

Aldershot • Brookfield USA • Singapore • Sydney

Published by
Dartmouth Publishing Company Limited
Gower House
Croft Road
Aldershot
Hants GU11 3HR
England

Dartmouth Publishing Company
Old Post Road
Brookfield
Vermont 05036
USA

British Library Cataloguing in Publication Data
Wagner, William Joseph
    Contractual Reallocation of Procreative
    Resources and Parental Rights: Natural
    Endowment Critique. – (Medico-Legal Series)
    I. Title II. Series
    347.304419

Library of Congress Cataloging-in-Publication Data
Wagner, William Joseph, 1951-
    The contractual reallocation of procreative resources and parental
    rights : the natural endowment critique / William Joseph Wagner.
        p.   cm. – (Medico-legal series)
    Includes bibliographical references.
    ISBN 1-85521-653-1
    1. Human reproductive technology–Law and legislation–United
    States. 2. Contracts–United States. 3. Human reproductive
    technology–Economic aspects–United States. I. Title.
    II. Series.
    KF3830.W34   1995
    344.73'0419–dc20
    [347.304419]   95-16700
                                                           CIP

Printed and bound in Great Britain by
Hartnolls Limited, Bodmin, Cornwall
ISBN 1 85521 653 1

CONTENTS

ACKNOWLEDGEMENTS

I am indebted to my secretary, Arthienyer L. Fraser, for her expert assistance in preparing the manuscript of the present book, and to my students, Erin O'Dell, Christina Saarlas, and Christine Bianchine, for their research assistance.

W.J.W.
December 10, 1994

This work, since revised, was first published in *Case Western Law Review*. Proper citation to the work includes reference to "Wagner, *The Contractual Reallocation of Procreative Resources and Parental Rights: The Natural Endowment Critique*, 41 Case W. Res. L. Rev. 1 (1990)."

INTRODUCTION

The theme of commercial markets whose expansion outpaces the development of social norms is recurrent in the American story.[1] Enthusiasm seizes the American consciousness as ideas and other resources become available for commercial exploitation and as markets for new products emerge. Today, the field of applied biology is fertile ground for this enthusiasm.[2] The instinct for commercial exploitation now extends to the most profound biological process, human reproduction.[3] In past eras, effective exploitation of new resources has depended upon the promulgation of legal forms guarding potential investors' expectations sufficiently to ensure adequate investment of capital.[4] The quest for a legal response to the new technologies of human reproduction has produced more than one model incorporating legal forms associated with expanding economic markets.[5] In particular, contract has been proposed as a basis for the reorganization and redirection of human reproductive behaviour.[6] Some advocates of contract equate the value of contract in this context with its value in more traditional commercial areas.[7] Other advocates do not acknowledge contract's commercial character, but propose it as a means of expressing individual reproductive identity[8] or distributing scarce resources among classes of previously disadvantaged individuals.[9]

Positions expressly placing the law of human reproduction in economic categories face considerable obstacles to acceptance.[10] As distinct from some areas of applied biology, human reproduction has inextricable links with fundamental facets of social and personal identity. An industry of human reproductive biology would fulfil tasks not on the margin of experimentation or innovation like most new areas of exploitation, but rather at the core of humanity's most ancient, universal, and personal wants.[11] Changes in the law enabling such an industry might well eliminate or transform accustomed aspects of personal and social life. Thus, the legal literature contains an element of caution concerning negative social consequences, a persistent counterpoint to the excitement regarding marketable innovation that is the leitmotif of much writing on law and the new reproductive technologies.[12]

Regardless of whether it relies on the categories of commerce or economics, any proposal using contract for ordering the new human reproduction requires examination in light of its deeper implications. A particular proposal may absorb the ordering of human reproduction into the commercial market-place, or may borrow contract principles from the commercial

1

market in an attempt to integrate them into the private realm of reproductive expression or fulfilment. However, the latter approach, no less than the former, unsettles conceptual boundaries long held basic to the legal ordering of central societal concerns.[13] Such concerns extend to the basis of rights,[14] the grounds for the legal coercion of individual choice and action,[15] the limits on alienation of fundamental aspects of human personality,[16] and the definition of the respective societal spheres of market, family, and politics.[17]

Assessment of the validity of contract proposals for responding to the new reproductive technologies has been made difficult by a myopic view of the relevant parameters. In most studies, the social context has been too narrowly and uncritically drawn. The context often encompasses only an artificially constructed class of consumers and a set of actions construed as choices among items of medical treatments.[18] Despite the potential for these proposals to reshape American law substantially, the implications for basic legal structures generally have not been explored.[19] Discussion usually has been restricted to the applicability of discrete legal doctrines or to the requirements of adjudication between certain specific kinds of disputants.[20] Consideration has not been given to the full spectrum of implicated societal values being advanced or subordinated.[21]

This book inquires into the meaning and value of contract as a principle for ordering technologically assisted human reproduction. The book seeks to provide an analytically sound definition of this contractual option for ordering the new reproductive technologies, an accurate statement of its current legal status, and an assessment of its theoretical cogency and political and practical appeal. The purpose of the book is the clarification and critique of contract-based proposals for a new legal ordering of human reproduction. On a more general level, it seeks to contribute to a sound conceptual framework for the ongoing discussion of the legal implications of new reproductive technologies.

Methodologically, the book first pursues a schematic understanding of several hypothetical applications of contract to the legal ordering of technologically assisted human reproduction. To facilitate this discussion a definition of contract is proposed. The book then develops a general taxonomy of legal approaches to the new reproductive technologies that builds on a critique of taxonomies proposed by others. The first chapter identifies the analytically distinct applications of contract within the taxonomy it proposes.

The inquiry's intermediate task is to describe the status of contract in the ordering of human reproduction under present law and under proposals for legal reform. This status is complex under existing law. Therefore, the second chapter develops, as a baseline, an analysis of the law of the marriage contract and the traditional non-enforcement of ordinary contracts within the domain of marriage and family. To comprehend the evolution the law has undergone in response to the new reproductive technologies, this chapter examines the contractual aspect of existing statutory schemes governing artificial insemination by donor,[22] as well as judicial and legislative responses to hired maternity contracts.[23] As a proposal for further legal reform, it explores the contractual aspect of a recently promulgated model statute: the Uniform Status of Children of Assisted Conception Act.[24] At each step, the analysis is related back to the taxonomic scheme the book offers at the outset. The chapter's purpose is to restate, within a unified analytical framework, the concrete choices facing courts and legislatures with regard to contract's role in ordering human reproduction.

The book's final aim is a normative evaluation of the basic options under existing law and of proposals for legal reform which apply contract to order human reproduction. As a prelude, the third chapter describes the contemporary sociological and technological conditions that urge reconsideration of the law's response to human reproduction.[25] It then evaluates contract normatively as an instrument of legal reform in the field under four key considerations: the basis for legally recognizing rights;[26] the grounds for enforcing promises;[27] the limits to alienation of rights or other aspects of personality;[28] and the balance among family, market, and politics, as spheres of human activity.[29] The conclusion of this normative evaluation is that there are no compelling reasons for, and many grounds that compel against, adopting ordinary contract as a core principle for ordering the new reproductive technologies.

Endnotes

1. In classic descriptions of the American character, the free market and wealth gained in the market often take precedence over other cultural values. De Tocqueville, for example, made the following comment:

> In Europe, people talk a great deal of the wilds of America, but the Americans themselves never think about them: they are insensible to the wonders of inanimate Nature, and they may be said not to perceive the mighty forests which surround them till they fall beneath the hatchet. Their eyes are fixed upon another sight: the American people views its own march across these wilds—drying swamps, turning the course of rivers, peopling solitudes, and subduing Nature. This magnificent image of themselves does not meet the gaze of the Americans at intervals only; it may be said to haunt every one of them in his least as well as in his most important actions, and to be always flitting before his mind . . . .
>   . . . .

It would seem as if every imagination in the United States were upon the stretch to invent means of increasing the wealth and satisfying the wants of the public. The best-informed inhabitants of each district constantly use their information to discover new truths which may augment the general prosperity; and if they have made any such discoveries, they eagerly surrender them to the mass of the people.

. . . .

If I were to inquire what passion is most natural to [Americans] . . . I could discover none more peculiarly appropriate to their condition than this love of physical prosperity . . . .

. . . .

. . . Carefully to satisfy all, even the least wants of the body, and to provide the little conveniences of life, is uppermost in every mind . . . .

. . . .

. . . The doctrine of interest rightly understood is not then new, but among the Americans of our time it finds universal acceptance: it has become popular there; you may trace it at the bottom of all their actions, you will remark it in all they say.
A. De Tocqueville, Democracy in America 292, 317, 339, 338, 333 (H. Reeve trans. 1946).

If there is an "American" story in literature, it attests not merely to a national preoccupation with commercial markets but also a notable ambivalence about the appropriate scope of their reach. *See, e.g.,* T. DREISER, THE FINANCIER (1946); S. LEWIS, BABBITT (1922). Literature reflecting ambivalence about the market-orientation of American consciousness often affirms a keen regard for the inalienability and indefeasibility of family loyalties and personal integrity. *See, e.g.,* J. CONRAD, NOSTROMO (1921); N. HAWTHORNE, THE SCARLET LETTER (1892); H. JAMES, THE GOLDEN BOWL (1904); H.B. STOWE, UNCLE TOM'S CABIN (1852). The same ambivalence is examined in a recent sociological study of the interplay between aggressive individualism and community solidarity in contemporary America. *See* R. BELLAH, R. MADSEN, W. SULLIVAN, A. SWIDLER & S. TIPTON, HABITS OF THE HEART: INDIVIDUALISM AND COMMITMENT IN AMERICAN LIFE (1985) (a compilation of four research studies of the relationship between public and private life in America).

Narrative jurisprudence stresses the importance of stories and myths such as these for organizing law in relation to basic values and the reciprocal effect of law as narrative, fashioning and orienting the cultural universe. *See* C. GEERTZ, LOCAL KNOWLEDGE: FURTHER ESSAYS IN INTERPRETIVE ANTHROPOLOGY 173 (1983) (law as a "distinctive manner of imagining the real"); J.B. WHITE, HERACLES' BOW: ESSAYS ON THE RHETORIC AND POETICS OF THE LAW (1985) (viewing law as a rhetorical and literary endeavor acting through language, culture, and community, thereby changing these facets of society); Cover, *The Supreme Court, 1982 Term - Foreword: Nomos and Narrative*, 97 HARV. L. REV. 4, 68 (1983) (the existence of legal institutions is dependent on narratives for meaning). For an application of the reasoning of narrative jurisprudence in the area of family law, see M. GLENDON, ABORTION AND DIVORCE IN WESTERN LAW 112-42 (1987). For an application of narrative jurisprudence to contract, see Dalton, *An Essay in the Deconstruction of Contract Doctrine,* 94 YALE L.J. 997, 999-1000 (1985).

In interpreting the meaning and value of proposed modes of distributing procreative resources and parental rights, the question arises: is this another story of the mastery of commercial markets or a tale of the inalienability and indefeasibility of family loyalties and personal integrity? The most famous passage from the *Baby M* case illustrates this conflict: "There are, in a civilized society, some things that money cannot buy. In America, we decided long ago that merely because conduct purchased by money was 'voluntary' did not mean that it was good or beyond regulation and prohibition." *In re* Baby M, 109 N.J. 396, 440, 537 A.2d 1227, 1249 (1988) (citing minimum wage laws, laws prohibiting gender-based

4

wage discrimination, child labour laws, and worker safety laws).

2. *See* C. GROBSTEIN, FROM CHANCE TO PURPOSE 135 (1981) (noting the emergence of "a larger and enlarging biotechnology, already palpable in agriculture and medicine, growing on the horizon in energy and materials production").

3. The growing number of entrepreneurs in this field includes Randolph and Richard Seed whose Chicago-based Reproduction & Fertility Clinic provides such services as surrogate embryo transfer and New York's Idant Corporation, a thriving interstate business that stores, sells, and distributes human semen. Shapiro, *New Innovations in Conception and Their Effects upon Our Law and Morality*, 31 N.Y.L. SCH. L. REV. 37, 44 n.42, 52 (1986).

4. This process was seen, for example, in England's enclosure movement which led to developments in the law of real property advantageous to the wool industry. T. MORE, UTOPIA 24-28 (E. Surtz ed. 1964); Hardin, *The Tragedy of the Commons*, 162 SCIENCE 1243 (1968) (analogizing from enclosure to the need to restrict reproductive rights as a preventive measure for overpopulation). More recently, it has been seen in the recognition of the patentability of primitive living organisms. *See* Diamond v. Chakrabarty, 447 U.S. 303, 307 (1980) (a genetically engineered bacterium capable of breaking down crude oil was deemed patentable, as a new and useful manufacture or composition of matter). Claims to an ownership interest in higher species and human tissue cultures also have been recognized. *E.g.*, Moore v. Regents of Univ. of Cal., 202 Cal. App. 3d 1230, 249 Cal. Rptr. 494 (1988) (the human donor of bodily tissue which gave rise to a patented cell line was held to have a property interest in his tissue and the cell-line that arose from it), *rev'd*, 51 Cal. 3d 120, 793 P.2d 479, 271 Cal. Rptr. 146 (1990) (invalidating property interest in excised human tissue); OFFICE OF TECHNOLOGY ASSESSMENT, PUB. NO. 5, 101ST CONG., 1ST SESS., NEW DEVELOPMENTS IN BIOTECHNOLOGY: PATENTING LIFE 12 (1989) (special report) (patent granted to Harvard University for a mouse that is highly susceptible to cancer).

5. This task has already begun, to some extent, in the related field of human organ and tissue exchange. *See* Andrews, *My Body, My Property*, HASTINGS CENTER REP. Oct. 1986 28, at 28 (discussing legal ramifications of declaring that body parts are property which can be bought or sold); Healey, *Legal Regulation of Artificial Insemination and the New Reproductive Technologies*, in GENETICS AND THE LAW III 139, 143 (A. Milunksy & G. Annas eds. 1984) ("One other aspect of the cultural transition is the increased commercialization in health care" reflected by "the financial rewards associated with the sale of organs or body parts"); Note, *Toward the Right of Commerciality: Recognizing Property Rights in the Commercial Value of Human Tissue*, 34 UCLA L. REV. 207, 212 (1986) (discussing an individual's right to exploit the commercial value of his body).

Comparable recognition or property interests in human gametes and embryos has been proposed. *See infra* note 257 Ch. 3. In contrast, model legislation in the area of "new human reproduction" appears to be intended to organize the labour market in a new area of the service economy. *See, e.g.*, Section of Family Law Adoption Committee and Ad Hoc Surrogacy Committee, *Draft ABA Model Surrogacy Act*, 22 FAM. L.Q. 123 (1988) [hereinafter *Model Surrogacy Act*].

6. The use of contract to organize what amounts to a market in procreative resources and parental rights has been proposed by academic commentators, *e.g.*, Hollinger, *From Coitus to Commerce: Legal and Social Consequences of Noncoital Reproduction*, 18 U. MICH. J.L. REF. 865 (1985) (arguing legal efforts to prohibit these procreative markets would be unwise); by governmental commissions, *e.g.*, 2 ONT. LAW REFORM COMM'N, REPORT ON HUMAN ARTIFICIAL REPRODUCTION & RELATED MATTERS (1985) [hereinafter ONTARIO COMM'N] (noting legal ramifications of private contractual arrangement for artificial incentives); and under proposed legislation, UNIF. STATUS OF CHILDREN OF ASSISTED CONCEPTION ACT § 5, 9B U.L.A. 154 (Supp. 1994) [hereinafter UNIF. STATUS ACT] (pro-

posing regulation of surrogacy agreements for the benefit of the child conceived).

7. *See, e.g.*, Posner, *The Ethics and Economics of Enforcing Contracts of Surrogate Motherhood*, 5 J. CONTEMP. HEALTH L. & POL'Y 21 (1989) (arguing that contracts of "hired maternity" no less than contracts routinely enforced by law in other areas, are entered into voluntarily, maximize value through market incentives, and promote the legitimate interests of the parties involved). In this book the practice generally known as "surrogate motherhood" is called "hired maternity." For a discussion of the significance of these terms, see *infra* note 190 Ch. 2.

8. *See, e.g.*, Note, *Rumpelstiltskin Revisited: The Inalienable Rights of Surrogate Mothers*, 99 HARV. L. REV. 1936, 1941-49 (1986) (discussing paternalistic views held by courts towards a woman's right to choose reproductive alternatives). Even in these cases the discussion is often implicitly organized around the idea of identifying and satisfying a market. *E.g.*, Robertson, *Embryos, Families and Procreative Liberty: The Legal Structure of the New Reproduction*, 59 S. CAL. L. REV. 942, 944-46 (1986) (discussing the factors driving the quest for alternative reproductive technologies, including both social and economic forces).

9. For a framework arranging the new reproductive technologies based on distributive concerns, see Dresser, *Social Justice in New Reproductive Techniques*, in GENETICS AND THE LAW III, *supra* note 5 Intro., at 159-74. The theme also appears in Robertson, *Procreative Liberty and the Control of Conception, Pregnancy, and Childbirth*, 69 VA. L. REV. 405, 428 (1983) ("a legal distinction based on the natural lottery of physical equipment is not reasonable").

10. The cognitive structure of human awareness of cultural, moral, and legal problems presupposes certain subliminal propositions which the mind resists abandoning. *See* L. FESTINGER, A THEORY OF COGNITIVE DISSONANCE (1957); P. JOHNSON-LAIRD, MENTAL MODELS (1983). Shifts in such subliminal cognitive commitments can occur on a global level within a culture. *See* T. KUHN, THE STRUCTURE OF SCIENTIFIC REVOLUTIONS 110-34 (1962).

11. Personal fulfilment in relationships with others must be distinguished from needs subject to fulfilment in discrete transactions. See E. ERIKSON, CHILDHOOD AND SOCIETY (1950); R. LIFTON, THE LIFE OF THE SELF (1976).

12. *See* Annas & Elias, *Social Policy Considerations in Noncoital Reproduction*, in GENETICS AND THE LAW III, *supra* note 5 Intro., at 147; Note, *Toward a Dignified Theory of Children: Prohibition of Collaborative Reproduction*, 19 Tex. Tech. L. Rev. 1091 (1988). *Compare* L. KASS, TOWARD A MORE NATURAL SCIENCE (1985) (viewing scientific advances in light of ethical considerations); P. RAMSEY, FABRICATED MAN: THE ETHICS OF GENETIC CONTROL (1970) (arguing that moral and religious considerations should always prevail in the context of the new reproductive technologies). The classic warning of the political and moral dangers posed by scientific intervention in the process of human reproduction was sounded by Aldous Huxley. A. HUXLEY, BRAVE NEW WORLD (1946).

13. This occurs at "the level of deep structure". Rosenfeld, *Justice and Contract: The Relation Between Classical Contract Law and Social Contract Theory*, 70 IOWA L. REV. 769, 808-09 (1985).

14. Despite some post-liberal critical re-evaluation, the notion of rights continues to be considered indispensable for understanding or evaluating the legal system. *See* R. DWORKIN, TAKING RIGHTS SERIOUSLY (1977); D. LYONS, RIGHTS (1979).

15. Liberalization of rules governing private conduct is not an adequate concept for describing the dilemma facing the legal system. The new reproductive arrangements are creating conflicts, in which someone suffers the "jurispathic violence" of a legally enforced defeat. Allen, *Privacy, Surrogacy, and the Baby M Case*, 76 GEO. L.J. 1759, 1761 (1988). On the meaning of "jurispathic", see Cover, *supra* note 1 Intro., at 40-44 (courts are

jurispathic insofar as they establish laws that reflect the community's story).

16. So thoroughgoing is this challenge that the antislavery amendment to the U.S. Constitution enters the discussion. *See* Means, *Surrogacy v. The Thirteenth Amendment*, 4 N.Y.L. SCH. HUM. RTS. ANN. 445 (1987).

17. The way that these arrangements are characterized transcends the individuals involved and serves morally and cognitively to organize our societal world. *See* Watson, *The Future of Asexual Reproduction*, in CONTEMPORARY ISSUES IN BIOETHICS 599, 605 (1978) (noting the general discomfort in society regarding new and proposed reproductive technologies, such as cloning). For an application of the idea of "spheres" of social life, see M. WALZER, SPHERES OF JUSTICE (1983).

18. For an example of this approach in a popular work, see L. ANDREWS, NEW CONCEPTIONS: A CONSUMER'S GUIDE TO THE NEWEST INFERTILITY TREATMENTS, INCLUDING IN VITRO FERTILIZATION, ARTIFICIAL INSEMINATION AND SURROGATE MOTHERHOOD (1984) (reviewing new infertility treatments for consumers). However, this approach imposes unacceptable methodological constraints on scholarly studies adopting it. *See, e.g.*, Dresser, *supra* note 9 Intro., at 159-60 (limiting the scope of analysis concerning the ethical and political considerations involved in the new reproductive technologies to problems arising in the health care field); Robertson, *supra* note 8 Intro., at 942-47 (confining the discussion of social pressures to problems arising from infertility, both medical and non-medical). One source of this truncated methodology is undoubtedly the breadth of the definition of health and the medical profession seen in some contemporary schools of bio-ethics and medicine. *See* Thomasma, *The Goals of Medicine and Society* in THE CULTURE OF BIOMEDICINE 4-54 (D. Brock ed. 1985) (assuming the role of the medical profession in society to include all aspects of social interaction).

The inadequacy of the approach becomes clear when one considers that the "[u]se of these technologies need not be confined—nor is it likely to be confined—to the scale of individual couples making private decisions, nor to treatment of infertility. Indeed, several proposals for additional uses have already been placed before the public." L. KASS, *supra* note 12 Intro., at 61.

19. *But see* Annas & Elias, *supra* note 12 Intro., at 148-52 (exploring "the most important policy issues raised by [the new reproductive] techniques").

20. For frequently cited contributions at this level, see Note, *Surrogate Motherhood and the Baby-Selling Laws*, 20 COLUM. J. L. & SOC. PROBS. 1 (1986) (examining the relationship between hired maternity and state adoption laws); M. FIELD, SURROGATE MOTHERHOOD (1988) (surveying various positions for dealing with hired maternity issues). However, "there comes a point in the moral discourse surrounding reproductive interventions when one must step aside from the casuistry of individual interventions and view the future possibilities and directions in aggregate and in the light of over-all convictions . . . ." R. MCCORMICK, HOW BRAVE A NEW WORLD? 334 (1981).

21. The need for a framework facilitating such consideration has been confirmed by many. *See, e.g.*, Wadlington, *Family Law Begs for Broad Review*, N.J.L.J., Feb. 18, 1988, at 31, col. 1, col. 4 (noting the lack of a clear public-policy framework within which alternative forms of reproduction can be evaluated in relation to fundamental questions of personal and societal values). A variety of academic legal commentators have attempted to provide a framework. *E.g.*, Eaton, *Comparative Responses to Surrogate Motherhood*, 65 NEB. L. REV. 686 (1986) (analyzing various studies on hired maternity and proposing guidelines to deal with common conflict situations); Hollinger, *supra* note 6 Intro., at 868 (suggesting the "urgent need for the creation and clarification of a legal framework within which contemporary efforts to produce or procure children can take place"); Robertson, *supra* note 8 Intro., at 939-1041 (proposing reproductive freedom as a framework for dealing with new

7

technologies); Note, *Redefining Mother: A Legal Matrix for New Reproductive Technologies*, 96 YALE L.J. 187 (1986) [hereinafter Note, *Redefining Mother*] (proposing a new reproduction issue framework based on stages in the procreative process).

Proposed frameworks often fail to assess concrete issues against a sufficiently broad background, either within family law or within the horizon of relevant social values. A particularly pervasive handicap is legalistic dependence on the "fundamental right/compelling state interest" framework of constitutional jurisprudence. Without a broader philosophical and jurisprudential justification, this dependence leads to begging all the most important questions. *See, e.g.*, Comment, *Baby-Sitting Consideration: Surrogate Mother's Right to "Rent Her Womb" for a Fee*, 18 GONZ. L. REV. 539, 552-65 (1982-83) (supporting a gestational mother's right to contract on constitutional grounds); Note, *supra* note 8 Intro., at 1936-55 (evaluating the constitutionality of statutory authorization for specific performance of hired maternity contracts); Note, *Prohibiting Payments to Surrogate Mothers: Love's Labor Lost and the Constitutional Right of Privacy*, 20 J. MARSHALL L. REV. 715, 735-45 (1987) (assessing the constitutionality of baby-selling laws).

A cost-benefit framework in this area also typically assumes more than it explains or justifies. *See, e.g.*, Robertson, *supra* note 9 Intro., at 423-27 (assessing the benefits of new reproductive technologies without considering the ethical questions raised). A number of governmental and professional committees and agencies have contributed studies, both nationally and internationally, that provide a foundation for working towards the goal. *See, e.g.*, ETHICS ADVISORY BOARD: DEP'T. OF HEALTH, EDUCATION, & WELFARE, REPORT & CONCLUSIONS: HEW SUPPORT OF RESEARCH INVOLVING HUMAN *IN VITRO* FERTILIZATION AND EMBRYO TRANSFER (1979) [hereinafter ETHICS ADVISORY BOARD]; OFFICE OF TECHNOLOGY ASSESSMENT, INFERTILITY: MEDICAL AND SOCIAL CHOICES (1988) [hereinafter OFFICE OF TECHNOLOGY ASSESSMENT]; COMITÉ CONSULATIF NATIONAL D'ETHIQUE POUR LES SCIENCES DE LA VIE ET DE LA SANTÉ, AVIS SUR LES PROBLÈMES ETHIQUES NÉS DES TECHNIQUES DE REPRODUCTION ARTIFICIELLE (1984) [hereinafter COMITÉ CONSULATIF NATIONAL]; Vatican Congregation for the Doctrine of the Faith, *Instruction on Respect for Human Life in Its Origin and on the Dignity of Procreation*, 16 ORIGINS 1 (1987) [hereinafter Vatican Congregation]. For a general analysis of such committee and agency statements, see Walters, *Ethics and the New Reproductive Technologies: An International Review of Committee Statements*, HASTINGS CENTER REP. June 1987, special supplement at 4; COMM. TO CONSIDER THE SOCIAL, ETHICAL, & LEGAL ISSUES ARISING FROM IN VITRO FERTILIZATION, REPORT ON THE DISPOSITION OF EMBRYOS PRODUCED BY *IN VITRO* FERTILIZATION (1984) [hereinafter WALLER REP.]; DEP'T OF HEALTH & SOCIAL SEC. REPORT OF THE COMM. OF INQUIRY INTO HUMAN FERTILISATION & EMBRIOLOGY (1984) [hereinafter WARNOCK REP.]; ONTARIO COMM'N, *supra* note 6 Intro. American Fertility Society, *Ethical Considerations of the New Reproductive Technologies*, 46 FERTILITY & STERILITY 1S-945 (1986) (suggesting roles Congress can play in the regulation of new reproductive technologies).

Ethicists also have generated voluminous commentary, but the value of their world is limited by a failure to understand the legal dimension. *E.g.*, P. SINGER & D. WELLS, MAKING BABIES: THE NEW SCIENCE AND ETHICS OF CONCEPTION (1985) (noting the lack of public consensus on the ethical issues raised by new reproductive technologies); TEST-TUBE BABIES: A GUIDE TO MORAL QUESTIONS, PRESENT TECHNIQUES AND FUTURE POSSIBILITIES (1982) (providing a wide-ranging discussion of the ethical problems associated with in vitro fertilization ("IVF"), while failing to examine the legal issues involved).

8

22. Critics have argued that existing law on artificial insemination by donor ("AID") is an inadequate point of departure in draft legislation to other new reproduction technologies. *See, e.g.*, Annas & Elias, *supra* note 12 Intro., at 149-50 (AID "is an unfortunate paradigm" because it leaves social issues unresolved). *See generally infra* text accompanying notes 149-88 Ch. 2.

23. Hired maternity has received the greatest publicity among issues of applied human biology. H. CLARK, THE LAW OF DOMESTIC RELATIONS IN THE UNITED STATES § 20.8 (2d ed. 1987). *See generally infra* notes 189-358 Ch. 2 and accompanying text.

24. UNIF. STATUS ACT, *supra* note 7 Intro.; *see infra* notes 359-403 Ch.2 and accompanying text.

25. The legal response to the new reproductive technologies is "likely to be a political and moral battleground for the rest of the century", Robertson, *supra* note 9 Intro., at 408.

26. *See, e.g.*, M. BAYLES, PRINCIPLES OF LAW: A NORMATIVE ANALYSIS 170-92 (1987) (defining contract rights as duties created by the terms of the contract).

27. *See, e.g.*, Goetz & Scott, *Enforcing Promises: An Examination of the Basis of Contract*, 89 YALE L.J. 1261 (1980) (discussing the extent and circumstances to which promises are enforceable and legally binding according to modern contract law).

28. *See, e.g.*, Radin, *Market-Inalienability*, 100 HARV. L. REV. 1849 (1987) (discussing the effect of market alienation on the rights of parties involved in prostitution, baby selling, and hired maternity).

29. *See, e.g.*, Olsen, *The Family and the Market: A Study of Ideology and Legal Reform*, 96 HARV. L. REV. 1497 (1983) (examining the ineffectiveness of efforts to reform the social role of women and arguing for the transcendence of the traditional dichotomy between market and family).

9

I. FRAMING THE DISCUSSION: THE ROLE OF CONTRACT UNDER HYPOTHETICAL LEGAL ALTERNATIVES FOR ORDERING HUMAN REPRODUCTION

Too often, the extensive literature on law and new reproductive technologies offers a survey of technological novelty, human anguish, and patches of legal doctrine, plausible enough perhaps yet somehow still askew.[1] Proposed legal solutions present pictures of law and reality confounding any coherent meaning for essential distinctions such as those between the public and the private, the personal and the impersonal, and the intimate and the arm's length.[2] In general, the discussion lacks adequate efforts to integrate the analysis within a larger framework of societal values, or within the system of law as a whole. Confusion about the meaning of basic terms pervades the literature.

A systematic review of the implications of a concept as basic to the legal system as contract for ordering the new reproductive methods should offer conceptual clarification to the general discussion. This exercise also provides a foundation for the substantive analysis and evaluation which are this book's ultimate goals. To do this, a definition of contract is needed.[3]

A. A Definition of Contract

Contract historically has been one of the central concepts, if not the central concept, defining the legal structure of liberal Western society.[4] A variety of developments, however, have led to uncertainty about the meaning, nature, and scope of contractual relationships.[5] The classical definition of contract, stated in perhaps its clearest form by Oliver Wendell Holmes, Jr., in the late nineteenth century,[6] has a considerable continuing influence on the general orientation of the legal system, even as it corresponds less and less with the way agreements are actually made and enforced.[7]

Holmes viewed contract as the enforcement of bargains made in a business or commercial setting[8] whether the promisee has actually invested in performing the bargain or otherwise relied on it.[9] Any promise which reasonably appeared to be "bargained for", that is, reciprocally exchanged for a "legal detriment" on the part of the promisee, was enforceable at law. The rule in business was *pacta sunt servanda*.[10]

11

In this view of contract, the value of individual autonomy requires the consistent legal enforcement of promises struck in the course of economic cooperation, without regard to the fairness of the bargain or the apparent wisdom of the joint project.[11] The criteria of enforcement are voluntariness, or consent, and cooperation in the form of business or commercial exchange. Freedom of individual action requires a corresponding non-enforcement of involuntary duties of kinship or social convention, with the exception of certain carefully defined family duties.[12] It also requires the non-enforcement of simple promises classified as "gratuitous".[13] Voluntary, cooperative exchanges of promises in family settings and social relationships are, in this view, non-enforceable, both for the sake of further validating the freedom of the individual and for exempting such settings and relationships from the intrusive mechanism of legal enforcement.[14]

As measured by the criterion of consent, contract obligation is distinguished from involuntary obligation in tort or criminal law. As measured by promise, it is distinguished from present gifts and barter. As measured by the criterion of commercial or business exchange, it is distinguished from both gratuitous promises and exchanges within family or informal social contexts. The justification for this distinction is the moral meaning attached to the autonomous choice of one party to induce a future act of will by another in a market setting.[15] Since the time of Holmes, more prosaic justifications have been tied to the evidentiary, cautionary, and channelling functions, which bargain effectively serves within society.[16]

This definition of contract is insufficient for two reasons. First, it presupposes a clear distinction between market and family as well as the appropriate role of contract in the context of family relationship, the very question contemporary developments in human reproduction put at issue. These presuppositions must be discarded in order for the definition to serve as a useful analytical tool. Second, the definition no longer fully corresponds to the law of contract as it has evolved since the time of Holmes. Contractual obligation may now be imposed based on a promise unsupported by a bargain, as long as the promise foreseeably induces measurable detrimental reliance on the part of the promisee[17] or, in certain narrow cases, as long as the promise is given with requisite formal attestation.[18] In addition, commercial bargain alone no longer guarantees the legal enforcement of a promise. A promise is unenforceable if obtained in an unfair bargain. "Contract without bargain" is mainly the product of the promissory estoppel doctrine; "bargain without contract" flows from the doctrine of unconscionability.[19]

In addition to the doctrine of unconscionability, state neutrality with respect to the enforcement of private bargains has been eroded on another front. In matters important to consumer welfare such as employment, housing, and insurance, the government may dictate some or all the terms of contract.[20] In the course of performance, the state may participate in the contractual relationship, through its regulatory structure, as though it were a third party to the agreement—for example, the involvement of the Department of Labour and the Internal Revenue Service in employer/employee arrangements. The existence of complex governmental regulation may make performance as much a matter of complying with governmental regulations as with the provisions of the contract itself—for example, under contracts implicating federal and state environmental protection laws.

As a consequence of the changing status of both bargain and consent as criteria of the enforceability of promises, further elements in Holmes's definition must be modified if a credible definition of contract is to be fashioned. The solution of the *Restatement (Second) of Contracts* is to define contract as any promise the law makes legally enforceable.[21] Contract becomes any consent given under conditions the law establishes for enforcement. Although the *Restatement* definition does not shatter doctrinal contradictions implicit in the cases, it is so clearly tautological as to be conceptually inadequate.[22] Consent is a necessary, though not a sufficient, element of any definition of contract. Some further criterion is required to establish what promises are enforceable as a matter of contractual obligation.

The idea of contract requires an element of collabouration between private parties. If state involvement eliminated all vestiges of exchange between private parties, the resulting legal form would no longer be contract. Thus, an activity coordinated entirely by the state, but involving the legal enforcement of consensual obligations by individuals, would not be contract, at least in the paradigmatic sense, although it would satisfy the *Restatement* definition.[23] In the view proposed here, government contracts for services of which the state is the only end user, such as military service, are contracts by analogy only.[24] Yet, because the state is no longer neutral about the content or fairness of contracts, a definition of contract treating it as a strictly private arrangement cannot be accepted either. In place of this strict notion of contract as private, it is necessary to substitute a more minimal requirement: to qualify as contract, a promise must look towards some form of cooperation between two persons, neither of whom, in principle, is required by law to be the state.[25]

A looser notion of reciprocity in some form of private cooperation may be substituted for bargain in the strict classical sense. Bargain remains as one, though not the only, form of reciprocity. Subsequent foreseeable reliance on a promise resulting in detriment to the promisee is also reciprocal, as is the formally attested simple promise given to another as a guarantee of performance.[26] This definition of contract is broad enough for it to begin to overlap with categories traditionally distinguishable from contract, such as intentional tort. However, it remains analytically distinct. Under the law of contract, so defined, legal obligation arises from any of a range of responses that a promise by one private person may elicit in another.[27] Within the broad class of cases covered by this definition, the law may further narrow the scope of promises subject to enforcement based on different policy considerations.[28]

In the present discussion, then, contract will be assumed to mean a promise that is legally enforceable because it satisfies the following conditions: it is given in furtherance of social reciprocity, whether in the form of a reciprocal bargain between promisor and promisee, promissory inducement of detrimental reliance by the promisee, or solemnly attested promissory assurance; neither party is an agency of the government functioning in a role that is distinctively and exclusively governmental; and the promise is otherwise of a kind that is enforced by law. Involuntary liabilities imposed by the state in its police power or under criminal law and non-promissory tort law are not contract. Voluntary duties undertaken in relation to an activity over which the state exercises a monopoly are not contract, nor are voluntary exchanges and other forms of future-oriented private cooperation that are not legally enforceable. The purpose of the present book is to understand and evaluate the potential role of contract, as defined, for the new legal ordering of human reproduction.

B. The Role of Contract in Two Existing Taxonomies of Legal Approaches to the New Reproductive Technologies

With "jurisprudence . . . poised on the brink of its evolutionary surge", an analytically sound map of alternative approaches in lawmaking with regard to artificially assisted human reproduction is a priority.[29] Two frameworks devised for this purpose merit review. One is proposed in the Ontario Law Reform Commission's *Report on Human Artificial Reproduction and Related Matters*.[30] The other is offered in an influential article by Professor Walter Wadlington.[31] Each framework utilizes contract. Although neither taxonomy fully coheres or even intends to account consistently for the potential role of contract, each offers an opportunity for critically discerning conceptual distinctions important to an analytically sound framework.

14

1. The Ontario Law Reform Commission Taxonomy

Charged by the provincial Attorney General with studying the legal implications of the new reproductive technologies, the Ontario Law Reform Commission published its conclusions in the *Report on Human Artificial Reproduction and Related Matters*.[32] The report recommends a unified legislative response to these technologies.[33] To facilitate this goal the Commission analysed several conceptual alternatives.[34] The importance of the Commission's analysis is underscored both by the Commission's prestige[35] and by the decisive impact of its conclusions on the content of the National Conference of Commissioners' Uniform Status of Children of Assisted Conception Act.[36]

According to the Commission's classification, legislative approaches to the new reproductive technologies can be placed on a spectrum defined at one end by a state preference for private intention and at the other by state preference for community norms of behaviour.[37] One type of legislative response would require consistently honouring private intentions; the Commission names this the "private ordering" option.[38] Another type, the "state regulation" model, would support community norms.[39] A third type, the "hybrid" or "flexible" approach, draws on both pure types interchangeably, as circumstances dictate.[40] Closer analysis discloses the role of contract in each of the three alternatives and the degree of conceptual soundness to be accorded the Commission's scheme.

a. The Private Ordering Model

In the private ordering model, the state restricts its purposes in the area of assisted human reproduction to furthering the intentions of private parties.[41] As envisioned by the Commission, such an approach imposes no restrictions on eligibility for available reproductive opportunities.[42] It does not screen participants or require medical supervision.[43] It requires no governmental approval or filing as condition for recognizing a parent-child relationship.[44] Individuals are free to choose gamete donors at will and to assign child custody, as they like.[45] The state intervenes in a parent-child relationship formed through assisted conception only in the event of parental neglect or abuse.[46]

The Commission suggests that the closest analogue to this approach under existing law is the "legal model of natural reproduction".[47] Existing law can hardly be characterized as laissez faire with respect to the initiation by individuals of reproduction.[48] Nevertheless, the law does assume the individual's right to initiate procreation without undue governmental

15

interference. Those who procreate without technological assistance need no special governmental approval to reproduce or to obtain recognition of the parent-child relationship.[49] The law intervenes in the "naturally" occurring parent-child relationship only in the exceptional cases of divorce or parental abuse.[50] Ancillary fertility treatments are free from special regulation where conception occurs through natural means.[51] The Commission believes natural reproduction provides a legal model of "private decision-making" and "state non-intervention"[52] that parallels its concept of "private ordering" for technologically assisted reproduction.

However, the analogy fails because the Commission includes contract as an essential element of the "private ordering" of the new reproductive technologies. According to the Commission, private ordering in the domain of technologically assisted reproduction includes the legal enforcement of contracts for the purchase and sale of gametes and for transfer of parental rights.[53]

The inclusion of contract cannot be considered an insignificant addition to the legal model of natural reproduction. This model establishes more than the attitude of the state toward individual choices to procreate. It determines the basis for recognizing parent-child relationships, and for legally resolving conflicting parental claims of the two or more adults who have contributed procreative "resources" to the conception of a child. Under received law, contract is excluded, at least nominally, from answering these questions.[54]

In the existing legal framework, families comprise an important constituent part of the private realm. Natural reproductive arrangements are so fundamentally private that public tools of law enforcement, like that of contract, remain presumptively excluded from their sphere.[55] By analogizing the private ordering option to the legal ordering of natural reproduction, the Commission appears to advance this sort of privacy. But this meaning of privacy does not correspond to the one that the Commissioners ascribe to the "private" ordering option. This option actually places the mechanism of the state within the sphere of "privacy" to decide disputes between parties. The meaning of privacy that matches the content of the Commission's "private ordering" model is one encountered in legal discussions of the market as a product of state-enforced private contract:[56] it is the privacy of *Lochner* v. *New York*.[57] The Commission purports to build the private ordering model by analogy to procreation in the natural family, when its implicit reference is to the commercial market-place.

b. The Model of State Regulation

At the other end of the spectrum, the Commission constructs a model of "state regulation".[58] In this approach, the state seeks primarily the enforcement of community norms of behaviour.[59] Individual preference is subordinate.[60] As applied to ordering artificially assisted reproduction, this approach may lead the state to regulate access to the new reproductive technologies;[61] dictate the medical context for their utilization;[62] and decide the legal status of the children conceived.[63] The Commission assumes that the overriding public value giving direction to this scheme is the best interest of the child.[64]

The Commissioners point to adoption law as analogous to their model of state regulation. Under existing adoption law, no one has a legal right to adopt a child.[65] Personal privacy is sacrificed under the scrutiny of the adoption screening process.[66] Every aspect of the adoption process from placement to final court approval is supervised by state authority.[67] Those who conform to community standards are generally approved for adoption, while those who do not conform are rejected.[68] The Commission observes that state regulation could be modulated to allow varying degrees of state control, and that its response to a given practice might range from outright prohibition to minimal oversight. As an existing analogue to the form of envisioned state regulation adjusted for more minimal control, the Commission cites the law on step-parent adoption.[69]

Analogizing a state regulatory scheme for the new reproductive technologies to the existing adoption agency framework ignores a crucial difference between adoption practice and proposed state regulation of new reproduction methods. Existing adoption law is premised on the state's parens patriae duty to protect the welfare of a child in being. It imposes burdens on affected adults strictly for this purpose. It does not address who has the right to reproduce or how reproduction ought to be pursued. If a legal structure modelled on adoption regulation were applied to control reproductive choices, state regulation would extend significantly beyond the scope of the existing parens patriae rationale and simultaneously conflict with state regulation of the marital contract as well as individual freedom to pursue informal, non-marital procreation.

Curiously, the Commission illustrates the stronger form of the model of state regulation by citing a form of "surrogate motherhood" contract.[70] The Commission envisions a contract requiring judicial validation at formation and judicial supervision during performance.[71] Even so, according to canons of "privacy" and "state regulation", it is surprising that a contract between two private persons who have initiated cooperation between

17

themselves should be considered a prime example of state regulation.[72] While the Commission supplies no critical note, the anomaly seems rooted in the dichotomy underlying the Commission's scheme of classification. This dichotomy exists between the state enforcement of private intention on the one hand and public community standards on the other.[73] Within this regime, the only salient trait distinguishing one legal alternative from another is the degree to which state standards are imposed: a heavily regulated contract falls necessarily within the model of state regulation.

c. The Preferred Approach

The Commission advocates a "hybrid" or "flexible" model. In this model, the state balances values of private choice and community norm.[74] The Commission reasons that the law ordinarily gives a presumption to individual freedom, and thus accords broad scope to private intention as expressed in contract.[75] However, when a countervailing interest is at stake, the law tilts to a regulatory approach.[76] In the case of new reproductive technologies, the welfare of the children provides a sufficient basis for regulation.[77] To the Commission, state regulation of artificially assisted reproduction is generally appropriate, and practices such as "surrogate motherhood" ought to be governmentally controlled.[78] Where experience shows that private ordering of a particular technology happens to increase the welfare of children the law may dispense with a regulatory approach and allow private ordering. The Commission asserts that this is the case with Artificial Insemination by Donor (AID) and may also be so with In Vitro Fertilization (IVF).[79]

The Commission has arranged the alternatives to place its preferred approach in the middle. Whether this framework has the conceptual integrity required to channel alternative approaches into a single scheme is open to debate. In distilled form, the Commission's hybrid approach seems to amount to state regulation, allowing private ordering only on an exceptional basis, as state assessment of the children's welfare makes appropriate.[80] The Commission, however, provides no general test for determining when the children's welfare justifies allowing private ordering. A more serious objection, conceptually, is that the relaxation of state regulation in favour of private ordering on a technology-by-technology basis appears self-contradictory. If the state makes a case-by-case determination, the model remains state regulation, even if it incidentally sanctions private agreements. The Commission, for instance, cites AID as the sort of private ordering that is permissible under its hybrid approach but fails to note that AID generally occurs within a strictly regulated scheme of state oversight.[81] The Commission's supposed third option is "state regulation" fortified by some indeterminate incidental concern for private preference.[82]

d. Summary Critique

One test of the functional validity and coherence of the Commission's framework is whether it succeeds analytically in ordering the new human reproduction by distinguishing basic options with respect to the role of contract. The dichotomy the Commission draws between private ordering and state regulation might imply a distinction based on contract. However, the inference does not obtain. Contract is a mode of ordering under all three alternatives. It serves equally as a method for enforcing both private choice and state interest in the welfare of the child. Not even the Commission's so-called private ordering option takes its form from the distinctive character of contractual cooperation between private persons; it is derived from an abstract validation of individual intention, treating contract as an incidental feature.[83] Where contract is mentioned in connection with any of the Commission's three models, no apparent significance is attributed to the choice of contract over any other mode of legal ordering. This is as true of the choice of contract over some more static form of ordering in the context of private ordering as it is of the choice of judicially supervised "surrogate motherhood" contracts in the context of state regulation. The Commission's framework fails to make meaningful analytical distinctions in the application of contract to the new reproductive technologies.

The framework suffers from a further, more fundamental analytical defect. The Commission builds on a dichotomy between laws facilitating private intention and laws implementing public interest. Roughly, this dichotomy underlies the debate of the past several decades on the merit of legal regulation of private, consensual sexual acts.[84] The dichotomy reduces the scope of relevant inquiry to the "vertical" issue of whether the state or the individual should decide. Extending this dichotomy to organize the discussion of legal responses to technologically assisted procreation is inappropriate. In the procreative context, there is a second, "horizontal" issue: resolution of conflicts between and among various adults over competing claims to the parent-child relationship. The law must choose some basis for resolving such "horizontal" conflicts. The dichotomy that the Commission borrows from the debate on the regulation of private consensual sex provides no meaningful basis for such a choice.

The Commission's failure to consider the need for distinctions regarding this horizontal conflict undermines the value of the dichotomy between public and private, even with respect to vertical conflicts of individual versus state.

19

The Commission's public ordering of reproduction yields enforcement of private hired maternity contracts. Its private ordering yields an unprecedented entry of the state into private family relationships for the purpose of enforcing exchanges among family members. The organization of the Commission's framework expressly depends on the distinction between public and private, but ends in obfuscating it. The Commission's inconsistencies ultimately produce a taxonomy which includes only one category, state action. The only question is whether the state should act to enforce bargains or act to enforce its own agenda. The only possible answer is that the state should act on its own agenda, while including some deference to private preference. In spite of the prestige of its drafters, the taxonomic scheme of the Ontario Law Reform Commission is a failure. Its particular danger is that it appears to facilitate ordered choice, while it, in fact, obscures important choices.

2. Wadlington's Taxonomy of Approaches

In a short article entitled *Artificial Conception: The Challenge for Family Law*, Professor Walter Wadlington proposes a separate taxonomy of legal responses to technologically assisted reproduction.[85] Departing from the dichotomous approach used by the Ontario Law Reform Commission, Wadlington constructs a tripartite framework that classifies putative legal responses as "static", "private ordering", or "state regulation".[86] While still imperfect, the Wadlington taxonomy represents a significant advance on that of the Ontario Law Reform Commission.

a. The Static Approach

In contrast to the Canadian report, Professor Wadlington distinguishes biological status from contract when analysing the bases for recognizing parent-child relationships.[87] Where the Commission treats both elements as aspects of private ordering, Wadlington makes biological status the key to a separate model which he terms the "static" approach.[88] Under this approach, legal recognition of "parenthood and all accompanying rights and duties" flows from biological relationship.[89] Legal validation of parental status and social role is premised on biology. The approach is "static" in that biological status which is not alterable by contractual exchange or other means determines legal status. Wadlington disapproves of this approach; the only benefit he concedes is that it engenders predictability of familial rights and duties in the context of assisted reproduction.[90] He advocates rejection of this model because it would defeat the intended transfer of parental rights in AID arrangements which he deems socially valuable. He also asserts that it would be detrimental in unspecified ways to the best interests of children.[91]

Within Wadlington's taxonomy, the "static" approach is intended to mirror received legal forms governing the family.[92] However, such forms derive only in part from biological relationship. They may also be based on marital relationship or de facto rearing bond, each of which, no less than contract, must be distinguished from biology.[93] More than one claimant will always be able to assert biological parenthood, making conflict between biological parents unavoidable. Persons other than the biological parents may be able to assert a rearing bond with the child and conflicts may arise in this connection as well. Some norm other than biology is needed to resolve these conflicts. Thus, Wadlington's definition of the "static" approach in exclusively biological terms suffers from a serious conceptual lacuna. Recognizing this gap, Bernard Dickens adds "social form" to biological relationship as a basis of static ordering.[94] Dickens observes, for example, that the "static ordering" approach may restrict reproductive technologies to married couples, and, in so doing, order procreative relationship according to social form rather than biology.[95]

Wadlington, Dickens, and others criticize the static approach for being a "rigid" concept that is socially conservative.[96] They also consider it "static" because it provides a rationale for obstructing legal change.[97] Proponents of the approach are said to wish to "discourage" the use of the new technologies.[98] The approach includes penalties that could be imposed upon children.[99] However, it is not accurate to characterize the "static" approach as especially rigid. Regardless of whether the results would be uniformly desirable, procreative relationships under this approach could be as wide-ranging as biology and extended social cooperation would allow. Rules for resolving post-natal conflicts would rest on biological ties, the de facto bond between the biological parents or between one biological parent and another person, and the psychological rearing bond between the biological or adoptive parent and child, rather than on contract or legislative decree.[100] Founded in equity, such rules would be inherently flexible compared to corresponding rules under an approach based on contract or state conferral.[101]

Every legal approach to procreation implies some form of penalty, whether implicit or express.[102] In the "static" approach, penalties would be implicit and would affect children where the emphasis on social form led to legally enforced definitions of legitimacy in terms of birth and parentage. Stressing legitimacy, however, is not essential to the "static" approach, but rather is only one option historically associated with a single version of it.[103] On the other hand, express penalties would probably be imposed on those transferring parental rights by illegal contract, just as they now are under statutes prohibiting baby-selling.[104]

Penalties under alternative approaches would be at least as intrusive and burdensome. Under a contractual model, for example, a so-called surrogate mother would be subject to subordinate and "illegitimate" status in relation to the wife who is destined to serve as the rearing mother.[105] Persons with natural claims on children who attempt to assert them in the face of contrary contractual provisions might be subjected to extreme penalties.[106] In fact, the only intrinsically "punitive" aspect of the static approach derives from disappointed expectations where procreative intent cannot be effected without contractually enforced exchange.[107] To this extent, alternative approaches would create comparable frustrations, but would allocate them differently.[108] Conceptually, the "static" ordering approach is not peculiarly punitive.

b. The Private Ordering Approach

"Private ordering" in Professor Wadlington's framework differs in an important respect from the private ordering of the Ontario Law Reform Commission. It dispenses with any analogy to the "legal model of natural reproduction", and is constructed exclusively by reference to contract. According to Wadlington, "private ordering" through contract "would allow individual decisionmaking to control the definition of parental rights and duties . . . ".[109] Private ordering also "[would] allow tailored agreements to meet specific needs according to the technique used and the parties involved".[110] Wadlington notes that some degree of commercialization in human procreation flows inevitably from this option.[111] As Bernard Dickens observes: "[i]t would . . . accommodate commercialism in the supply of sperm, ova, and surrogate services; and compel recognition in principle of whatever arrangements private persons may determine among themselves to govern the conception, prenatal carriage, birth, and custody of children".[112] Wadlington correctly concludes that the model does not require the exclusion of other approaches, but does demand predictability of enforcement within its allotted scope.[113] While Wadlington fails to address the broader implications of private ordering, he greatly enhances its value as an analytical tool by plainly identifying it with contract.

State enforcement of rights and duties, in this view, is justified by reference to the meaning and value of promises made in pursuit of private social cooperation. By allotting such promises the power to preempt the meaning and value of both social form and biology, this model directly advances individual autonomy.

22

c. The State Regulation Approach

In its broad outlines, Wadlington's version of state regulation mimics that of the Canadian Commission.[114] In both versions, the state decides who will have access to the technologies and regulates conduct to ensure the health and adequate rearing of children.[115] Wadlington goes beyond the Ontario Commission to differentiate several forms or styles of government regulation.[116] Government regulation might be delegated to the medical profession.[117] At an extreme of bureaucratization, the state might institute a super adoption agency, coordinating and supervising all artificially assisted human reproduction.[118]

As Bernard Dickens notes, state regulation can be further categorized in terms of whether it utilizes inducement[119] or proscription.[120] The proscriptive approach is exemplified by a Florida statute prohibiting the sale of human embryos.[121] An example of inducement is the sort of AID statute that legally recognizes party allocation of parental rights and duties on condition that insemination occur through the mediation of a licensed physician.[122] An entire regime of "state regulation" can be imagined, in which private initiative in compliance with state regulation effectively redistributes rights and duties, otherwise statically ordered. Punishment under this "inducement" approach would be the implicit discomfort of being subject to the rules of static ordering.

Wadlington, like the Ontario Law Reform Commission, favours the model of state regulation.[123] But he does not manage, any more than does the Commission, to account for the difference between a model grounded either statically or through private ordering but subject to state regulation and one that is grounded in the positive power of government.[124] Wadlington's version of the state regulation approach fails to define the roles biological status, social status, and contract are to have in conjunction with or subordinated to state power.

d. Assessment

Wadlington's tripartite framework is conceptually more coherent than the Ontario Law Reform Commission's simplistic dichotomy between state interest and private intention. Wadlington's categories allow valid distinctions among legal approaches according to their mode of resolving horizontal conflicts between individuals, as well as vertical conflicts between individuals and the state, and give contract an analytically distinct role on both levels. Yet, to its credit, the Ontario Law Reform Commission's otherwise inadequate taxonomy is grounded in a unified analytical inquiry,

23

having set out to distinguish among answers to a single question—the goal of state action. Wadlington's framework lacks this analytical unity. It is not always clear what one question each of his three approaches is designed to answer. At various times, this issue appears to be the proper role of government, the basis of parental rights, or the per se value to be accorded to the new reproductive technologies. The undeniable functional value of the categories of "biology", "contract", and "the state" for distinguishing among relevant legislative proposals indicates that, analytically, these categories are at least close to being appropriate. To form the basis of a serviceable taxonomy, these categories require more express and consistent integration into a unified field of analytical inquiry.

C. A Unified Field of Analysis for the Legal Ordering of the New Reproductive Technologies

In recent decades, the legal ordering of human sexuality in general has come to be associated with the particular issue of the propriety of state interference in private, consensual sex acts.[125] The Ontario Law Reform Commission is not alone in analysing the legal response to the new reproductive technologies in these terms.[126] Issues of sexuality, privacy, and the propriety of state intervention are important and incidentally relevant but not the essence of the problem posed for the law by the new reproductive technologies.

The advent of the new reproductive technologies raises three different, more fundamental issues concerning: the right to initiate the procreation of a human person and to acquire the necessary biological resources for the purpose,[127] the right to form and maintain a parent-child relationship,[128] and the standard to be used in resolving conflicts among rival claims to a particular parental relationship.[129] The one question unifying the diverse ways of ordering the new reproductive technologies, then, concerns the basis of rights on each of these three levels. A valid analytical framework for mapping the relevant legal options discloses the many ways in which this question can be answered. Closer consideration of the three contexts within which the question arises will aid in the construction of such a framework.

Until the arrival of the new technologies, the right to initiate the procreation of a human being was limited to those with the requisite native fecundity. To be deemed legitimate, procreation was further restricted to the confines of civil marriage.[130] Non-legitimate procreation was, nonetheless, available to any fertile couple.[131] Because the new technologies allow the initiation of procreation by a person lacking native fecundity, a fertile partner, or both, these technologies force the formerly abstract question of when, on

24

whose part, and with what third party assistance society should honour an intention to procreate.

Hypothetically, the right to initiate procreation could be allocated by society in several analytically distinct ways. The right might be recognized in the state only; or, conversely, it might be limited to private parties. The right also might be shared by both the state and individuals. If private persons have the right, it might be recognized only in couples who naturally possess the full complement of genetic resources necessary to procreate within a relational bond suited to rearing children. In the alternative, the right to initiate procreation might be recognized in persons who, either individually or as a couple, have at least a partial complement of genetic resources; or it might be recognized in any individual or couple who intended to rear the child procreated, without reference to whether they had even a partial complement of the requisite resources. Finally, the right might be recognized in any person, without regard to complement of resources or intention to rear the resulting infant.

In order for parties with less than the full complement of procreative resources to have the right to procreate there must be a reallocation at least of gametes and gestational capacity outside the marriage relationship. Redistribution could be left to informal social cooperation, accomplished by enforcing contractual exchanges, or effected by state decree.[132] By whatever means accomplished, redistribution presents unique problems of legal ordering. Unlike procreation within a marital relationship, any form of procreation by redistribution brings together contributors, each of whom may feel a personal stake in the procreative project, while sharing no general community of interest for reaching shared decisions. The need to adjudicate conflicts regarding control over the procreative process and disposition of extracorporeal gametes and embryos is foreseeable.[133] Contributors alienating the physical resources needed for a procreative project initiated by another may feel a natural claim of identity and relationship with the resulting child.[134] The child may, in later years, wish to assert a claim against one of the contributors.[135] The law will have to resolve conflicting claims of identity and relationship. To the extent that redistribution is enforced by contract or state conferral, there exists the possibility of legal coercion that invades the bodily privacy and autonomy of the contributors and divides intimate emotional relationships between natural parents and children.

Although the right to assert a parent-child relationship was once considered a simple corollary of the right to initiate procreation, the new reproductive technologies sharpen the distinction between the two rights and urge independent inquiry into the former. At one time, it was assumed that,

25

although the right to a parent-child relationship might exist without participation in procreation, as in adoption, a role in procreation necessarily gave rise to parental rights.[136] Under the new reproductive regime, a role in procreation may be foreseen without the concomitant right to assert a parent-child relationship.[137] Thus, the new technologies invite broad reconsideration of the basis of a right to a parent-child relationship. In the abstract, there are five imaginable bases of the right: state conferral, original intention to initiate procreation, biological contribution whether genetic or gestational, de facto rearing bond whether gestational or postparturient, or contractual assignment. These diverse grounds for recognizing a parent-child relationship might exist in combination, or one of them might be enacted to the exclusion of the others.

The third fundamental question which the emergence of technologically assisted reproduction raises is how to resolve conflicts among competing claims to the same parental relationship. Plainly, the more restrictive the law is in recognizing a right to initiate procreation or to assert a claim to a parent-child relationship, the fewer conflicts will arise. Yet even at its most restrictive, the law on technologically assisted reproduction will be called upon to resolve a greater diversity of conflicts than arose prior to the emergence of the new technologies.[138] Prior to the advent of the new reproductive technologies, a single progenitor and single progenitrix might be at odds, following a divorce or conception out of wedlock. Either or both biological parents might come into conflict with a party who enjoyed a psychological or nurturing bond with the child.[139]

With the new technologies, the legal claimants who might come into conflict include all of the following: genetic father(s) or mother(s);[140] gestational mother;[141] custodial parent;[142] contractual parent;[143] parent by original procreative intent;[144] and parent by right of state conferral.[145] To the extent that these parties have legally cognizable claims, these claims may come into conflict, and the law must be able to resolve them. In resolving disputes, the law may hold that one party's claim simply cancels another's; in the alternative, it may differentiate the parent-child relationship into its constitutive elements, including formal status, custody and right of visitation, and allocate these piecemeal among disputants. The latter approach defines disputes in a way that minimizes stakes and maximizes flexibility in finding remedies. Further, the law could favour ad hoc adjudication, based on secondary criteria concerned with the character and conduct of the parties and concerned with the best interest of the child or some other equitable standard; it could prefer a constitutional or statutory framework establishing priorities based in either fundamental rights or social

26

policy; or it could choose to enforce priorities and rights established by contract.

Devising a valid taxonomy of alternative legal approaches to the new reproduction is a matter of identifying alternative modes of response to the single question underlying the three foregoing sets of problems. As stated above, this question centres on the basis for the legal recognition of rights. Analysis of the alternatives that emerge upon consideration of the legal ordering of the three foregoing problems discloses three values that might serve as that basis. These values are state conferral,[146] individual autonomy,[147] and natural endowment.[148] They resemble the categories employed by Professor Wadlington, but differ in at least three important ways. First, conferral by the state is not the same as regulation by the state. Rights may be based on contractual transfer or natural endowment, and yet may be heavily regulated. On the other hand, rights conferred by the state may be relatively unregulated. Second, individual intention is recognized largely by enforcing contractual expectation, but it also may exist as a basis for recognizing rights, even in the absence of a contract.[149] Third, natural endowment differs from biological relationship. It includes biological ties of genetic contribution and gestation, but also subsumes sexual bonding that brings together a full complement of procreative resources, and de facto bonding between child and primary adult caretaker. Parties with such a bond do not require redistribution of procreative resources through the compulsion of contract or state decree.

D. A Taxonomy of Alternatives in the Legal Ordering of the New Reproductive Technologies

The following taxonomy classifies diverse legal approaches to the new reproductive technologies according to consistent modes of allocating procreational rights, parent-child relationships, and resolution of conflicts over parental rights. The three alternative modes comprising this taxonomy are grounded in: 1) state conferral, 2) individual autonomy and 3) natural endowment. Each mode can be further subdivided into strong and moderate types. The strong type exemplifies the guiding value in close to pure form. The moderate type qualifies its approach under the influence of one or both of the two remaining values. Classification is a relative rather than absolute matter, even where the type is "strong", since legal ordering in this area will virtually always require some subordinate reference to one or both of the two values not chosen as primary. A "moderate" model acknowledges a secondary value in a consistent and principled manner.

27

1. The State Conferral Model

One approach to the consistent legal ordering of the new human reproduction would be to assume that the state confers the right to initiate procreation, form a parent-child relationship, or assert precedence in a conflict over parental rights.[150] In its strong form, this approach would lead the state to exercise the right to initiate procreation and rear children, delegating component tasks to individuals. By definition there could be no conflicts over parental rights. In its moderate form, the approach would lead the state to confer these rights on private persons, according to the pattern of regard for individual autonomy, natural endowment, or any other value that it deemed to advance public policy.

a. Strong Type: A Reproductive Bureaucracy

In the event the state itself were to exercise the right to procreate and rear children, a substantial bureaucracy would necessarily arise. The ensuing type of ordering for procreation could be termed reproductive bureaucracy.[151] The nearest analogue under existing law would be the organization of the standing armed forces. If the state undertook this exercise on an exclusive basis, society would come to resemble the vision of Aldous Huxley's *Brave New World*[152] or, perhaps, Plato's *Republic*.[153] Reproductive bureaucrats could be expected to pursue genetic engineering.[154] A paradoxical feature of the approach is that it removes natural endowment as a basis of parental rights but is likely to posit a form of genetic endowment as a goal of state action. Many suppose the approach ineluctably leads to or flows from totalitarianism.[155] The darkest fears aroused by the new reproductive technologies are that they may lead society in this direction.[156] In the present political culture, it is not likely that the state would take direct control of the procreation and rearing of children. For now, the question at most is whether the state might do so in the limited case of technologically assisted procreation. It might, for example, expand the bureaucracy of adoption to encompass the initiation of technologically assisted reproduction. In this limited context, it might license individuals or couples who gain approval, and oversee the procreative process or assign parental status to individuals on the basis of bureaucratic norms.[157]

b. Moderate Type: State Conferred Status

In a more moderate approach, the state would not itself exercise the rights of procreation and child rearing, but instead would confer such rights on others. This type of response would be concerned, most fundamentally, with positively redefining parenthood so that it would be a state conferred status rather than the contribution of natural endowment.[158] If it elected to pursue consistent secondary recognition of individual autonomy, the state would then delegate most of the organization of reproductive behaviour to private contract, rather than pursuing it directly by bureaucracy. Within this framework, the state might limit and direct behaviour through licensing requirements.[159] The reproductive aspect of marriage itself might be distinguished and redefined in these terms. The state might intervene to supervise and enforce the performance of the appropriate private agreements.[160]

Under the moderate form, parental status would be conferred upon meeting formal, state-promulgated criteria. Through these criteria, the state might give significant secondary weight to elements of natural endowment reinterpreted as a eugenics or social engineering goal or as individual intention expressed in contract.[161] The primary object of such criteria, however, would be bureaucratic certainty and predictability with respect to state enforcement of property rights, bureaucratic entitlements, and parental duties.[162] The application of the moderate state conferral model would represent further progress in an existing trend whereby the law absorbs even the ordering of the "private" sphere into a master calculus of public purposes. If an analytically consistent ordering were to be distilled from the state regulation model proposed by the Ontario Law Reform Commission and Professor Wadlington, it would likely fit here. As the subsequent discussion of current law suggests, this second type of state conferral, after removing evasions and subterfuge, is receiving serious consideration in reforming the law of human procreation.[163]

2. The Individual Autonomy Model

An alternative ordering of technologically assisted reproduction would consistently base legal rights to procreate, to assert a parent-child relationship, and to successfully assert parental rights on the value of the autonomous intention of the individual.[164] Anyone capable of forming the intent to procreate would have the prima facie right to initiate procreation.[165] Any necessary redistribution of procreative resources would occur through contract. The intentions of the contracting parties would be used to justify the enforcement of this redistribution, as well as to justify the allocation of parental status, rights, and duties. In its strong type, the autonomy model would be given a laissez faire formulation, permitting the rise of industry and commerce in human procreation. In its moderate type, the autonomy model would be given a consumer rights formulation, restricting the redistribution of procreative resources in ways beneficial to consumers.

29

a. Strong Type: Laissez Faire

In its strong form, the individual autonomy model would enforce all contractual redistributions of procreative resources. The contractual rights of the party with the original procreative intent would override any claims to parental rights by those contributing gametes or gestational capacity, even where the intending party had made no biological contribution to the child. In order to bring this strong type of individual autonomy into existence, the law would have to reject the notion of parental rights as a function of natural endowment, and reconstrue them as arising from the appropriation of procreative resources. Rights flowing both from an original procreative intent and from natural endowment with procreative resources would be fully alienable. All relevant exchanges would be permitted on a commercial basis.[166] Market forces would tend to give rise to a procreation industry allocating differentiated functions to the most efficient provider. The same forces would organize a commercial market-place for resources and products, allowing roles for brokers and middlemen.[167] Eugenic engineering would be employed to create more desirable babies at lower cost.[168] Within this framework, commercial eugenic services would also eventually be sought by couples having a full natural endowment of procreative resources, as well as by those seeking reallocations of basic procreative resources.[169] The procreative process also might be exploited commercially in order to produce and distribute human organs, tissues, and other products, rather than to bring children to term.[170]

A structural premise of the model is that, once a child is born into a commercially arranged relationship, it would no longer be subject to commercial exchange.[171] Whether this premise would remain in place in a society actually implementing the values implicit in the laissez faire approach is a valid question. As long as the premise is observed, however, the rearing parents would have no right of rejection on delivery, but would perhaps be allowed damages for breach of warranty. Some assume that general reliance on money damages, rather than specific performance, would follow the option's commercial logic.[172] The party-in-possession, typically the gestational mother, could refuse to deliver the child or to waive parental rights, but at the cost of paying money damages. Money damages, when added to the intrinsic cost of raising a child, would render breach a rare occurrence. In addition, the right to breach in order to convey the child to someone willing to pay more money is logically implied, but practically courts would seem unlikely to go so far. It is more probable that, even in the laissez faire approach, courts would premise any "right" to breach and pay money damages in lieu of delivery upon the party's continuing intention

30

to retain a relationship with the child. Thus, the advantage of the party-in-possession would not be alienable.

In practice, then, under the strong type of the individual autonomy model an original intention to procreate would override rights grounded in natural endowment by operation of the enforcement of contract. However, custody of the child at birth might prevail over either claim, as long as the party-in-possession is willing to pay money damages, and this latter option is non-alienable. But, this balance would seem unstable. Courts are more apt to respond by eliminating the right of the party-in-possession to resist specific performance. Alternatively, they might respond by strengthening the right of the party-in-possession to resist delivery by making the party's obligation voidable, thus removing the penalty of money damages. The latter would represent a substantial moderation of and departure from the strong form of the individual autonomy model. The adoption of this laissez faire approach in the United States is conceivable.[173]

b. Moderate Type: Consumer Rights

In its moderate form, the individual autonomy model would restrict the redistribution of a complete complement of procreative resources and a fortiori the redistribution of parental rights to persons who intend to rear the child themselves; that is, to consumers.[174] It might place a ceiling on the price of procreative resources to prevent full commercial competition.[175] Or it might restrict the ability to contract to individuals who possess at least a partial complement of procreative resources, or to married individuals.[176] All of these restrictions would be designed to prevent the emergence of a full-fledged industry and commerce of procreation. They would reduce the incidence of commercialized procreative exchanges and restrict the ability of the parties to those exchanges that did occur to achieve goals and control outcomes. Individual autonomy would remain the leading value in this moderate type, as in the strong type of the model, but state conferral aimed at distributing advantages in conformity with a particular vision of society would be given consistent effect as a moderating value.[177] Some degree of moderation also might be exercised by consistent respect for the informal social cooperation and, perhaps, even the biological relationships which have a primary role in the third model.[178] However, "intention" to procreate would be given more or less of a priority over contribution out of natural endowment in establishing priorities to parental rights. At the outer limit of the individual autonomy model, the right of contractual exchange might be eliminated altogether, and original procreative intention alone might be vindicated by means of a system of public notice filing, leaving redistribution to informal cooperation.[179]

31

The consumer approach to individual autonomy ordering would also emulate the various consumer protections that have developed in twentieth-century contract law generally. The law would dictate the terms of contracts, impose disclosure requirements, and strike down onerous terms.[180] Parties selling procreative resources would be protected by labour protection legislation.[181] Professional classes of doctors, psychologists, and lawyers, bound by fiduciary standards, would be brought in as intermediaries.[182] Couples and, perhaps, even individuals procreating through reallocative exchanges would be given public affirmation. The validity of assent by parties alienating procreative resources and parental rights would be the focus of concern.[183] State regulation to safeguard at least the minimal interests of the child would be admitted. The consumer rights type of approach joins state conferred status as one of the primary contenders for present enactment in the United States.

3. The Natural Endowment Model

The third basis on which the law might recognize procreation rights, parent-child relationship, and precedence in conflicts over parental rights is status derived from natural endowment of genetic or gestational relationship, or de facto relationship of nurturance. No enforced redistribution of procreative resources by contract or government decree would be permitted.[184] In its strong type, this model would take further steps to channel procreation into normative social forms based on the natural configuration of the couple in possession of a complete complement of procreative resources. In its moderate type, the model would validate informal, non-commercial redistributions of procreative resources, for the sake of allowing, if not encouraging, a more polymorphous form of social organization.

a. Strong Type: The Traditional Family

The recognition of rights related to procreation, parent child relationship, and precedence in conflicts over parental rights under the strong type of the natural endowment model is based on "natural endowment". Natural endowment means both the disposition of procreative resources, which can be commanded without violation of tort and criminal law and without resort to governmental power, and the de facto bond an adult has with a child by virtue of a nurturing relationship.[185] Under this approach, the law would refrain from lending state power to the reallocation of procreative resources, either through state conferral or contract enforcement. The law might also actively choose to discourage partners from resorting to an informal redistribution of procreative resources.[186] At a minimum, the law would

32

actively encourage the exclusive pursuit of procreation within the confines of the marital relationship or other envisioned formal relationships suited to rearing children, monogamous marriage being only one. Entry into such a relationship by marital consent is the distinguishing application of contract within the natural endowment model. This continuing linkage between procreation and marriage or other formal rearing relationships would reduce both the numbers and kinds of diverse claimants to parental status. Mechanisms for the resolution of conflicting claims would favour the social form over biological relationship.[187]

This model generally starts from the assumption that lineage or de facto nurturance is the appropriate basis for the recognition of parental rights. In its pure form, it adds an assumption that the cooperative relationship leading to procreation ought to serve simultaneously the rearing of the child conceived. The strong type of the model posits the importance of a stable rearing relationship to the welfare of the child, and gives priority to rights that flow from formal marriage over those which flow from biological parenthood. In this form of ordering, dyadic and triadic personal relationships, as basic building blocks of community and personal identity, enjoy a priority over the autonomy of the individual.[188] The value of state conferral enters to the limited extent of justifying the enforcement of marital prerogatives over rights based in biological relationship out of a policy preference for securing the adequate rearing of children.

This type of approach corresponds to the traditional law of the family and, to a certain extent, continues to define the law's treatment of attempted reallocations of procreative and parental rights.[189] The new reproductive technologies complicate the facts of human procreation to such an extent that the continued validity of this approach requires a renewal of the theoretical justification of its goals and a practical rethinking of the appropriate juridical means for achieving them. Proponents would see the value of alternative models mainly for the perspective they lend in this process of renewal and rethinking.

b. Moderate Type: Informal Social Cooperation

When moderated by the secondary concern for the value of individual autonomy, the natural endowment model might encourage, or at least might not discourage, informal redistributions of procreative resources, as long as they occur without the benefit of legal enforcement and are not unambiguously meretricious.[190] Donors presumably would be motivated by non-monetary benefits or altruism.[191] In this type of approach, a policy encouraging or at least allowing donations would be in delicate equipoise with one not allowing monetary exchanges.[192] Individuals would make gifts or barters that they might try to revoke, but which the law might treat as irrevocable for reasons other than respect for the expectations generated by the transaction. Parties cooperating informally to share procreative resources would give contractual appearance to ancillary exchanges. At times, they would attempt to circumvent the ban on commercial bargains for procreative resources by various forms of subterfuge. Faced with reliance, the courts would feel pressure, in equity, to give limited enforcement to certain bargains.

By encouraging redistributions while not recognizing either contract, governmental decree, or social form as a basis for resolving conflicts among claimants to parental rights, the law would make conflict resolution more complex. In this moderate type of the model, the value of individual autonomy among adult participants is given priority over the value of stability and uniformity in the rearing of children.[193] At the same time, lineage and de facto bonds of nurturance remain the base of parental rights. As a consequence, the law would need to adjudicate among diverse claimants with conflicting demands to a parent-child relationship.

To direct the resolution of these conflicts, the law would probably adopt several standing adjudicatory rules. For instance, it might distinguish between custody, visitation rights, and parental status, being the most cautious about granting the first, and quite liberal in recognizing the last. It would tend to favour the gestational mother, as the party in a de facto nurturing bond with the baby at birth, in allocating custody. It would develop rules for deciding what kinds of informal custody allocations on birth required the state's parens patriae supervision to protect the best interests of the child. It would tend to require records of genetic parentage and ensure at least qualified access to children born as a result of informal redistributions of procreative resources.[194] The informal social cooperation type of the natural endowment model would tend to provide a middle ground between the traditional family and the alternatives available under the individual autonomy model. As such, it may have appeal to those who find the traditional model too rigid and alternative models objectionable because of perceived statist or commodifying tendencies.

E. Summary: The Diverse Roles for Contract in the Legal Ordering of the New Reproductive Technologies

In the context of this book, the primary reason for developing the foregoing taxonomy is to disclose the analytically distinct roles contract might assume in the legal ordering of the new reproductive technologies. Insofar as the issue is one of individualized contractual allocation of procreative resources and parental rights, the taxonomy yields four diverse roles assignable to contract. Contract, for example, would have a subordinate role in the moderate type of state conferral. Under this approach, party exchanges would require state validation at the time of formation and would be subject to government supervision in their performance. The private bargain, properly validated, would trigger the conferral by the state of parental status. By contrast, contract would have its most central role in the strong type of the individual autonomy model, reorganizing human procreation into a form virtually indistinguishable from existing commercial markets. Here, enforcement of bargains reallocating natural or purchased endowments of procreative resources and parental rights would be justified categorically. A third role that could be assigned contract is seen in the moderate type of the same model. There, contract's commercial character would be moderated by respect for the value of state conferral, bestowing protections and benefits according to a particular, liberal vision of society. State regulation would probably give rise to professional agencies that channel and socialize bargains. A fourth, "shadow" role would be found within the moderate type of the natural endowment model. In that setting, contract would assume some role on the periphery of informal exchanges aimed at redistributing procreative resources, whether through ancillary agreement, subterfuge, or equitable enforcement of de facto bargains. When contract is proposed as a means of ordering the new reproductive technologies, it is proposed in one of the four foregoing senses. In contrast to these individualized contractual reallocations, the strong type of the natural endowment model applies contract in a specialized sense as a means of introducing public accountability to voluntary personal arrangements for the long-term pooling of procreative resources and rearing of children. This last approach resolves the specific issues raised by the new reproductive technologies, not through contract, but through considerations of status moderated by equity.

Concrete legal proposals are likely to be ambiguous, and subject to differing interpretations. A given proposal may contain elements of more than one type. Furthermore, within the scheme itself, each moderate type, with a reversal of emphasis, can be transmuted into an instance of the moderate type of an altogether different model. The moderate type of state conferral can shift into the moderate form of individual autonomy and vice versa, depending on the relative weight given to the element of state validated contract. The moderate form of individual autonomy and the moderate form of natural endowment also might be transmuted by altering the extent to which the state permits equitable enforcement of reliance interest in the context of exchanges of procreative resources. Thus, the taxonomy is not so much for definitively classifying particular legal proposals as for mapping the broad generic alternatives against which particular legal proposals may be evaluated.

Endnotes

1. *See* Allen, *supra* note 15 Intro., at 1759 ("[there is] a search for agreement about the paradigms of social experience to which surrogacy-related roles and transactions are properly analogized."); Healey, *supra* note 5 Intro., at 140 ("[M]any areas of legal ambiguity and uncertainty" exist in the literature). Family law as a whole, moreover, has been said to be in "conceptual disarray". Weyrauch, *Metamorphoses of Marriage*, 13 FAM. L.Q. 415 (1979). The present objective is not to return to a rigid conceptual framework that restricts authentic human flourishing. *See* Olsen, *supra* note 29 Intro., at 1560 (the traditional dichotomy between family and market has had a destructive effect on various strategies intended to improve the lives of women). Rather, the aim is coherence, as measured by the quality of discourse about a particular pressing societal problem, and it presumes that prescriptive and constructive coherence are meaningful goals.

2. The descriptive and predictive value of the distinction between public and private has been questioned. *See* Kennedy, *The Stages of the Decline of the Public/Private Distinction*, 130 U. PA. L. REV. 1349, 1357 (1982) (noting the blurring of the private/public distinction and questioning its continued utility); Rakoff, *Contracts of Adhesion: An Essay in Reconstruction*, 96 HARV. L. REV. 1174, 1215-20 (1983) (questioning the value of the distinction between public and private as it pertains to contracts of adhesion). The claim here is not that there should be a priori conceptual content to the terms "public" and "private", but that legal proposals can be assessed by how well they create a social universe that can be coherently described in basic terms.

3. The purpose of the definition offered here is a formal analysis of the hypothetical range of applications contract could have in resolving a potential source of social disorder. The definition is formal and presupposes a minimal underlying orientation to certain broad values. However, the value and meaning of contract for ordering the new reproductive technologies will vary depending on how this simple formal definition is given further and more explicit content in relation to important substantive values. *See infra* text accompanying notes 150-194 Ch. 1.

Arthur Corbin provides a realist's salutary caution against formalist misunderstandings at this juncture:

Definitions [of contract] have been constructed by almost all writers on law
and in many thousands of judicial opinions . . . . It is a very common error to
suppose that legal terms, such as contract, have one absolute and eternally
correct definition. The fact is that all such terms have many usages, among
which every one is free to select. One usage is to be preferred over another

only in so far as it serves our necessity and convenience.
1 A. CORBIN, CORBIN ON CONTRACTS § 3 (1952) (footnote omitted). Friedman suggests that most textbook definitions are not particularly helpful in isolating the societal meaning or value of contract. L. FRIEDMAN, CONTRACT LAW IN AMERICA 15 (1965).

4. For example, contract was the subject of the first American legal casebook, C. LANGDELL, A SELECTION OF CASES ON THE LAW OF CONTRACTS (1871); L. FRIEDMAN, *supra* note 3 Ch. 1, at 211. The foundational insights underlying contract's central role in liberal Western society were made by Adam Smith. A. SMITH, AN INQUIRY INTO THE NATURE AND CAUSES OF THE WEALTH OF NATIONS (1776). On the central role of contract, see generally E. FARNSWORTH, CONTRACTS § 1.2 (1982) (noting that a free enterprise economy relies on direct bilateral exchanges between individuals); J. HURST, LAW AND ECONOMIC GROWTH 301 (1984) (noting that contracts express self-interest and advance public policy by putting economic resources to use); W. SEAGLE, THE HISTORY OF LAW 253-72 (1946) (discussing the preeminent place of contracts through ancient and classical periods and into its maturity in modern times).

5. *See generally* G. GILMORE, THE DEATH OF CONTRACT (1974) (arguing that contract is becoming subsumed within tort law).

6. O.W. HOLMES, THE COMMON LAW 289-307 (1938). Gilmore argues that classical contract theory was "pieced together" most notably by Holmes "in broad philosophical outline", but also by Williston, who gives a "meticulous, although not always accurate, scholarly detail" of the theory in his 1920 treatise. G. GILMORE, *supra* note 5 Ch. 1, at 14. The pivotal role Gilmore assigns Holmes has been criticized. Speidel, *An Essay on the Reported Death and Continued Vitality of Contract*, 27 STAN. L. REV. 1161, 1170-71 (1975). While Gilmore's emphasis on Holmes may be exaggerated, the exaggeration is illuminating. What distinguishes Holmes from his immediate procursors is his willingness to generalize about the formal requirements of contract, without relying on the historic scope of the actual common law forms. *Cf.* C. LANGDELL, A SUMMARY OF THE LAW OF CONTRACTS §§ 45-47 (1880) (discussing elements needed to assume proper consideration for contract formation). One does not have to accept Holmes' formalism to benefit from the leverage his ahistorical formulations provide for explorations of what the law was, is, or may become. Holmes, of course, defies easy categorization, being simultaneously a precursor of the formalists and realists. E. BODENHEIMER, JURISPRUDENCE 114-16 (1962).

7. For an explanation of the idea that legal concepts can exert a "gravitational" pull upon the deep structures of the legal system, transcending their particular application, see G. CALABRESI, IDEALS, BELIEFS, ATTITUDES, AND THE LAW (1985).

8. O.W. HOLMES, *supra* note 6 Ch. 1, at 289-307. The justification of contract enforcement was closely linked to its economic productivity. E. FARNSWORTH, *supra* note 4 Ch. 1, § 1.3. In the classical theory, bargains were understood to be enforceable formally within a scope narrowly circumscribed by "legality". In a typical treatise of the classical era, sections on "consideration" and "agreement" were matched by sections on the limits of "form", "capacity", and "consent", as well as "legal object". *E.g.*, *Id.* § 1.1; J. LAWSON, THE PRINCIPLES OF THE AMERICAN LAW OF CONTRACTS AT LAW AND EQUITY 3 (1893). Blackstone's earlier explanation of the scope of the legal object of contract essentially remained current:

> The last species of offences which especially affect the commonwealth are
> those against the public *police* or *economy*. By the public police or economy
> I mean the due regulation and domestic order of the kingdom, whereby the
> individuals of the state, like members of a well-governed family, are bound
> to conform their general behavior to the rules of propriety, good neighborhood,
> and good manners, and to be decent, industrious, and inoffensive in their

respective stations.

4 W. BLACKSTONE, COMMENTARIES ON THE LAWS OF ENGLAND 162 (W. Lewis ed. 1897) (emphasis in the original). As objects which were to be considered illegal or against public policy, Blackstone included clandestine and bigamous marriage contracts. *Id.* at 163-65. A fundamental feature of the enforcement of promises in the classical scheme was thus the limitation of its application to exchanges that fit within the sphere of the commercial bargain.

9. The idea of the "simple contract" was classically defined as "a bargain", and, as such, distinguished from its close cousins, promises under seal and negotiable instruments. *E.g.*, C. ASHLEY, THE LAW OF CONTRACTS § 3 (1911). Holmes' paradigm is a promise to "transport a cask of brandy to Cambridge." O.W. HOLMES, *supra* note 6 Ch. 1, at 290. Williston begins his treatise by distinguishing the bargained for exchange as being "of much greater importance", than other types of enforceable promises such as those under seal. 1 S. WILLISTON, THE LAW OF CONTRACTS § 2A (3rd ed. 1957); *see also* E. FARNSWORTH, *supra* note 4 Ch. 1, § 1.1 (discussing the importance of an exchange between the parties in terms of evaluating a contract's enforceability).

10. Literally, "agreements are to be kept". The maxim is "[a]n abbreviated form of the rule stated in Justinian's Code 2, 3, 29, an expression of the principle that undertakings and contracts must be observed and implemented". D. WALKER, THE OXFORD COMPANION TO LAW 912 (1980). For a general discussion of the principle associated with the maxim, see Note, *Pacta Sunt Servanda*, 41 COLUM. L. REV. 783, 783-85 (1941) (arguing that a theory of practiced dependability controls the development of contract law).

11. C. LANGDELL, *supra* note 6 Ch. 1, § 148. This is expressed in the maxim that a "peppercorn" is adequate consideration for a promise. 2 W. BLACKSTONE, *supra* note 8 Ch. 1, at 440. The pure value of certainty concerning future expectation is an essential aspect of contract, in this view. As such, contract is defined as excluding present barters and donations. A. CORBIN, *supra* note 3 Ch. 1, § 4 (1952); E. FARNSWORTH, *supra* note 4 Ch. 1, § 1.1.

12. "In essence, the role of modern contract can be summarized as the concurrent dissociation of organic relationships and the recombination of abstracted monads into external relationships of limited association entailing narrowly circumscribed forms of social cooperation." Rosenfeld, *supra* note 13 Intro., at 810; *see also* E. FARNSWORTH, *supra* note 4 Ch. 1, § 1.1 (discussing the law's primary concern with an exchange between parties in order to give rise to an enforceable contract).

13. The emergence of the non-enforceability of gratuitous promises under the common law appears originally to have presupposed the concurrent enforcement of such promises, in at least some circumstances, within the ecclesiastical courts, under designation as *fides facta*. H. POTTER, HISTORICAL INTRODUCTION TO ENGLISH LAW AND ITS INSTITUTIONS, 450 (4th ed. 1958). Yet the classical treatment of common law contract makes it axiomatic that bargains are enforceable, and gratuitous promises are not. E. FARNSWORTH, *supra* note 4 Ch. 1, §§ 1.1, 2.5; J. LAWSON, *supra* note 8 Ch. 1, § 91.

14. "'Purposive contracts' . . . neither affect 'the status of the parties nor give rise to new qualities of comradeship' but aim solely 'at some specific (especially economic) performance or result.'" Kronman & Posner, *Notes and Questions*, in THE ECONOMICS OF CONTRACT LAW 261-62 (A. Kronman & R. Posner eds. 1979) (quoting M. WEBER, LAW IN ECONOMY AND SOCIETY (E. Shils & M. Rheinstein trans. 1954)); *see* E. FARNSWORTH, *supra* note 4 Ch. 1, § 2.2. The nonenforcement of contract obligation within the confines of the marital relationship was, until recently, well settled. See, *e.g.*, Balfour v. Balfour, [1919] 2 K.B. 571, 121 L.T.R. 346, 88 L.J.K.B. 1054, 35 T.L.R. 609, 63 Sol. J. 661 (C.A.) (holding that a husband's promise to pay his estranged wife's living expenses is not intended to be a legally enforceable bargain). For reference to the thesis of Sir Henry Maine that the move-

ment of progressive societies is away from familial relationship and towards contract, see *infra* note 77 Ch. 3.

15. *See* P. ATIYAH, THE RISE AND FALL OF FREEDOM OF CONTRACT 713 (1986) (noting that the market rewards those who articulate their future needs); *see also infra* text accompanying note 99-102 Ch. 3.

16. *See* Note, *Consideration and Form*, 41 COLUM. L. REV. 799, 800-06 (1941) (discussing formalities historically associated with contracts). Earlier in history, only written promises made under seal were enforceable at law as opposed to promises exchanged in commercial bargains. The seal fulfilled these same functions. E. FARNSWORTH, *supra* note 4 Ch. 1, § 2.16.

17. RESTATEMENT (SECOND) OF CONTRACTS § 90 (1979). Gilmore credits Corbin with demonstrating that Holmes had distorted the common law cases and with responsibility for the corrective inclusion of § 90 in the *Restatement*. G. GILMORE, *supra* note 5 Ch. 1, at 64.

18. Although the seal is either no longer recognized, or merely creates a presumption of consideration, see RESTATEMENT (SECOND) OF CONTRACTS § 96A statutory note, topic 3 (1979) (tables of relevant state laws), a modern trend has acknowledged formal contracts where adequate attestation exists. MODEL WRITTEN OBLIGATIONS ACT, 9C U.L.A. 378 (1957) requires the enforcement of any writing that contains an express statement that it is intended as legally binding. This proposal has been enacted only in Pennsylvania. Uniform Written Obligations Act, PA. STAT. ANN. tit. 33, §§ 6-8 (Purdon 1967). In New York promises are enforced as long as they are written, signed, and recite some past benefit received. N Y. GEN. OBLIG. LAW § 5-1105 (McKinney 1989). New Mexico makes written promises binding without consideration. N.M STAT. ANN. § 38-7-2 (1987). Lord Mansfield attempted to make a written promise binding without consideration, but was reversed by his successors on the bench. Pillans and Rose v. Van Mierop and Hopkins, 3 Burr. 1663, 97 Eng. Rep. 1035 (K.B. 1765).

19. On promissory estoppel, under RESTATEMENT (SECOND) OF CONTRACTS § 90, see generally Feinman, *Promissory Estoppel and Judicial Method*, 97 HARV. L. REV. 678 (1984) (tracing the development of promissory estoppel doctrine and its relation to broader developments in contract law). Even in commercial settings, the doctrine has led to the enforcement of promissory obligation where bargain is absent. *See, e.g.*, Drennan v. Star Paving Co., 51 Cal. 2d 409, 333 P.2d 757 (1958) (defendant's estimate used in plaintiff's bid on construction contract held enforceable as an irrevocable offer); Hoffman v. Red Owl Stores, 26 Wis. 2d 683, 133 N.W.2d 267 (1965) (plaintiff given franchise for a store based on reliance on defendant's promises).

On unconscionability, under U.C.C. § 2-302 and RESTATEMENT (SECOND) OF CONTRACTS § 208, *see generally* J. CALAMARI & J. PERILLO, THE LAW OF CONTRACTS §§ 9-37, 9-38, 9-39, 9-40 (3d ed. 1987) (discussing the language, history and application of U.C.C. §2-302); Eisenberg, *The Bargain Principle and Its Limits*, 95 HARV. L. REV. 741, 752-54 (1982) (reconciling U.C.C. § 2-302 and the bargain principle); Leff, *Unconscionability and the Code-The Emperor's New Clause*, 115 U. PA. L. REV. 485 (1967) (analyzing the purpose, language, and result of U.C.C. § 2-302); Speidel, *Unconscionability, Assent and Consumer Protection*, 31 U. PITT. L. REV. 359 (1970) (applying U.C.C. § 2-302 to consumer sales and the burden of proof). For important early cases illustrating unconscionability, *see, e.g.*, Williams v. Walker-Thomas Furniture Co., 350 F.2d 445 (D.C. Cir. 1965) (discussing factors involved in determining unconscionable clauses); Henningsen v. Bloomfield Motors, Inc., 32 N.J. 358, 161 A.2d 69 (1960) (arguing that disclaimer of implied warranty by automobile manufacturer is against public policy).

20. See J. CALAMARI & J. PERILLO, *supra* note 19 Ch. 1, § 1-3 (noting increased legislative restrictions on contractual freedom); E. FARNSWORTH, *supra* note 4 Ch. 1, § 1.7 (discussing the evolution of government limitation on contract in the twentieth century); Linzer, *The Decline of Assent: At-Will Employment as a Case Study of the Breakdown of Private Law Theory*, 20 GA. L. REV. 323 (1986) (discussing court-imposed restrictions on private law); Rehbinder, *Status, Contract, and the Welfare State*, 23 STAN. L. REV. 941 (1971) (discussing the beneficial effects of governmental interference in the evolution of private law).

21. "A contract is a promise or a set of promises for the breach of which the law gives a remedy, or the performance of which the law in some way recognizes as a duty". RESTATEMENT OF CONTRACTS § 1 (1932). The definition is retained in the Second Restatement. RESTATEMENT (SECOND) OF CONTRACTS §1 (1979). It is derived from Williston, the principal drafter of the first *Restatement*: "A contract is a promise, or set of promises, to which the law attaches legal obligation". 1 S. WILLISTON, *supra* note 9 Ch. 1, § 1. The Uniform Commercial Code defines contract as the total legal obligation resulting from the parties' agreement, which, in turn, is defined as bargain. U.C.C. §§ 1-201(3), (11) (1989).

22. For other criticism of the *Restatement* definition, see G. GILMORE, *supra* note 5 Ch. 1.

23. RESTATEMENT (SECOND) OF CONTRACTS § 1 (1979).

24. Where the state functions in a role that is not distinctively and exclusively governmental, such as buying or selling goods, hiring clerical staff, or contracting to construct buildings, it enters into a contract. However, where the state acts in a role exclusively reserved to it, either intrinsically or by governmental decree or enactment, its arrangements are better viewed as administrative than as contractual. Examples would include employment relations with elected officials and military personnel and agreements to buy defence equipment. However, the Supreme Court of the United States has held that "[w]hen the United States enters into contract relations, its rights and duties therein are governed generally by the law applicable to contracts between private individuals". Lynch v. United States, 292 U.S. 559 (1933).

25. In adoption proceedings, consent is given but is not an application of contract. *In re* Adoption of Anonymous, 286 A.D. 161, 165, 143 N.Y.S.2d 90, 94 (1955).

26. Fuller & Perdue, *The Reliance Interest in Contract Damages*, 46 YALE L.J. 52, 71-72 (1936). Standard treatises distinguished between simple contracts, which were bargains, and formal contracts under seal. Gradually the latter have disappeared. Now, an equivalent form may be returning, based not on the value of honour, but rather on a pragmatic value. Negotiable instruments were and are a thriving alternative based on formality. U.C.C. §§ 3-305, 3-306, 3-408 (1989) (providing formalities for negotiable instruments). The definition proposed here is not unlike "the relations among parties to the process of projecting exchange into the future". I. MACNEIL, THE NEW SOCIAL CONTRACT 4 (1980); *see also* Gordon, *Macauley, Macneil and the Discovery of Solidarity and Power in Contract Law*, 1985 WIS. L. REV. 565, 569.

27. In the definition offered here, contract is a promise given in the setting of socially recognized cooperation. Therefore, narrower justifications for enforcement founded on expectation or reliance interests and the like need not be considered, although they may play a decisive role in the scope society gives promissory obligation. Goetz & Scott, *supra* note 27 Intro., at 1261-62.

28. As demonstrated in the final chapter of this book, some normative theories of contract are quite selective in the precise forms of social cooperation they deem to warrant contractual obligation. These may allow fewer exceptions which Gilmore referred to as the new "formalism". G. GILMORE, *supra* note 5 Ch. 1. However, the standard treatment of contract assumes, as does present legal practice, that alienability by contract is restricted wherever

it "is reasonably designed to attain or encourage accepted social or economic ends". D. FESSLER & P. LOISEAUX, CONTRACTS: MORALITY, ECONOMICS AND THE MARKETPLACE: CASES AND MATERIALS 812 (1982). Earlier authors treated such limits to contract under the heading of "illegality", later authors generally treat it under "public policy". A. CORBIN, *supra* note 3 Ch. 1, § 1375. Most contemporary discussions assume a background of historical flux in the types of transactions that have "marched in and out of the area of contract". The early nineteenth century saw the scope of this field expand and "grow fat" with the "spoils of other fields". However, contemporary public policy developments have limited the ambit of contract, making it a residual field. Skepticism about this trend culminated in the legal realism of the 1950s. L. FRIEDMAN, *supra* note 3 Ch. 1, at 111-18, 184-85.

29. Dickens, *Surrogate Motherhood: Legal and Legislative Issues*, in GENETICS AND THE LAW 111, *supra* note 5 Intro., at 187. Walter Wadlington notes that the new reproductive technologies have the potential to serve as a catalyst for reordering family law generally. Wadlington, *Baby M: Catalyst For Family Law Reform*, 5 J. CONTEMP. HEALTH L. & POL'Y 1 (1989); Wadlington, *supra* note 21 Intro.; Wadlington, *Artificial Conception: The Challenge for Family Law*, 69 VA. L. REV. 465, 507-11 (1983) [hereinafter Wadlington, *Artificial Conception*].

30. ONTARIO COMM'N, *supra* note 6 Intro. For a less successful framework proposed by a governmental study, see the scheme of the Office of Technology Assessment, which melds "static", "private ordering", "inducement", "regulatory", and "punitive" categories borrowed eclectically from other schemes, into a loose pastiche. Its inducement and punitive categories should, for example, actually be considered modes of implementing a "regulatory" approach. OFFICE OF TECHNOLOGY ASSESSMENT, *supra* note 21 Intro., at 285-88.

31. Wadlington, Artificial Conception, *supra* note 29 Ch. 1.

32. ONTARIO COMM'N, *supra* note 6 Intro., at 1.

33. *Id.* at 105. Other governmental and professional bodies have made similar, if somewhat less schematic and often more ethically-oriented recommendations. *See, e.g.*, COMM. TO CONSIDER THE SOCIAL, ETHICAL & LEGAL ISSUES ARISING FROM IN VITRO FERTILIZATION, REPORT ON DONOR GAMETES IN IVF (1983), COUNCIL FOR SCIENCE AND SOCIETY, HUMAN PROCREATION: ETHICAL ASPECTS OF THE NEW TECHNIQUES [hereinafter DUNSTAN REP.]; ETHICS ADVISORY BOARD, *supra* note 21 Intro.; ROYAL COLLEGE OF OBSTETRICIANS & GYNECOLOGISTS, REPORT OF THE ROYAL COLLEGE OF OBSTETRICIANS & GYNECOLOGISTS ETHICS COMMITTEE ON IN VITRO FERTILISATION OR EMBRYO REPLACEMENT AND TRANSFER (1983); WALLER REP., *supra* note 21 Intro.; WARNOCK REP., *supra* note 21 Intro.; American Fertility Society, *supra*, note 21 Intro., at Supp. 1.

34. ONTARIO COMM'N, *supra* note 6 Intro., at 105-30.

35. One commentator claims that "[t]he Ontario Report is remarkably thorough and may well serve as the basis for comprehensive legislation in this area". Eaton, *supra* note 21 Intro., at 703 (1986).

36. UNIF. STATUS ACT, *supra* note 6 Intro., § 5-6, at 93-96. In its "Alternative A", this section requires the court to approve hired maternity agreements before they can be valid, closely following the recommendations of the Law Reform Commission. ONTARIO COMM'N, *supra* note 6 Intro., at 239-62.

37. ONTARIO COMM'N, *supra* note 6 Intro., at 106-7.

38. *Id.* at 106.

39. *Id.*

40. *Id.* at 107.

41. *Id.* at 107-8.

42. *Id.* at 109.

41

43. *Id.*

44. *Id.*

45. *Id.*

46. *Id.* at 110.

47. *Id.* at 108.

48. *See generally* H. CLARK, *supra* note 23 Intro., §§ 2.12 (dealing with marriage eligibility criteria related to reproductive function), 4.1-4.5 (dealing with strictures against illegitimacy).

49. *Id.* §§ 4.1-4.5.

50. ONTARIO COMM'N, *supra* note 6 Intro., at 108.

51. *Id.*

52. *Id.*

53. The Ontario Commission explicitly utilizes contract in the allocation of gametes and parental rights:

> The private ordering model would conceivably permit a gamete donor to contract for the sale of sperm or ova on condition that he or she would bear no legal relation to any child resulting from the use of such gametes . . . . [A]rtificially conceived children would be placed and named in accordance with private agreements.

Id. at 109.

54. *See* H. CLARK, *supra* note 23 Intro., §§ 19.10, 20.4. (The court may in its discretion entirely disregard any contract between natural parents allocating custody of a child.)

55. *See, e.g.*, Custody of a Minor, 378 Mass. 732, 743, 393 N.E.2d 836, 843 (1979). *See generally* E. FARNSWORTH, *supra* note 4 Ch. 1, § 5.4 (discussing the traditional unenforceability of contracts related to marriage); S. GREEN & J. LONG, MARRIAGE AND FAMILY LAW AGREEMENTS 209 (1984) (noting the traditional invalidation of agreements in which sexual relations serve as consideration).

56. *See infra* notes 236-239 Ch. 3 and accompanying text.

57. 198 U.S. 45 (1905). In striking down labour legislation governing the working hours of bakers, Mr. Justice Peckham reasoned that:

> It seems to us that the real object and purpose were simply to regulate the hours of labour between the master and his employees (all being men, *sui juris*), in a private business, not dangerous in any degree to morals or in any real and substantial degree, to the health of the employees. Under such circumstances the freedom of master and employee to contract with each other in relation to their employment, and in defining the same, cannot be prohibited or interfered with, without violating the Federal Constitution.

Id. at 64; *see also* Adkins v. Children's Hospital, 261 U.S. 525 (1923) (fifth amendment protects liberty of contract for labour); Coppage v. Kansas, 236 U.S. 1 (1915) (legislation relating to labour contract violates liberty of contract); Adair v. United States, 208 U.S. 161 (1908) (legislation restricting employer position in labour contracts is an unjustifiable interference in the liberty of contract); Allgeyer v. Louisiana, 165 U.S. 578 (1897) (states cannot abridge the right of citizens to contract outside its boundaries).

58. ONTARIO COMM'N, *supra* note 6 Intro., at 110-11.

59. *Id.* at 110

60. *Id.*

61. *Id.* at 133.

62. *Id.* at 135.

63. *Id.* at 133.

64. *Id.*

65. *See* Adoption of a Minor, 386 Mass. 741, 438 N.E.2d 38 (1982); Child & Family Services Act, Part VII, ONT. REV. STAT. ch. C.11, §136 (1990); ONTARIO COMM'N, *supra* note 6 Intro., at 111.

66. ONTARIO COMM'N, *supra* note 6 Intro., at 113.

67. *Id.* at 111-12.

68. *Id.* at 113.

69. *Id.* at 115. Minimal regulation might be employed if artificially conceived children are viewed as having a presumptively closer bond with intended parents, than do children with prospective adoptive parents. *Id.* at 116-17.

70. *Id.* at 233-36. *See generally* Knoppers & Sloss, *Recent Developments: Legislative Reforms in Reproductive Technology*, 18 OTTAWA L. REV. 663, 696-718 (1986) (discussing the "judicialization of pregnancy").

71. ONTARIO COMM'N, *supra* note 6 Intro., at 234-35, 249-55.

72. Brest, *State Action and Liberal Theory: A Casenote on Flagg Brothers v. Brooks*, 130 U. PA. L. REV. 1296, 1323 (1982) (contrasting natural rights and positivist theories of privacy with state action).

73. ONTARIO COMM'N, *supra* note 6 Intro., at 106-7, 110-11.

74. *Id.* at 107, 118-30.

75. *Id.* at 119.

76. *Id.*

77. *Id.* at 120.

78. *Id.* at 120, 122.

79. *Id.* at 121-22.

80. *Id.*

81. *See, e.g.*, UNIF. PARENTAGE ACT § 5, 9B U.L.A. 301 (1987). *See generally infra* text accompanying notes 149-88 Ch 2.

82. The influence of libertarian principles expands where a public or governmental consensus on the relevant issues is lacking, even within a framework generally reliant on state conferral. ONTARIO COMM'N, *supra* note 6 Intro., at 119.

83. *Id.* at 107.

84. *Compare* P. DEVLIN, THE ENFORCEMENT OF MORALS (1968) (so long as it is based on deeply held public standards, the law can enter any private realm of morality) *with* H.L.A. HART, LAW, LIBERTY AND MORALITY (1963) (rejecting Devlin since there is no necessary relationship between the preservation of society and the enforcement of society's morality). Whether or not it is considered persuasive on a given issue, the basis for governmental regulation of sexual conduct is a general concern for public morality. *See* Bowers v. Hardwick, 478 U.S. 186 (1986). By contrast, the purpose of governmental regulation of the new reproductive technologies would be to regulate the dominion of one person over another who is emerging and unemancipated, as well as the formation of the basic unit of social life: the parent-child relationship.

85. Wadlington, *Artificial Conception*, *supra* note 29 Ch. 1, at 496-7.

86. *Id.*

87. *Id.* at 496-503.

88. *Id.* at 496.

89. *Id.*

90. "Strict adherence to this approach might eliminate some existing confusion about paternal status". *Id.*

91. *Id.*

92. *Id.*

93. *See infra* text accompanying notes 132-42 Ch. 2 (discussion of adoption); *infra* text accompanying notes 124-5 Ch. 2 (discussion of step-parent adoption).

94. Dickens, *supra* note 29 Ch. 1, at 193.

95. *Id.*

96. Wadlington, *Artificial Conception, supra* note 29 Ch. 1, at 496; Dickens, *supra* note 29 Ch. 1, at 193.

97. Wadlington, *Artificial Conception, supra* note 29 Ch. 1, at 496; Dickens, *supra* note 58 Ch. 1, at 193.

98. Wadlington, *Artificial Conception, supra* note 29 Ch. 1, at 496.

99. *Id.*; Dickens, *supra* note 29 Ch. 1, at 193 (possible penalties include denial of inheritance rights in the estates of members of the child's social family).

100. To some degree family law already embodies these rules. *See infra* text accompanying notes 120-23 Ch. 2. The more informal the social cooperation that society chooses to tolerate in conjunction with procreation, the greater the care required in formulating principles for resolving conflicts among proliferating claimants to parental rights.

101. Society, to some extent, would have to tolerate more ad hoc adjudication of conflicts, based on some general standard such as the "best interests of the child". Society also would have to tolerate complex intimate or domestic relationships among adults and children, leading to an increase in the number and kind of conflicts with a diminishing ability on the part of courts to provide "clean" solutions.

102. The formal imposition of penalties is only one kind of legal penalty. Judge Calabresi has stressed the punitive impact of the many indirect burdens allocated by the law. G. CALABRESI, THE COSTS OF ACCIDENTS 111-13 (1970).

103. *See generally* H. KRAUSE, ILLEGITIMACY: LAW AND SOCIAL POLICY (1971) (reviewing the distinctions in legal status between legitimate and illegitimate children); Hafen, *The Constitutional Status of Marriage, Kinship, and Sexual Privacy—Balancing the Individual and Social Interests*, 81 MICH. L. REV. 463, 494 n.135, 495-96 (1983) (describing the dilemma of providing effective inducements to adults to structure child rearing units in the interests of children while not unduly penalizing individual children).

104. At least twenty-four states have such laws. *See* Note, *supra* note 20 Intro., at 8 n.34.

105. This was the source of much sympathy for Mary Beth Whitehead. *See, e.g.*, Pollitt, *Contracts and Apple Pie: The Strange Case of Baby M*, THE NATION, May 23, 1987, at 667 (criticizing the trial court's decision to terminate the parental rights of a biological mother).

106. They might, for example, be charged with "kidnapping" for attempting to assert their natural parental relationship. *See* H. CLARK, *supra* note 23 Intro., §§ 11.2, 12.4.

107. *See, e.g.*, Robertson, *supra* note 8 Intro., at 1002-3.

108. These frustrations include conflicts with those who wish to assert natural parental rights notwithstanding prior assent to a contrary contractual understanding, *e.g.*, *In re* Baby M, 109 N.J. 396, 411-17, 537 A.2d 1227, 1235-37 (1988), and children who want a relationship with their biological parents. *See* Beyer & Mlyniec, *Lifelines to Biological Parents: Their Effect on Termination of Parental Rights and Permanence*, 20 FAM. L.Q. 233 (1986).

109. Wadlington, *Artificial Conception, supra* note 29 Ch. 1, at 496.

110. *Id.*

111. *Id.* at 496-7.

112. Dickens, *supra* note 29 Ch. 1, at 193-4.

113. Wadlington, *Artificial Conception, supra* note 29 Ch. 1, at 496.

114. *Id.* at 497, 503-12; ONTARIO COMM'N, *supra* note 6 Intro., at 110-17.

115. Wadlington, *Artificial Conception, supra* note 29 Ch. 1, at 497.

116. *Id.* at 506.

117. *Id.*

118. *Id.* at 507.

119. Dickens, *supra* note 29 Ch. 1, at 194-6.

120. *Id.* at 195.

121. FLA. STAT. ANN. § 873.05 (West 1994).

122. *E.g.*, UNIF. PARENTAGE ACT, *supra* note 81 Ch. 1.

123. Wadlington, *Artificial Conception, supra* note 29 Ch. 1, at 507-12. *See generally* Knoppers & Sloss, *supra* note 70 Ch. 1, at 667 (the institutionalization of reproductive technology requires the elaboration of an administrative and regulatory framework).

124. It is generally assumed that even a model relying heavily on contract would entail regulation aimed at limiting the number of offspring per donor and recipient, screening for diseases, and keeping records. *See* OFFICE OF TECHNOLOGY ASSESSMENT, *supra* note 21 Intro., at 244.

125. *See supra* note 84 Ch. 1. For an example of recent Supreme Court jurisprudence on the subject, see Bowers v. Hardwick, 478 U.S. 186 (upholding Georgia's criminal sodomy law as applied to homosexual activity), *reh'g denied*, 478 U.S. 1039 (1986).

126. ONTARIO COMM'N, *supra* note 6 Intro., at 107; *cf.* Knoppers & Sloss, *supra* note 70 Ch. 1, at 667 (examining mechanisms to regulate reproductive industry without impinging on personal choice).

The present inquiry is distinct from the issue of regulating the relationship between a couple and a third party which does not grant the third party any rights in the embryo, foetus, or child but does grant custody of the embryo during fertilization and prior to implantation, as in arrangements with commercial sperm and embryo banks. *See* ONTARIO COMM'N, *supra* note 6 Intro., Recommendation 17, at 277. A further concern beyond the scope of the present inquiry is regulation of technologically assisted reproduction to advance public health. *See* Knoppers & Sloss, *supra* note 70 Ch. 1, at 685 (limiting use to minimize genetic disorders caused by procreation within prohibited degrees of consanguinity); Vetri, *Reproductive Technologies and United States Law*, 37 INT'L & COMP. L.Q. 505. 520 (1988) (discussing donor selection, maximum use of donor sperm, and record keeping; *see also infra* text accompanying note 12 Ch. 3.

127. This question has been raised, in a more general way, in recent proposals that prospective parents be subject to a licensing requirement. *See* Mangel, *Licensing Parents: How Feasible?*, 2 FAM. L.Q. 17 (1988). Within the scope of the new reproductive technologies, the right to acquire "resources" contributing to a successful human gestation must be distinguished analytically from the simple right to initiate procreation with the resources the couple has in its given pool of such resources. *See* S. GREEN & J. LONG, *supra* note 55 Ch. 1, at 58. Transactions involving procreative resources, moreover, require management by third parties. These tertiary relationships generate their own legal problems outside the scope of the present study, which touch on contract and property issues. *See* OFFICE OF TECHNOLOGY ASSESSMENT, *supra* note 21 Intro., at 24. Such problems call for "regulation" and are often discussed in the context of a general "regulatory model" for responding to the new reproduction, e.g., Robertson, *supra* note 8 Intro., at 987-1000, but they are essentially unrelated to the three fundamental questions concerning basic human relationships under consideration here.

128. To say that the distinction between initiating procreation and asserting a parent child relationship is analytically necessary is not to say that it ultimately can or should be validated morally or legally. Hired maternity arrangements have been criticized because they "are designed to separate in the mind of the surrogate mother the decision to create a child from the decision to have and raise that child". Krimmel, *The Case Against Surrogate Parenting*, HASTINGS CENTER REP., Oct. 1983, 35 at 35, *reprinted in* BIO-ETHICS 658 (R. Edwards &

G. Graber eds. 1988); *see also* Robertson, *supra* note 9 Intro., at 411-13 (distinguishing the physical ability to procreate from the mental capacity to raise a child).

129. The question is similar to traditional disputes over child custody, with the significant exception that competing claimants are at greater "arms' length", never having shared in a marriage or even coital relationship.

130. *See* H. KRAUSE, *supra* note 103 Ch. 1, at 10 (defining illegitimate offspring as those children born outside of marriage, including offspring resulting from adulterous unions); *infra* text accompanying notes 21-2, 78-9, 108-31 Ch. 2.

131. H. KRAUSE, *supra* note 103 Ch. 1. The Supreme Court of the United States has long recognized procreation as an individual right. Skinner v. Oklahoma, 316 U.S. 535, 541 (1942) (prohibiting sterilization of prisoners).

132. Distinctions can be drawn among those approaches that prohibit transfers, involve free present gifts and exchanges, result in governmental coercion on behalf of individuals, and bring about governmental coercion to further governmental objectives.

133. *See* Davis v. Davis, 842 S.W. 2d 588 (Tenn. 1992), *cert. denied*, 113 S. Ct. 1259 (1992); *see also* Capron, *Alternative Birth Technologies: Legal Challenges*, 20 U.C. DAVIS L. REV. 679, 687-89 (1987) (discussing unanswered questions surrounding the legal and moral status of extracorporeal gametes and embryos).

134. See Hollinger, *supra* note 6 Intro., at 922 (1985) (discussing the feelings of sperm donors toward their unknown children); Eisenman, *Fathers, Biological and Anonymous, and Other Legal Strangers: Determination of Parentage and Artificial Insemination of Donor Under Ohio Law*, 45 OHIO ST. L.J. 383, 396 (1984) (noting that a donor father may establish a legal parent child relationship under Ohio law, if the donor learns the child's identity).

135. *See* Eisenman, *supra* note 134 Ch. 1, at 387; *see, e.g.*, Alma Soc'y, Inc. v. Mellon, 601 F.2d 1225 (2d Cir.), *cert. denied*, 444 U.S. 995 (1979) (suit brought by adult adoptees challenging New York statute sealing adoption records except on showing of good cause); J. TRISELIOTIS, IN SEARCH OF ORIGINS: THE EXPERIENCES OF ADOPTED PEOPLE (1973); Klibanoff, *Genealogical Information in Adoption: The Adoptee's Quest and the Law*, 11 FAM. L.Q. 185 (1977).

136. This was not true in slavery, where the child was disposable as a chattel of the mother's owner. Means, *supra* note 16 Intro., at 447-49.

137. For example, under section 5 of the Uniform Parentage Act: "the donor of semen ... is treated in law as if he were not the natural father of a child thereby conceived". UNIF. PARENTAGE ACT, *supra* note 81 Ch. 1, at 301.

138. Reproduction was something undertaken by couples. Now that there may be a third party involved, the law must resolve a more complex and potentially conflicting set of relationships. *Surrogate Mother Carries Child for Genetic Parents*, Wall St. J., Aug. 28, 1985, at 25, col. 6.

139. This status of "psychological parent" is determined strictly by the child's sense of relationship. J GOLDSTEIN, A. FREUD, & A. SOLNIT, BEYOND THE BEST INTERESTS OF THE CHILD 97-101 (1979) [hereinafter BEYOND THE BEST INTERESTS].

140. "[I]t is now possible for a child to have five parents: a genetic and rearing father and a genetic, gestational, and rearing mother". Annas & Elias, *supra* note 12 Intro., at 148. Another commentator has suggested that twelve combinations of "parental" cooperation among a number of adults are possible. W. O'DONNELL & D. JONES, THE LAW OF MARRIAGE AND MARITAL ALTERNATIVES 236 (1982); *see also* C. GROBSTEIN, *supra* note 2 Intro., at 43 (discussing technologies available that could result in offspring with four distinct genetic parents).

141. The discrete occurrence of gestational motherhood occurs in ovum donation and embryo transfer. The first child successfully gestated after embryo transfer was born on February 3, 1984 in Los Angeles. Shapiro, *supra* note 3 Intro., at 51. The gestational mother may or may not also be the intended mother. W. O'DONNELL & D. JONES, *supra* note 140 Ch. 1, at 236.

142. This role has been called "social parent", Knoppers & Sloss, *supra* note 70 Ch. 1, at 707, or "psychological parent", W. O'Donnell & D. Jones, *supra* note 140 Ch. 1, at 236.

143. *See, e.g.*, *In re* Baby M, 109 N.J. 396, 537 A.2d 1227 (1988).

144. The person who has the original intent to create a child would be deemed to have a potentially alienable right to rear the child. The ground for recognizing the intending party's claim could be understood in personal terms of donation to the resulting child or as a proprietary interest, like filing a patent. In either case, a claim could be asserted by filing a genetic description of the intended child in advance of conception. *See* Note, *Redefining Mother*, *supra* note 21 Intro., at 189.

145. This claim resembles claims under existing adoption law, although the adoptive parent may also have become the child's psychological parent by the time of conferral.

146. State conferral becomes a final ground of justification under positivism. Brest, *supra* note 72 Ch. 1, at 1297. The justification may in turn make reference to some value beyond the power of law, such as the shared value attributed to survival. H.L.A. HART, THE CONCEPT OF LAW 186-89 (1961). Such a value might be described in terms of welfare. However, state conferral, rather than welfare, is the salient value underlying this model, since the state decision validates both the object, what counts as welfare, and the means, allocation of parental rights.

147. The value of individual autonomy tends to be the guiding value of political liberalism, and, thus, it appears especially plausible as a basis for legal reform to those whose thinking has been shaped by liberal premises. For the classic defence of the liberal position, see J.S. MILL, ON LIBERTY 66-83 (R.B. McCallum ed. 1946). A legal proposal would not fall within the individual autonomy model by incidentally advancing individual autonomy in a general sense, but by consciously applying legal mechanisms for the purpose of securing individual autonomy. This is the value underlying the role of contract in Professor Wadlington's private ordering option.

148. More particularly, natural endowment refers to the relationships that arise from the voluntary pooling of procreative resources or from natural bonds of commitment formed through care and nurturance. Honouring this value impedes the application of the legal mechanism to further the choices of either the state or individuals. A philosophical justification for this value can be found in natural law theory. *See* J. FINNIS, NATURAL LAW AND NATURAL RIGHTS 225 (1980). However, it also can be derived as a subordinate element in liberal theory. *See* J. RAWLS, A THEORY OF JUSTICE (1972) (individual endowments of intellect and other gifts may be employed to advance individual life plans, but social institutions need only accept this arbitrary distribution to the extent it benefits all).

149. A system both based on individual autonomy and featuring inalienability is imaginable. Knoppers & Sloss, *supra* note 70 Ch. 1, at 707. However, when contract is given further content in relation to individual autonomy it fosters a particular vision of social cooperation, one which in fact coincides more closely with the classical bargain theory of contracts.

150. Obviously, positing this development raises theoretical questions about the role and nature of the state, which are beyond the scope of the present discussion. One point of departure for consideration of such questions would be Nozick's defence of the minimal state. *See* R. NOZICK, ANARCHY, STATE, AND UTOPIA (1974) (the minimal state views people as individuals with inviolate rights rather than as resources to achieve some notion of social utility).

151. On the perils of the bureaucratizing tendencies of modern society, see P. BERGER, TO EMPOWER PEOPLE: THE ROLE OF MEDIATING STRUCTURES IN PUBLIC POLICY (1977); P. BERGER & H. KELLNER, SOCIOLOGY REINTERPRETED: AN ESSAY ON METHOD AND VOCATION (1981).

152. Huxley describes a society in which the central government bureaucracy "decants" children. A. HUXLEY, *supra* note 12 Intro., at 1-32.

153. Plato prescribes state control of reproduction among the Guardian class in Book IV of *The Republic*:

> How are we to get the best results? You must tell me, Glaucon, because I see you keep sporting dogs and a great many game birds at your house; and there is something about their mating and breeding that you must have noticed.
>
> . . . .
>
> . . . Are you not careful to breed from the best so far as you can?
>
> . . . .
>
> It follows from what we have just said that . . . there should be as many unions of the best of both sexes, and as few of the inferior, as possible, and that only the offspring of the better unions should be kept . . . .
>
> . . . .
>
> We must, then, institute certain festivals at which we shall bring together the brides and the bridegrooms . . . .
>
> . . . .
>
> Moreover, young men who acquit themselves well in war and other duties, should be given, among other rewards and privileges, more liberal opportunities to sleep with a wife, for the further purpose that, with good excuse, as many as possible of the children may be begotten of such fathers.
>
> . . . .
>
> As soon as children are born, they will be taken in charge by officers appointed for the purpose . . . . The children of the better parents they will carry to the crèche to be reared in the care of nurses living apart in a certain quarter of the city. . . .

PLATO, THE REPUBLIC 158-60 (B. Jowett trans. 1945).

154. For more current expositions of the policies of eugenics, see EUGENICS: THEN AND NOW (C. Bajem ed.) (Benchmark Papers in Genetics No. 5, 1976); M. HALLER, EUGENICS: HEREDITARIAN ATTITUDES IN AMERICAN THOUGHT (1963). Eugenics as a term was coined in 1883 by Charles Darwin's cousin, Sir Francis Galton. *See* Allen, *Feats to Concoct the Flawless Being*, INSIGHT, July 11, 1988, at 8.

155. *See, e.g.*, Vatican Congregation, *supra* note 21 Intro., at 9 (cautionary conclusions of the Vatican Instruction on Reproductive Technologies).

156. A strong theme in the feminist response to the new reproductive technologies has been the apprehension that men will use the technologies to subordinate women in a new political order in which "biology" once again defines destiny. Margaret Atwood's novel, *The Handmaid's Tale*, is a fictional example. In Atwood's Republic of Gilead, after a fertility crisis, the state assumed responsibility for procreation, a new puritanism was introduced, and women were classified as wives, procreative concubines, and mistresses. M. ATWOOD, THE HANDMAID'S TALE (1985). Gena Corea's nonfiction mirrors the same concern, if not against the same apocalyptical background. G. COREA, THE MOTHER MACHINE: REPRODUCTIVE TECHNOLOGIES FROM ARTIFICIAL INSEMINATION TO ARTIFICIAL WOMBS (1985); Corea, *The Reproductive Brothel*, in MAN-MADE WOMEN: HOW NEW REPRODUCTIVE TECHNOLOGIES AFFECT WOMEN 38 (1987). A recurrent fear is expressed that the technologies may become a masculine tool harmful to women. M. WARREN, GENDERCIDE: THE IMPLICATIONS OF SEX

SELECTION (1985); Wikler, *Society's Response to the New Reproductive Technologies: The Feminist Perspective*, 59 S. CAL. L. REV. 1043, 1045-46 (1986). For a discussion of overlapping bioethical concerns, see L. KASS, *supra* note 12 Intro., at 61.

157. *See*, ONTARIO COMM'N, *supra* note 6 Intro.; Wadlington, *Artificial Conception*, *supra* note 29 Ch. 1.

158. In a given case, it would have to be carefully discerned whether the law or legal proposal actually rests on the value of state conferral, as opposed to those of individual autonomy or natural endowment, with state regulation as a constraint to protect the welfare of children parens patriae. Mangel, *supra* note 127 Ch. 1; *see also infra* notes 26-32 Ch. 3 and accompanying text.

159. LaFollette, *Licensing Parents*, 9 PHIL. & PUB. AFF. 182 (1980); *see infra* text accompanying notes 359-403 Ch. 2 (discussing Uniform Children of Assisted Conception Act). Contract in this context, would be valued for its usefulness in advancing goals elected by the state.

160. This is proposed in recent model legislation. *See, e.g.*, UNIF. STATUS ACT, *supra* note 6 Intro., § 5; *see also infra* text accompanying notes 359-403 Ch. 2.

161. *See infra* text accompanying notes 21-24 Ch. 3.

162. *Cf.* UNIF. STATUS ACT, *supra* note 6 Intro., at 87-8 (emphasizing the urgent need for a legal framework defining the rights and status of children of technologically assisted conception).

163. Respecting AID, see *infra* text accompanying notes 149-88 Ch. 2; regarding hired maternity, see *infra* text accompanying notes 189-358 Ch. 2.

164. This concept of intention only superficially resembles that of "private ordering" in the Ontario Law Reform Commission's framework. Here, individual intention represents a value justifying a given legal ordering. In the Law Reform Commission framework, it is no more than one goal, among others, of state action. *See supra* notes 41-57 Ch. 1 and accompanying text. As the concept is used here, it is closer to Wadlington's idea of "private ordering", since in most applications the vindication of the value would be pursued through the enforcement of contract.

165. For a discussion of the need for a minimum level of mental capacity in order to qualify for procreative rights, see Robertson, *supra* note 9 Intro., at 411-13.

It has been argued that individual choices in reproduction should be independent of any claim or consent of other adult procreative contributors. In this view, parental responsibility would flow strictly from an abstract choice to assume a parental role. The advent of reproductive technology will force a larger reform within family law along these lines and pursuant to values which are thought to have their own appeal independent of the exigencies of these particular technological arrangements. *See* Knoppers & Sloss, *supra* note 70 Ch. 1, at 707.

166. Organizing the discussion around the incidence of infertility implies that the framework for analysis is identifying, fostering, and regulating a market. Individual autonomy in choosing whether and how to satisfy private preferences is the implicit coordinating value. Some commentators make this value explicit. *E.g.*, Landes & Posner, *The Economics of the Baby Shortage*, 7 J. LEGAL STUD. 323 (1978).

167. Posner, *supra* note 7 Intro., at 23-30 (using a free-market analysis to support the enforceability of hired maternity contracts).

168. "Baby selling may seem logically and inevitably to lead to baby breeding, for any market will generate incentives to improve the product as well as to optimize the price and quantity of the current quality level of the product". Landes & Posner, *supra* note 166 Ch. 1, at 345 (footnote omitted). The market that would take hold under this scheme could be used for private concerted efforts aimed at the eugenic transformation of society, such as the

Repository for Germinal Choice in Escondido, California. *See The Sperm-Bank Scandal*, NEWSWEEK, July 26, 1982, at 24 (reporting on a sperm bank where donors are Nobel prize winners). Arguments have been made that the culling of embryos in the quest for the "perfect" child may be justified as a fundamental constitutional right. *See* Robertson, *supra* note 9 Intro., at 431-2.

169. Eventually, reproductive technologies will be developed which allow "genetic diagnosis and manipulation techniques that could be applied to the general population as well as big business for those involved in banking or storage techniques and furthermore, big business for those doing research on human genetic material in the absence of the implementation of . . . proposed reforms . . . ". Knoppers and Sloss, *supra* note 70 Ch. 1, at 718; *see also* Powledge, *Commerce and the Future of Gene Transfer*, in GENETICS AND THE LAW III, *supra* note 5 Intro., at 75, 79 (noting the Seed brothers' ambitions to genetically engineer embryos for profit); Allen, *supra* note 154 Ch. 1, at 8 (describing the practice of Dr. Mark Geier who strains spermatozoa to ensure female offspring at a ratio of 24/25). Further commercial involvement in non-reallocative human reproduction can be expected when embryo biopsy, the analysis of particular genes within individual embryos, is transferred to the medical establishment, an event which is likely to occur "within the next decade . . . ". *Embryo Biopsy May Be Standard Procedure Within Next Decade*, DRUG RESEARCH REP., THE BLUE SHEET, July 20, 1988, at 8, 8 [hereinafter *Embryo Biopsy*].

170. This use is currently forbidden. National Organ Transplant Act, 42 U.S.C. § 274e (1988). But, one theme of academic discussion appears to support it. *See* Robertson, *Fetal Tissue Transplants*, 66 WASH. U.L.Q. 443 (1988) (arguing that conceptions planned to obtain fetal tissue for transplants are defensible ethically and legally); Terry, *Politics and Privacy: Refining the Ethical and Legal Issues in Fetal Tissue Transplantation*, 66 WASH. U.L.Q. 523 (1988) (arguing that fetal tissue transplant issues have been subsumed unnecessarily under the abortion debate); Note, *Retailing Human Organs under the Uniform Commercial Code*, 16 J. MARSHALL L. REV. 393 (1983) (proposing that the shortage of organs available for transplant could be alleviated by a U.C.C.-governed market). Partial ectogenesis might even be undertaken for body parts. *See* C. GROBSTEIN, *supra* note 2 Intro., at 46-48. It has already been reported, for instance, that a couple conceived a child for use for sibling bone marrow transplant. *A Healthy "Bone Marrow Baby" Is Born to Ayalas*, L.A. Times, April 6, 1990, at B1, col. 2. Taking another step, such a project would entail the abortion of the child and the harvesting of its marrow for the use of another. If the implicated transactions were permitted, a market for human organs would follow. *E.g.*, *Man Desperate for Funds: Eye for Sale at $35,000*, L.A. Times, Feb. 1, 1975, § 2, at 1, col. 3; *100 Answer Man's Ad for New Kidney*, L.A. Times, Sept. 12, 1974, at 4, col. 2.

171. Posner, *The Regulation of the Market in Adoptions*, 67 B.U.L. Rev. 59 (1987).

172. *See, e.g.*, *id*. Compare Ulen, *The Efficiency of Specific Performance: Toward a Unified Theory of Contract Remedies*, 83 MICH. L. REV. 341, 365 (1984) (arguing that specific performance can be an effective remedy if the parties know it will be used) *with* Yorio, *In Defense of Money Damages for Breach of Contract*, 82 COLUM. L. REV. 1365, 1385-86 (1982) (arguing that money damages are a better remedy than specific performance because they are more flexible and efficient).

173. Feminist literature expresses concern that the generally superior economic power possessed by men will cause the free operation of market forces in the area of reproductive exchanges to lead to the subordination of women. See G. COREA, *supra* note 156 Ch. 1, at 2; Wikler, *supra* note 156 Ch. 1 , at 1044.

174. This was the thrust of the ABA Section on Family Law's proposed Model Surrogacy Act. *Model Surrogacy Act*, *supra* note 5 Intro. The Model Act was rejected by the ABA House of Delegates. *Infra* note 359 Ch. 2.

175. There is generally "a strong tendency to disallow payment for profit", but profit is often distinguished from expenses, lost income, and lost opportunities. and even compensation for pain and suffering. *See* Knoppers & Sloss, *supra* note 70 Ch. 1, at 715.

176. Extracorporeal embryos generate their own unique problems of legal ordering, quite apart from any attempt at their reallocation. Andrews, *The Legal Status of the Embryo*, 32 LOY. L. REV. 357, 396 (1986); Willis, *Quickening Debate over Life on Ice: Do Orphaned Embryos Have Legal Rights*, TIME, July 2, 1984, at 68.

177. Such a vision might be feminist if women's consumer preferences are made the norm. Andrews, *Surrogate Motherhood: The Challenge for Feminists*, 16 LAW, MED. & HEALTH CARE 72, 77 (1988). But, Wikler would seem to be correct in noting that although the feminist and consumer approaches "voice similar concerns", each ultimately "has a different, though overlapping, constituency, and ultimately supports a different set of policies". Wikler, *supra* note 156 Ch. 1, at 1054.

178. Voidability would further rely on informal dispute resolution, rather than judicial enforcement. Restrictions might be placed on initiation or procreation except where at least one of the intending rearing parents is also a biological parent.

179. "[F]iliation, the establishment of a parent-child relationship as recognized under law, could in *all* births be voluntary, intentional and consensual and legally sanctioned rather than legally imposed or presumed. Parents could then, in the context of reproductive technologies, be those individuals who together or singly choose to contribute gametes for the creation of an embryo so as to conceive and raise a child." Knoppers & Sloss, *supra* note 70 Ch. 1, at 707 (emphasis in original).

180. *See, e.g., Model Surrogacy Act, supra* note 5 Intro.

181. *Id.*

182. A bureaucratizing trend towards the "medicalization of reproduction" has been noted All committee and agency reports on hired maternity call for psychological testing and counselling of applicants. Knoppers & Sloss, *supra* note 70 Ch. 1, at 679.

183. *See infra* notes 211-226 Ch. 3 and accompanying text.

184. Contracts with the technological facilitators of conception and gestation must be distinguished from those attempting to reallocate parental rights or procreative resources. *See* Shapiro, *supra* note 3 Intro., at 44 n.43 (describing terms of agreement between patron and world's largest sperm bank).

185. *See* BEYOND THE BEST INTERESTS, *supra* note 139 Ch. 1, at 5-26 (1973) (discussing child placement based on a biological and psychological relationship). The recognition of rights may be contingent on the prior termination of the natural parents' rights. Smith v. Organization of Foster Families for Equality and Reform, 431 U.S. 816 (1977) (reversing a lower court holding that foster parents have a right to a hearing before a child is placed with its natural parents or in another foster home). Under the traditional family model, only legally sanctioned expectations about relationships with natural offspring are encouraged. *See* Hafen, *supra* note 103 Ch. 1, at 504 (kinship and marriage create a "justifiable expectation" of performance that gives them a unique place in laws relating to social relationships).

186. *See* Rice, *A.I.D.— An Heir of Controversy*, 34 NOTRE DAME L. REV. 510 (1959) (recommending the criminalization of AID).

187. The family groupings arising from reallocations of procreative resources and parental rights under the new reproductive technologies are distinguishable from "blended" families arising after divorce or death. The latter are adaptations to unplanned and unwished challenges. The former are created as an intended and desired effect. Krimmel, *supra* note 128 Ch. 1, at 35-37. The Oregon AID law, OR. REV. STAT. §§ 109.239, 109.243 (1989), provides, for example, that the donor has no legal right, obligation, or interest with respect to the child. Consequently, a contract to acknowledge paternity and permit the biological

father to adopt in the context of hired maternity is not enforceable. Oregon Attorney General's Opinion, 1989 Ore. AG LEXIS 26 (April 19, 1989).

188. The existing structure of American family law has been said to be built around ties of "blood, marriage and adoption". Hafen, *supra* note 103 Ch. 1, at 493. The fact that state regulation is heavily implicated in the strong type of natural endowment should not be mistaken for similarity to the state conferral model. The state merely encourages the formation and public validation of "natural" reproductive and rearing units and discourages any sort of alienation of procreative resources. This action preserves the significance of public validation as decisive in resolving conflicts with third parties. To that extent, schemes for solemnization of marriage and legitimization of births can be compared to schemes for the "perfection" of contingent property interests. *See, e.g.*, U.C.C. § 9 (1989).

The traditional family in American law and society is composed of a monogamous pair which both reproduces and rears its children. Reynolds v. United States, 98 U.S. 145 (1878) (determining that a federal law criminalizing bigamy in American territories was constitutional). In other cultures, the family is polygamous or, rarely, polyandrous. Such families fall within the strong type of the natural endowment model, as it is set forth here, for the societies in which they occur, as long as the multiple individuals participating in the family's reproductive projects also continue as part of the family as a formal social unit, during rearing.

189. *See* M. GLENDON, THE TRANSFORMATION OF FAMILY LAW: STATE, LAW, AND FAMILY IN THE UNITED STATES AND WESTERN EUROPE 85-110 (1989); W. WEYRAUCH & S. KATZ, AMERICAN FAMILY LAW IN TRANSITION (1983).

190. *See generally* Note, *Developing a Concept of the Modern "Family": A Proposed Uniform Surrogate Parenthood Act*, 73 GEO. L. REV. 1283 (1985) (discussing obstacles to enforcement). The boundary between this moderate form of the natural endowment model and that of individual autonomy is defined by the scope given to state coercion in the form of enforcement. However, the absence of some control on unenforceable monetary exchanges would move society implicitly towards the alternative individual autonomy model. Quite apart from legal enforcement of contract promises, *de presenti* monetary exchanges in the area of procreation, themselves, are widely seen as generating moral issues. Knoppers & Sloss, *supra* note 70 Ch. 1, at 681. "Sperm donors have [typically] received from twenty to seventy dollars for each donation. Payment has been deemed compensation for lost time, transportation, costs, and inconvenience. It has not been seen as a direct payment for the gametes". *Id.* at 683 (footnote omitted). The payment of fees, as opposed to expenses, is prohibited in adoption. *E.g.*, OR. REV. STAT. § 109.311(2) (1989).

According to some, the law has moved "toward a definition of the family which is not necessarily related to genetic ancestry". Knoppers & Sloss, *supra* note 70 Ch. 1, at 690. Even if this trend is true, one alternative to genetic contribution exists as a basis for parental rights within the natural endowment model: nurturance. Under existing law, even where provision is made for waiver of parental rights by biological parents the continuing recognition of a residual parental relationship arising from genetic contribution remains a separate issue for some. The frequently proposed requirement that permanent records of genetic parentage be maintained is just one example. At present, this requirement has been enacted in Sweden. Knoppers & Sloss, *supra* note 70 Ch. 1, at 696.

191. *See* Smith, *Wombs For Rent, Selves for Sale?*, 4 J. CONTEMP. HEALTH L. & POL'Y 23, 26 (1988) (arguing altruistic motives in some hired maternity arrangements sufficient to preclude a ban on such arrangements altogether).

192. This "middle-ground alternative" requires proving paternity and showing by clear and convincing evidence that custody is in the child's best interest. *See generally* NEW YORK STATE TASK FORCE ON LIFE & THE LAW, SURROGATE PARENTING: ANALYSIS & RECOMMENDATIONS FOR PUBLIC POLICY 137 (1988) [hereinafter NEW YORK STATE TASK FORCE] (proposing an evidentiary standard of clear and convincing evidence in addition to the substantive standard of the child's best interests); Clark, *New Wine in Old Skins: Using Paternity Settlements to Facilitate Surrogate Motherhood*, 25 J. FAM. L.Q. 483 (1986-87) (proposing paternity suit settlements in which the child's best interests are equal to those of the parents).

193. Existing rules defining paternity and step-parent adoptions provide an adequate basis for ordering conflicts that may arise. NEW YORK STATE TASK FORCE, *supra* note 192 Ch. 1, at 42-44, 234. Certain recent trends in American social organization and American law appear to sacrifice stability of child rearing for the sake of greater autonomy for the individual adult. It is generally recognized, however, that at some point, rules of static ordering must enter for the sake of securing the best interests of children. *See, e.g.*, Hafen, *supra* note 103 Ch. 1, at 544. One argument is that, in conflicts generated by the new reproductive technologies, the mother's bond with the child at birth should prevail in determining rearing rights, with her husband being legally entitled to step-parent adoption, terminating the sperm donor's rights. Another argument is that the consummation of voluntary contemporaneous exchanges can be given legal validation through paternity suit settlements. *See generally* Clark, *supra* note 192 Ch. 1. If new arrangements for reproduction are recognized on this de facto basis, without requiring the intervention of legally enforced expectations grounded in individual autonomy or state conferral, it is, perhaps, not unfair to treat them as variants on the "blended family". *See* Erickson, *The Feminist Dilemma over Unwed Parents' Custody Rights. The Mother's Rights Must Take Priority*, 2 LAW & INEQUALITY: J. THEORY & PRAC. 447 (1984) (arguing that mothers' rights should be paramount in custody decisions); Robertson, *Surrogate Motherhood: Not So Novel After All*, HASTINGS CENTER REP. Oct. 1983, at 3, 4, reprinted in BIO-ETHICS, *supra* note 128 Ch. 1, at 645-57 (stating that "what matters is not *whether* but *how*" custody matters are settled); Bartlett, *Custody Preference Should Go to Mother*, N.J.L.J., Feb. 18, 1988, at 29, col. 3 (advocating custody rules similar to those for step-parent adoption); Palmer, *No Rights For Sperm Donors*, N.J.L.J., Feb. 18, 1988, at 29, col. 1 (advocating basing custody decisions on the nurturing bond).

194. Because it entails positing a legal right in open conflict with an existing nurturing relationship, gestation, hired maternity is a less ambiguous departure from the natural endowment model than is AID. For this reason, most studies simply "dismiss . . . [hired maternity contracts] outright as contrary to public policy". Knoppers & Sloss, *supra* note 70 Ch. 1, at 708. On the waiver of constitutional rights, see Rubin, *Toward a General Theory of Waiver*, 28 UCLA L. REV. 478, 487 (1981).

II. THE ROLE OF CONTRACT IN ORDERING REPRODUCTION UNDER EXISTING LAW AND PROPOSALS FOR LEGAL REFORM

In evaluating a legislative proposal, relevant points of reference include hypothetical alternatives, legal status quo, and normative arguments in favour of the proposal as the basis for change. The previous chapter laid out hypothetical alternatives; the next will consider normative arguments. This chapter explores contract's role in the ordering of human reproduction under current law. To attain clarity without obscuring the complexity of this inquiry, it develops the relevant legal role of contract in three parts. As a baseline, it depicts the role of contract in the law of marriage. It then shows the contract dimension of the legal response to practices of artificial insemination by donor and hired maternity. Finally, it portrays the operation of contract in a significant recent statutory proposal for reform of law on procreation: the Uniform Status of Children of Assisted Conception Act.[1] From this basis, the status of contract under current law and in existing proposals for law reform can be analysed to discern its place within the study's taxonomy of hypothetical legal alternatives.

A. The Role of Contract in the Existing Law of Marriage

Notwithstanding substantial changes in law and society, the law of marriage so far remains central in the law's ordering of human procreation.[2] Marriage is a complex reality, variously interpreted and valued. Depending on the observer and the question raised, marriage may be understood in anthropological, sociological, psychological, religious, or legal terms.[3] In legal terms, marriage is usually defined as a type of contract.[4] At the same time, the law treats marriage as more than, or other than, contract, in that it sharply limits the scope of enforcement of contracts that would modify, compete with, or substitute for marriage; channels benefits to the marital unit; and otherwise organizes society around marital status.[5] For the purposes of the present inquiry, this seeming paradox must be resolved to yield a unified statement of contract's role under the law of marriage and procreation. This chapter sets forth the content and limits of the legal notion of marriage as contract and the role of the marriage contract in the establishment of rights to initiate procreation, assert a parent-child relationship, and claim priority in conflicts over parental rights.

1. Marriage as Contract: Content and Limits of the Idea

Marriage is defined as contract at common law and, in many states, by statute.[6] The shifting sociological content of marriage creates uncertainty about exactly what the legal concept means and how it should function.[7] Nevertheless, the concept of marriage as contract remains embedded in the law of domestic relations. A common obstacle to understanding contract's nature and role in this shifting context is the mistaken apprehension that the contract of marriage is a species of contract in the sense embodied in the enforceable commercial bargain.[8] In legal history, the concept of the marital contract antedates the emergence of contract in its general or ordinary form by several centuries, and has never been assimilated into the latter framework, even though recently the differences between the two may have blurred.[9] Historically, the contract of marriage is not a subset of contract as an enforceable commercial bargain, but a distinct branch on the phylogenic tree. Marriage, of course, is a contract within the formal definition developed earlier in this study.[10] The issue is whether the implicit acquisition of the right to initiate procreation and claim a parental relationship through the marriage contract can be equated with the acquisition of the same rights in discrete transactions, through ordinary contract.

Legal history is the most helpful guide to a precise understanding of marriage as contract. In the medieval canon law, from which English law on the subject derives, marriage acquired its legal definition as contract in a period of reform and development that lasted from the twelfth to the fourteenth centuries.[11] This movement was the outgrowth of the trend within the Western Church towards a unitary system of law that began with the Gregorian Reform of the eleventh and twelfth centuries.[12] By the mid-fourteenth century, a fully developed juridical notion of marriage in the form of contract was firmly in place in the canon law of England.[13]

By conceiving of marriage as a contractual bond or *vinculum*, the canonists made juridical assessment of the existence of a marriage more certain and more uniform.[14] Medieval canon lawyers desired certainty and economy in such determinations for three reasons. Marriage had become more important, being expressly understood as a sacrament.[15] Church lawyers felt the need to be able to say, with precision, whether or not the sacrament in a given case had been effectuated. The exchange of consent by the spouses had come to be understood by theologians as the external sign of the sacrament's invisible working through grace in their souls.[16] By formulating the exchange of consent in the formal juridical terms of contract, the canonists were in a better position to justify a judgement that the sacrament had actually been conferred in a particular case.

In addition, the incorporation of the doctrine of marital indissolubility into the law of the period made it critical that canon lawyers be able to decide whether a valid existing marriage was an impediment to the recognition of a subsequent union.[17] The earlier codification of Roman law by Justinian, for example, had not made indissolubility a feature of the law, even though it was an important feature of Christian belief.[18] During the middle ages, betrothals formalizing future, arranged marriages sometimes came into conflict with clandestine marriages entered against the will of families.[19] The idea of marriage as a contractual bond facilitated judgments regarding the indissoluble nature of either the betrothal or the clandestine marriage.[20] Finally, property rights and social rank hinged on the categorization of resulting births as legitimate or illegitimate. Concern with assigning status based on legitimacy was longstanding.[21] Confusion wrought by clandestine marriages aggravated the task of ascertaining a child's status. Ease and certainty in assessing the existence of a marriage meant equal ease and certainty in assigning rights based on the legitimacy of offspring.[22]

The notion of the marital contract adopted by canonists between the twelfth and fourteenth centuries was founded on the already existing notion that consent was the distinctive element bringing marriage into being. From at least the time of Justinian, the Western Church had made consent the legal basis of marriage, although prior to the fourteenth century consent was not contractual, but rather a more loosely defined "union" or "sharing of life".[23] In continuing to base marriage on consent, the Church was implicitly rejecting other available alternatives. In the medieval period, the customs of more recently Christianized northern and central European tribes made marriage derive not from consent, but from public acknowledgement of the bride's transfer from the protection of her father to that of her husband.[24] The form of public acknowledgement prescribed generally related to the beginning of cohabitation. In keeping with this tradition, Gratian suggested that sexual consummation, and not consent, brings the marriage into being.[25] Peter Lombard opposed Gratian's view, arguing that marriage begins with the exchange of consent.[26] Canon law settled the issue in favour of Lombard and the tradition of marriage as consent descending from Justinian.[27]

It should be evident that legal choices dating to the medieval and ancient treatment of marriage continue to give content to the law's use of the concept of contract to define marriage even today. This concept still ensures that marital status arises through the consent of the partners, rather than by the transfer of the bride as ward or chattel, by family alliance, or by consummation.[28] Conceptualizing marriage as contract also continues to aim at placing the marital relationship within society's juridical control. While the importance of classification as either legitimate or illegitimate is decreasing, the concept of the marriage contract still furthers judicial economy in enforcing child support obligations against fathers.[29]

One prominent feature that today distinguishes marriage contracts from commercial bargains is the requirement in most jurisdictions that the formation of the marriage contract be solemnized.[30] Legal history of the postmedieval period discloses the requirement's significance. In England the requirement goes back to Lord Hardwicke's Act, also known as the Marriage Act, enacted by Parliament in 1753.[31] The Act ended common law marriages in England by providing that marital consent could be legally given only according to public ceremonial norms prescribed by the Church of England. An ancillary purpose seems to have been to marginalize religious nonconformists, but the primary one was the elimination of abuses associated with clandestine marriages.[32] To achieve this purpose, the Roman Catholic Church had promulgated similar legislation at the conclusion of the Council of Trent.[33]

The requirement of solemnization by a public ceremony after the announcement of banns was intended to bring the marriage contract more fully within the juridical control of ecclesiastical and civil authorities. Goals included giving notice of marital status to potential victims of bigamy and ensuring stability in the transfer of property and assignment of status to children.[34] Solemnization advanced both goals by reducing public confusion regarding the existence and validity of marriages.[35] States making no allowance for common law marriages, in effect, follow the policy established by Lord Hardwicke's Act.[36] States which, in the tradition of the original American colonies, allow common law marriages, follow the notion that simple mutual consent, rather than solemnization, brings a marriage into being.[37] The requirement of solemnization, where it exists, does not alter the consensual nature of marital obligation, but reflects the special interest the state takes in the publication of such consent.

With the secularization of Europe following the Protestant Reformation and, later, the French Revolution, the concept of marriage as contract acquired a new meaning. Originally used to distinguish the external sign from the inner sacramental reality of marriage in Christian theology, the concept was adapted by some Northern European states to justify civil jurisdiction over marriage without regard to its "inner" religious significance for some.[38] In England, the contractual character of marriage was used to justify removing the solemnization of marriage from the generally exclusive authority of the Church of England.[39] In the American context, the idea of marriage as a civil contract continues to support state jurisdiction over marriage, notwithstanding the religious significance of the relationship for many groups.[40]

Legal history, thus, discloses that conceptualizing marriage as contract subjects the marital relationship to juridical control, grounds legal recognition of the marital relationship and the status that flows from it in the consent of the parties, and places such regulation in the hands of the state, independent of the Church. History shows that the consensual reality of marriage has been experienced as a uniquely private reality. The private nature of the marital relationship is seen in the religious meaning found in marital consent, in one form or another, through much of its history. At the same time, the contractual form of marriage and the requirement of solemnization arose to take the relationship from the realm of strictly private ordering into that of public regulation. The choice of contract, as a conceptualization making marriage amenable to public regulation, was an alternative to legal forms treating the bride as chattel and the marriage as an exchange or transfer of status between extended family groups. The concept of marriage as contract both furthers individual freedom to choose a partner and allows society to hold the individual publicly accountable in relation to both partner and offspring.

Contract is now commonly understood in the ordinary sense of commercial bargain described earlier.[41] Contract, in this sense, is distinguishable from the marriage contract both in content and history. Nevertheless, the marriage contract in some sense has always shared certain features with ordinary commercial contract.[42] Recent changes accentuate such common features. By turning from a historical to a functional analysis of the two kinds of contract under existing law, more specific conclusions can be reached about the nature and extent of the contemporary intersection between them. Identifying this intersection establishes the limits to the validity of equating "marriage as contract" with the more general contemporary usage of "contract". More importantly, it pinpoints the relative discontinuity that proposals for reordering human procreation under legally enforceable bargains would bring into the area of family law.

As it now functions, the marriage contract, like the paradigm case of the ordinary contract, arises from the exchange of assent.[43] Its formation, like that of ordinary contract, gives private individuals the power of the mechanism of state enforcement.[44] While the terms of the marriage contract are said to be largely dictated by law, the same is true, if to a lesser degree, of other contracts or agreements that give rise to ongoing associations. The terms of the business partnership agreement, for example, are prescribed, to a certain degree, by law, and these prescribed terms flow from the character of the association that happens to be the subject of contract.[45] As a class, such contracts do not attempt to provide for exchanges of cash for a disposable commodity, but rather to provide rules for determining equity participation growing out of a joint, for-profit undertaking. The freedom of the marriage partners to vary the terms governing ownership of, control over, and disposition of common property upon dissolution of the marriage by death or divorce may not be as great as that of the partners in an ordinary business partnership.[46] Yet spouses enjoy some of the same sort of freedom through antenuptial agreements, which are enforced with increasing latitude.[47] While money damages, generally the mode of enforcing ordinary contracts, are not available for a breach of the marriage contract, they are available for breach of promise to marry, an agreement ancillary to marriage.[48] The division of property and award of alimony on the dissolution of a marriage may function, at times and to a limited extent, like compensatory damages for breach of contract.[49]

If ordinary contract is generally understood as a mechanism for freely reallocating resources to accord with changing party preferences, the marital contract, then, differs substantially in theory from ordinary contract, since the marital contract gives rise to a status which in principle is not intended for reallocation.[50] With the universal enactment of no-fault divorce, the two kinds of contract, however, move considerably closer, even in this fundamental respect.[51] Under the no-fault system of divorce, parties may bilaterally or unilaterally rescind marriages at will and may shift their resources into other marriage arrangements.[52] Although the terms between the parties may be dictated in part by state policy while marriages last, and although the relationship places various ancillary limitations on the partners' freedom of contract in the interim, the ability to dissolve the arrangement at will aligns the marital contract more closely with ordinary contract.[53]

Along with no-fault divorce, other recent legal developments diminish the distinction between marital and ordinary contracts.[54] One of these developments is a trend towards enforcing domestic agreements, entered into in lieu of marriage.[55] Generally, marriage contracts assign rights and duties with respect to support on the basis of spousal status. Entitlement to the marital res is assigned by the same means either as community property or under equitable distribution. Attempts by the marriage partners to reassign, as between themselves, such rights, duties, and entitlements by contract are generally unenforceable.[56] In the event that a couple forgoes marriage and lives together, the court now may enforce contractual arrangements the couple implicitly, or even expressly, makes regarding support and entitlement to property, at least in the context of property settlement on dissolution of the relationship.[57] Previously, courts uniformly refused to enforce any claim to a property entitlement or service obligation growing out of unmarried cohabitation.[58]

The result of this development is that contractual redistributions are now enforced within a sphere previously closed to ordinary contract, on the sole condition that the parties refrain from publicly solemnizing their relationship as marital. In recognizing such "anuptial" agreements, courts create pressure to expand the recognition given to antenuptial and nuptial agreements entered into by parties who formally marry.[59] Additional pressure comes from a gradual evacuation of specific, gender-based content in the roles the law prescribes for spouses.[60] Spouses, increasingly, are left to give shape to their relationship, according to their own informal agreements, bargains, and exchanges. A movement exists to make these informal agreements, bargains, and exchanges legally enforceable through individualized antenuptial or nuptial contracts.[61] Its acceptance might open the way for making marital or extramarital procreative exchanges a subject of individualized nuptial contracts, as well as of contracts with third parties.

Even allowing for the partial convergence of marriage and ordinary commercial contract, in light of recent legal developments, the contemporary marriage contract continues to function differently from ordinary contract in three notable ways. One difference is the unique character of human sexual expression as a subject matter of the marriage contract. Apart from marriage, contract enforcement is withheld by the law from exchanges of sexual expression.[62] Courts will not enforce any promise supported by such consideration. Contracts to buy and sell sex are considered prostitution and are unenforceable.[63] For example, mention of sexual expression in an antenuptial agreement may render the agreement unenforceable as "meretricious". Courts enforce the property aspects of such domestic arrangements but refuse to enforce their sexual aspects.[64] Within the marriage contract, by contrast, sexual expression is in some way related to the essence of the agreement. Sex was once understood to be the consideration lending the agreement its basic structure as a bargain.[65]

Although still a part of the marriage contract, sexual expression now plays a more loosely defined role, with respect to both the presumed structure of the "contract" and the rights and duties of the partners.[66] Even when sexual expression most explicitly defined the exchange under the marriage contract, its exchange took place as part of an integrated personal relationship involving an obligation of undivided mutual support.[67] The policy underlying both the voidness of the exchange of sex by ordinary contract and the licitness of marriage as a means of this exchange has been to oppose the alienation of sexual expression as commodity.

A second difference between marital and ordinary contract is that the marriage contract gives rise to status that is a pervasive reference in the legal ordering of American society. This status continues to be counted as fundamental in judicial and legislative allocation of benefits and burdens, and attribution of rights and duties.[68] Legal recognition of marital and related status fosters a general societal acknowledgement of such status.[69] The status consequences of marriage affect the spouses *inter se*, and they affect the status of the spouses *ad extra*. *Inter se*, the spouses relinquish their status, relative to each other, as rights-bearing individuals, in that they lose, to some extent, the ability to contract with one another.[70] In relation to the world *ad extra*, under the old common law, the wife relinquished her status as a bearer of rights, since her legal identity merged into her husband's.[71] She lost the ability to contract with others, and, to a limited degree, her accountability under the criminal law.[72] At the same time, the couple gained a corresponding immunity from state interference. This right was understood as quasi-sovereignty, which the husband enjoyed over the family unit.[73] The woman's marital incapacity, of course, was lifted long ago by statute.[74] The concept of the family unit being grounded in the legal personality of one of the spouses has been relinquished. Married couples continue, nonetheless, to enjoy a certain joint legal status.[75] In addition, both state and private employers distribute significant economic benefits based on marital status.[76] Jurisprudence developed by the Supreme Court of the United States adds a layer of constitutional protection to the couple's immunity from state interference, where their decisions concern choices regarding the education and welfare of children.[77]

The status consequences of the marriage contract most relevant to the present inquiry relate to the parent-child relationship. As will be discussed more fully below, the marital contract may form the basis for subsequent recognition of the spouses' status as legal parents, and of the child's status as legally cognizable offspring of the marriage.[78] Further, the generic rights and duties, which the state reads into a contract between spouses, are inextricably related to presumptions about the welfare requirements of children who may be born of the marriage.[79] Societal benefits flowing to married couples are also justified by reference to the welfare requirements of children.[80]

The third difference between the marriage contract and ordinary contracts is the unique nature of the state's interest in the marital relationship. The state has a substantial interest in channelling sexual expression into relatively stable, non-promiscuous unions.[81] State recognition of the marital contract as the exclusive basis for regulating exchanges related to sexual expression as well as state licensing and solemnization requirements is best understood by reference to this purpose.[82] The state also has a substantial interest in the reproduction and rearing to adulthood of the population. Its eligibility and licensing requirements for marriage are more fully understood in the context of this second aim.[83] Eligibility for entering the marriage contract is restricted to heterosexuals in monogamous relationships.[84] It is denied to persons too proximately related by degree of consanguinity.[85] The age of capacity traditionally is geared not to the general age of contractual capacity, but rather to sexual maturity and some lesser capacity for assent.[86] All of these facts are explained by the state's interest in channelling procreation by favouring the formation and preservation of select, long-term sexual and procreative relationships, rather than short-term reallocations of sexual and procreative resources.

Jurisprudence on sex, marriage, and family handed down by the Supreme Court over the past thirty years has tended to destabilize at least two of these three distinctive features of the marital contract. It is no longer clear how far society may go in making the marital contract the basis for deciding questions of societal status, nor the extent to which the state may regulate procreation and sexual expression. In a line of cases that begins with *Griswold* v. *Connecticut*,[87] the Court began a reconceptualization of the marriage relationship in terms of a zone of protected privacy.[88] This zone of privacy encompasses a limited right allowing a marital couple to shape their relationship free from state interference.[89] The contract of marriage itself, in this view, becomes a form of personal expression, the entry upon which the state may not broadly regulate, even for the public welfare.[90] This line of cases also suggests that sexual expression, both within and apart from marriage, should be similarly protected from state interference,[91] although the Court itself has drawn away from this conclusion.[92]

These cases place in question the permissible role of the marriage contract in determining rights relating to procreation and parental status. The right to initiate procreation, for example, has been held by the Court to reside, not in the couple, but in the individual.[93] The right to decide whether the life of a foetus should be terminated in abortion resides exclusively in the mother.[94] The issue arises of conflict between the individual members of the couple over the life or death of the extracorporeal embryo.[95] The loosening of the relationship between the marital contract, on the one side, and procreative rights and parental status, on the other, has also been accentuated by a second line of Supreme Court cases, in which the equal protection rights of unmarried fathers and children born out of wedlock are held to restrict the state's right to take illegitimacy or marital status into account in making laws.[96] The state generally may not claim a rational basis for defining any class of beneficiaries under law to include legitimate, but exclude illegitimate children.[97] This rule does away with a significant inducement to limit procreation to marital relationships which historically had accompanied the rise of contract as a conceptualization of the marriage relationship.[98]

In addition, the state's ability to require that a natural father enter a marital contract with the child's mother before recognizing the father's paternal rights is now restricted.[99] States may, however, condition their recognition of paternal rights on the prior establishment of a relationship of care and support between the biological father and the child.[100] Several issues contribute to the Court's discounting of the traditional legitimating function of the marital contract.[101] The development of scientific tools, making direct proof of paternity feasible, may be one contributing cause, since, historically, one function of the marriage contract has been to establish an irrebuttable presumption of paternity, direct proof of paternity having been unavailable.[102]

According to some interpretations, the reasoning of these Supreme Court cases compels the virtual abandonment of the law of the marriage contract. In this view, the strictly individual rights of sexual and procreative expression give rise to a zone of privacy protecting these social activities from government intrusion; governmental attempts to shape conduct through the terms and conditions of the marriage contract would violate individual rights,[103] just as distinguishing among children according to legitimacy is a violation.[104]

If the Supreme Court jurisprudence on the marriage contract eventually draws the implications of past cases to this far-reaching conclusion, modes of sexual and procreative activity will become more diverse and, thereby, the array of conflicts greater. At the same time, the law will redraw the traditional rules for resolving conflicts in the area.[105] One solution would be to rank individual claims as being more or less fundamental constitutionally. Then, no doubt could arise as to which claim takes precedence in a conflict, as, for example, the claim of the pregnant woman to abort the foetus now trumps the father's claim to preserve its life.[106] The other solution would be to allow the parties to order their relationships by ordinary contract and then resolve conflicts according to terms agreed upon by the parties in advance.[107]

To summarize, the contract of marriage differs from ordinary contract in providing an exclusive, non-commodifying channel for the exchange of sexual expression; establishing marital and parental status which are allowed wide-ranging societal effect; and, in both these and other respects, fulfilling

64

basic state interests. Recent trends in the law blur these distinctive characteristics. One trend has moved the marital relationship further away from contract, dissolving it into privacy and the polymorphous natural relationships of informal social cooperation. The result of this trend is that de facto elements of status, including genetic relationship, informal cooperation, and emotional bond, replace juridical elements of status as an alternative basis for resolving disputes. A second countervailing trend has reinforced the contractual dimension of marriage, but has done so in the sense of ordinary contract, blurring marriage as a relationship of personal fealty. In particular, divorce and remarriage, as well as the broader application of prenuptial and anuptial agreements, have made marriage function more like ordinary contract. Arguments have been made to accelerate this trend, to allow parties to enforce bargains within the confines of marriage itself. According to this latter trend, diverse forms of contract-based obligation, either as a matter of state conferral or individual autonomy, are seen as filling the vacuum created by the erosion of gender-based marital roles and the privacy immunity the Supreme Court has conferred upon reproductive choice.

2. The Role of the Marriage Contract in Defining Rights to Initiate Procreation, Establish a Parent-Child Relationship, and Assert Precedence in Disputes over Parental Rights

The discussion thus far has focused on marriage's general meaning as a form of contract. A brief further exploration of the marriage contract with a narrower analytical focus on the question of its relevance for procreation allows a more fully elaborated statement of the marriage contract's role in that relevant context. As the new reproductive technologies underscore, the legal ordering of procreation requires an analysis of three fundamental considerations: the initiation of the procreation of a new human being and the acquisition of biological resources necessary thereto, the formation and maintenance of a parent-child relationship, and the resolution of conflicts among rival claims to a particular parental relationship. Ascertaining the role of the marriage contract for the ordering of human procreation is a matter of describing its role in each of these areas.

Historically, the right to initiate procreation was effectively recognized by law only for couples within a contract of marriage. The only way to initiate procreation was sexual intercourse and, in jurisdictions forbidding fornication and adultery, sexual intercourse was technically deemed reserved to marriage.[108] Restrictions on the right of marriage have been clearly aimed at regulating procreation.[109] The law, however, has never seriously attempted to enforce directly the restriction of procreation to marriage.

Rather, it has provided a positive inducement to parents to reproduce only within the marital boundaries, by characterizing offspring born outside them as illegitimate. The disadvantages of illegitimacy weigh more heavily on the mother, but also affect the parental rights of the father.[110] Through the marriage contract, individuals have acquired a joint status that has ensured an affirmative legal and social response to their procreating. The right to procreate has not been acquired as an incident to the contract itself. It has arisen from the public acknowledgement of a relational status between a man and a woman.

With the gradual demise of status based on legitimacy, this system of inducement has largely disappeared.[111] Prohibitions on extramarital intercourse are also being withdrawn.[112] The Supreme Court has identified the right of procreation as belonging to the individual.[113] In a very real sense, the law can no longer be said to premise the right to initiate procreation on the status flowing from the existence of a marriage contract.[114] It seems more accurate to say that the right to initiate procreation now belongs to individuals without regard to marital status, while the law generally aims to encourage the exercise of the right within a marital relationship. Some interpretations of Supreme Court jurisprudence would see a pattern of evolution tending towards the abandonment of even this linkage between marital status and a right of procreation.

The marriage contract continues, nonetheless, to guarantee the recognition of a personal relationship within which procreation can occur. It functions as a legally sanctioned means of obtaining the procreative resources necessary to produce a child.[115] The marriage contract itself contains only the implicit expectations that go along with the exchange of sexual intercourse. In certain circumstances, the failure to meet these expectations may be grounds of annulment.[116] Immunity from legal liability for forcible intercourse was once subject to being viewed as a kind of implicit, albeit morally offensive, remedy of "self-help", where the failure of procreative expectation grew out of the partner's withholding of intercourse.[117] Even under the expanding effect allowed nuptial and antenuptial agreements, more directly commodified expectations regarding procreative resources within marriage are not enforceable.[118] Generally, the enforcement of expectations concerning procreation under the marriage contract has been indirect. Barriers to divorce and remarriage, and duties of postmarital support, while they existed, served as inducements to make procreative resources available to the present marriage partner.[119]

In the case of paternity, the contract of marriage was, and to some extent still is, at times a condition to the legal recognition of a parent-child relationship. Where recognized, the natural father's claim was subject to

66

being legally terminated if the child was assumed into another legitimate family unit either by adoption by a stepfather[120] or, by operation of the marital presumption, through the mother's prior marriage contract with another.[121] The absence of a marriage contract with the child's mother continues to have some residual power to prejudice a natural father's ability to establish a parent-child relationship with his offspring. In general, however, his right is now guaranteed against the most arbitrary forms of invalidation.[122] The mother's right to assert a parent-child relationship with her offspring has never been contingent on the existence of the marriage contract, although her right to establish the relationship has not always been upheld against a challenge by the father.[123]

The marriage contract is not, as such, a means for acquiring a right to a parent-child relationship with a biologically unrelated child already born.[124] At most, it may create an advantage in obtaining state recognition of step-parent status under the liberalized step-parent adoption laws existing in many states.[125] Assignments of custody, visitation, or parental status are not enforceable as such under a separation or divorce agreement,[126] much less through any other form of agreement.[127] In sum, far from being a device that allows the acquisition of the right to a parent-child relationship as a form of property, the marriage contract generates a triad of status-based personal relations.

Establishing precedence in disputes over parental rights is generally outside the scope of the marriage contract. Where two or more adults contend for precedence in asserting a parental relationship, a litigant may seek visitation privileges, custody rights, or exclusive parental rights through the termination of such rights in another.[128] With the possible exception of the family compact doctrine, none of these goals may be attained by advance provision appended to the marital contract.[129] Courts generally resolve such questions only once the child's custody is cast into doubt.[130] At most, the marital status of a party may be deemed indirectly relevant to the child's best interest, and so may result in precedence in a conflict over parental rights.[131]

Paralleling the law of marriage, the existing law of adoption is premised on the proposition that neither parental rights nor precedence in conflicts over parental rights may be obtained by contract.[132] Some states do permit private adoptions, thereby allowing the assignment of parental rights with court approval.[133] However, it has been held that such an assignment is not properly considered contractual. The court may terminate the parental rights of the child's natural parents after a finding of voluntary waiver, unfitness, or abandonment.[134] The reallocation of parental status, in this context, is grounded in the implied or express waiver of the natural parent

67

together with the needs of the child. It is undertaken by the state in its parens patriae power, on a case-by-case basis.[135]

Private adoption, sometimes called grey market adoption, in effect permits an informal exchange between the natural mother and the adoptive parents, consisting of payment of the mother's expenses during pregnancy and child birth for the waiver of the mother's parental rights.[136] Neither side of the exchange is enforceable without court consent to the exchange.[137] Enforcement of grey market adoption agreements is not justified by reference to party expectation but rather by most effectively advancing the child's interests.

Black market adoptions yield the mother a profit in addition to costs and expenses.[138] Often much of this profit is captured by an intermediary.[139] Such arrangements are viewed as contractual and therefore are void as against public policy.[140] They also subject the parties to criminal penalties in some jurisdictions, under so-called "baby-selling" statutes.[141] Many jurisdictions forbid even grey market adoptions, requiring that all adoptions of minors be conducted through agencies licensed by the state. In these jurisdictions, the state takes an active parens patriae role in identifying the best available placement for adoptees.[142]

In sum, the marriage contract is traditionally the only legally sanctioned and even indirectly enforceable method of completing the complement of resources necessary for procreation. As such, it avoids the commodification of procreative resources, by allowing their transfer only within an integrated relationship of fealty that has the form of mutual personal support.[143] Historically, a couple's mutual decision to enter a relationship of fealty has been construed as a contractual bond, for the sake of grounding state recognition of rights and duties arising from it in the free consent of the parties and otherwise making the relationship amenable to some degree of juridical control. In this vein, the marriage contract was once a prerequisite for initiating procreation without incurring the disability of illegitimacy. It continues to be legally preferred, but is no longer the only rightful basis for undertaking human procreation. The marriage contract as such does not serve to permit the acquisition of either a parent-child relationship or even precedence in a conflict over parental rights. While both the marriage contract and ordinary commercial contract fall within the broad outlines of the generic definition of contract offered at the outset, the relationship of the marriage contract to human procreation stands in sharp opposition to commodified exchanges by commercial contract. The marriage contract places procreation within an enduring personal relationship. Commercial contract, by contrast, would make procreation subject to the vagaries of transactional bargain.

3. The Place of Marriage in this Study's Taxonomy

In order to relate the existing law of the marriage contract explicitly to the categories of the taxonomy developed in Chapter I, it is necessary to identify the primary value which underlies it: state conferral, individual autonomy or natural endowment. Despite the considerable state regulation currently imposed on the marriage contract, state conferral, at least formally, has not supplied this value. Even though the right to initiate procreation was once limited to marriages recognized by the state, the marriages in question came into being by consent of the parties. Despite the contractual form of marriage, neither is individual autonomy, as expressed in ordinary contract, the underlying value. Partners to a marriage contract are limited to the choice of whether or not to enter a status relationship, at least with respect to marriage's procreative aspect. In all three contexts under consideration—initiation of procreation, establishment of the parent-child relationship, and priority in conflicts over parental rights—the primary value embodied in the law of the marriage contract is natural endowment. In each context, legally recognized rights are based on genetic relationships which come into being through the long-term pooling of procreative resources by couples possessed of the full complement of necessary resources, or by a legal presumption that such pooling has occurred. Within the limits of this value choice, the law of the marriage contract generally favours the stability of family units for the sake of nurturance over an unwavering deference to biology. In this study's taxonomy, the traditional marriage contract falls, not surprisingly, within the natural endowment model, under the type of the traditional family.[144]

Evolution of the law of the family over the last thirty years complicates this picture. One trend has been the dissolution of the law of the marriage contract into an individual privacy right. This has left the law of human procreation under the model of natural endowment, but moved it towards informal social cooperation. A second trend has begun to replace the law of the marriage contract with ordinary contractual obligations tailored to the individual preferences of the parties. To the extent that this latter trend gains juridical acceptance, it will move the legal treatment of procreation from the model of natural endowment to that of individual autonomy.[145] Current marriage contract law suggests three divergent paths of evolution: the law might seek to restore the formal order provided by the traditional family, it might allow further relaxation in the direction of informal social cooperation, or it might move to a new formal order based on the model of individual autonomy. If individual autonomy serves as the vector of new development in family law, it may ultimately yield a deeper reliance on the value of state conferral. Charting the adjustments which the law has already made or which have already been proposed in an emerging societal response to the new reproductive technologies will allow an exploration of these evolutionary alternatives.

B. Existing Legal Adaptations to the New Reproductive Technologies

As a legal ordering principle for sex and procreation, the law of the marriage contract in recent decades has come to coexist, in tension, with privacy rights beyond restriction by the marital contract and autonomy rights enforced through ordinary contract. All sides of this equation are evident in adaptations to the law in response to the new reproductive technologies. The first and most widely enacted adaptation relates to AID.[146] Significant adaptations in the law relating to hired maternity, or surrogate motherhood, have been undertaken recently.[147] Both practices separate genetic parenthood from the marital relationship as well as the rearing function. Hired maternity also severs ties between genetic and gestational motherhood. Both practices entail a redistribution of procreative resources to which the law must respond.[148] In principle, such redistribution could be legally prohibited; if permitted, its pursuit might be channelled in several ways, including by informal social cooperation, government decree, or contract. The direction the law has actually taken with respect to these options serves to further define the role of contract in the current legal ordering of human procreation.

1. The Law of Artificial Insemination by Donor

The first recorded instance of artificial insemination by donor in America took place in the 1880s.[149] Estimates of AID births vary, owing to the confidentiality of the procedure, although most accept that the number is generally acknowledged to be growing.[150] In the ordinary case, AID involves one or more exchanges that are implicitly contractual,[151] but the law of contract has not generally shaped the current legal status of AID. That status is provided by domestic relations law. Litigation, for the most part, has been between divorcing marriage partners, rather than between the ultimate parties to the AID exchange: the sperm donor and the conceiving woman. Most commonly, divorcing husbands have argued that in undergoing AID the wife committed adultery,[152] or that, as a product of AID, a child is illegitimate and not entitled to paternal support.[153] Although courts at first upheld these arguments under the traditional law of the marriage contract, they eventually refused to do so, at least in more progressive jurisdictions.[154] Now, substantial precedent holds that the absence of sexual intimacy in AID legally removes the practice from the scope of adultery, and that a husband who consented in advance to the procedure is estopped from denying paternity of a child conceived by AID.[155]

The first legislation regarding AID in the United States was enacted in Georgia in 1964.[156] The National Conference of Commissioners on Uniform State Laws accelerated the trend when it promulgated the Uniform Parentage Act in 1973.[157] Over thirty states now have such legislation; at least seventeen having enacted the Uniform Parentage Act.[158] The Act provides that any child conceived by AID shall be treated as the legitimate offspring of the mother's husband, on condition that a licensed physician supervises the insemination and the husband consents.[159] To be considered valid, the husband's consent must be signed by both husband and wife and certified by the physician.[160] The Act provides that "[t]he donor of semen . . . is treated in law as if he were not the natural father of a child thereby conceived".[161] States with AID laws other than the Uniform Parentage Act generally adopt the Act's basic pattern.[162] Where such legislation exists, AID is not treated as adultery by the wife.[163]

When placed beside the law of the marriage contract, this ordering exhibits a certain continuity. The legitimating function of the woman's marriage agreement, for example, resembles the traditional marital presumption of paternity.[164] On closer consideration, an element of discontinuity also appears. If the marriage agreement is understood as a contract, then the mutual consent of husband and wife to AID, certified by the physician, has the form of a bilateral modification changing one of the marriage contract's essential terms.[165] Under the Act, this modification requires solemnization, no less than does the marriage contract. The solemnizing agency is simply the medical establishment, rather than civil authority or church.[166] The discontinuity lies in the disengagement of the procreative decision from the totality of common life and relationship promised in the underlying marriage agreement.[167] In effect, the couple is permitted to dispose of the procreative decision through a discrete bargain, exchanging the husband's acknowledgement and support for paternal rights in the child.

The element of discontinuity is heightened in states that do not require the mother to be married as a precondition to the annulment of the parental status of the sperm donor.[168] In those jurisdictions, the natural father's rights are terminated, apparently without consideration of whether the child will have an opportunity to become a member of a traditional family unit.[169] Laws formerly permitting the mother of an illegitimate child to consent unilaterally to its release for adoption are inapposite, since they only denied the natural father rights in order to ensure the child's membership in a complete family unit.[170] The termination of parental rights based on abandonment or waiver is not analogous either, since it depends on adjudication and occurs only subsequent to the birth of the child.[171]

Case law and statutes alike generally focus on the mutual consent of the mother and her husband as decisive to the AID transaction's legal character.[172] In the case of an unmarried woman who conceives by AID, there is, however, no such mutual consent within a marriage to distract attention from the more fundamental exchange occurring between the woman and the sperm donor. The donor gives semen and a waiver of his parental rights in the resulting child. The woman gives cash and immunity from liability for child support. Such an arrangement more fully and explicitly commodifies the procreative decision.[173]

An exchange occurring outside the scope of an AID statute is generally held unenforceable as an illegal attempt to assign custody by private agreement.[174] Neither the mother's reliance nor her expectation interest justifies depriving a child of the paternal relationship.[175] The removal of sexual intimacy does not change the general rule that rights and duties of parents cannot be altered by ordinary contract.[176] By contrast, where there is compliance with AID legislation, such as the Uniform Parentage Act, the intentions of the parties are executed.[177]

In at least one respect, the woman and donor enter an exchange that clearly entails reciprocal future obligations. If it is assumed that the agreement comes into existence when the donor delivers his semen and thereby accepts the unilateral contract offer of the physician or sperm bank, the recipient at that moment assumes a binding obligation to perform by paying the proffered cash and preserving the donor's anonymity.[178] The donor may be under an obligation of warranty.[179] There can be no doubt that AID occurs through a transaction in the form of a contract, or, more precisely, through a series of two or three contracts. The physician contracts to treat the woman for infertility, promising to treat her with professional competence, while she promises to pay for medical services, including the costs of the semen sample. The physician, then, contracts with a sperm bank, which in turn contracts with the sperm donor. Or, more likely, the physician contracts directly with the sperm donor, promising money and confidentiality in exchange for semen.[180]

The critical question for the present inquiry is whether the parties' relinquishment of rights, particularly to parental status, creates a contractual obligation per se. Under the Uniform Parentage Act, the pair is not agreeing to forbear from asserting rights, as they might in the settlement of a legal claim;[181] they separately consent to a present waiver of legal status making the future assertion of right bootless. Their waivers are binding, because consent is given under formal circumstances prescribed by the state.[182]

The Act attempts to blunt even the appearance of an ordinary contractual exchange by requiring that the transaction be channelled through a medical intermediary.[183] This procedure circumvents open conflict with the policy which would render private AID contracts unenforceable.

Notwithstanding its external form, the Act is susceptible to an interpretation that it validates contractual exchanges even on the ultimate question of parental rights. In the ordinary case, the conduct facilitated by the Act indisputably entails contractual exchange of semen for cash and anonymity. The Act facilitates these exchanges by guaranteeing that party expectations regarding the reciprocal waiver of rights related to parental status will be enforced.[184] While the Act provides that the transaction must be mediated by a third party, ostensibly to avoid the appearance of contract, such mediation serves the goal of anonymity, which presumably would be part of the parties' bargain in any case.[185] The state's allocation of parental status depends on the parties' consent. An argument can be made that enforcement of party waiver under the Act is grounded in the contractual exchange of consent, on the condition that it be formalized according to the demands of the statute. The formalities of the statute may be interpreted as a subterfuge covertly to relax a societal policy against the contractual transfer of parental rights[186] or as paralleling the requirement of solemnization in the context of marriage.[187] This latter interpretation yields the paradox of a form of "solemnization" that does not publicize the relationships involved, but rather further privatizes them under the discreet offices of the medical establishment.

If current AID legislation is assigned a category within the taxonomy proposed earlier based on its superficial characteristics, it belongs within the moderate state conferral model. Looking beyond the surface characteristics to the contractual reading just propounded, it might belong instead in the moderate form of the individual autonomy model, although that model ultimately tends to be more expressly contractual. From the perspective of the strong form of the natural endowment model, AID statutes undermine the traditional family by legally sanctioning extramarital procreation. From the perspective of the moderate type of informal social cooperation, such laws would be viewed as no more than tie-breaking devices in disputes arising between those cooperating in informal procreative reallocations. In this view, they would be held, as unduly restrictive in some jurisdictions, discriminating improperly against unmarried women. This last assertion is generally accompanied by the belief that, as between the mother and the sperm donor, only the mother's rights merit recognition because she has arranged for non-coital conception.[188]

73

2. The Current Legal Status of Hired Maternity

The decline in the number of babies eligible for adoption in the mid-1970s led to the formation of arrangements whereby women agreed to be artificially inseminated or, more recently, to undergo surrogate embryo transfer and to transfer custody of the resulting child to an "intending couple" at birth.[189] Couples who had been unable to become pregnant because the wife was infertile or otherwise unable or unwilling to achieve pregnancy comprised the participants. The practice has been called "surrogate motherhood", "surrogation", or "motherhood for hire". Here, it will be referred to as hired maternity.[190] By 1989 approximately 1000 children had been born through this practice and hundreds more were expected.[191]

Hired maternity received extensive publicity in litigation occurring between 1986 and 1988 over the fate of the Whitehead/Stern baby.[192] Both the social acceptability and the legal status of the practice fuel ongoing controversy.[193] Initially, public opinion failed to show a negative ethical assessment of hired maternity.[194] Courts and legislatures, however, reacted strongly, making hired maternity contracts one of the most controversial topics in family law.[195] Litigation has yielded a series of judicial holdings respecting the status of hired maternity under existing law.[196] Legislative enactments in at least nineteen states have further shaped that status.[197] Important governmental and agency reports consistently acknowledge the troubling ethical character of hired maternity.[198] Contemporary legal developments in the status of hired maternity establish, for now, the outer boundaries of the role of contract in the legal ordering of human procreation.

a. The Case Law on Hired Maternity

Contracts for hired maternity have elicited judicial responses within a variety of procedural settings and with diverse substantive outcomes. Substantive issues have included whether the contract should be completely void and unenforceable or whether, if not unenforceable, its force should extend to the assignment of parental rights and duties, be conditioned on its non-commercial character, or be subject to avoidance by the birth mother or to other policing mechanisms in the child's best interests.

(1) Cases Holding Hired Maternity Contracts Enforceable

The strongest judicial validation of hired maternity, to date, occurred in the trial court's holding *In re Baby M.*[199] In that well-publicized case, the genetic father initiated legal action through an ex parte application seeking enforcement of the hired maternity contract, when the birth mother resisted the transfer of custody and termination of her parental rights.[200] Stressing that the power of the parent was subject to the power of the king under early common law, the trial judge held the birth mother's parental rights subject to judicial termination on the ground of a binding contractual promise to waive them.[201]

According to the court, the genetic father's promise to pay entitled him to the enforcement of the birth mother's reciprocal promise to terminate her rights and transfer custody of the child.[202] For the sake of ensuring the genetic father the benefit of his bargain, her promise was held subject to specific enforcement from the moment of conception.[203] Prior to conception, the genetic father presumably had a right to money damages upon breach, but no right to specifically enforce the act of insemination.[204]

Notwithstanding its sweeping validation of contract principles, the court did not treat the enforceability of the hired maternity contract as entirely unqualified. It recognized the birth mother's constitutional right of abortion as beyond abridgment by contract.[205] It also acknowledged that specific enforcement of the contract, terminating the birth mother's rights and transferring custody, was subject to a determination of the child's best interests.[206] Assuming that the latter factor is all that really distinguished the holding from the strong, laissez faire form of the individual autonomy model, the court provided no clue as to how such a determination of best interests could be made within the framework it advanced. The only means imaginable is a strong presumption that specific performance is generally in the child's best interest. In sum, Judge Sorkow's opinion leans heavily towards the strong form of individual autonomy and relies on basic contract principles.

In *Surrogate Parenting Associates* v. *Commonwealth ex rel. Armstrong*,[207] a case decided before the enactment of Kentucky's statute making hired maternity contracts unenforceable, the Kentucky Supreme Court ruled against a challenge by the State Attorney General of the legality of a commercial "surrogacy" agency. In reaching its holding, the Court addressed the status of hired maternity contracts under then existing law.[208]

The Attorney General relied on Kentucky's law against baby selling in arguing that hired maternity contracts violated public policy. The Court interpreted that policy, however, as one of ensuring valid maternal assent to the waiver of parental rights.[209] Since the new practice did not entail the sort of pressure associated with unwanted pregnancy or the financial burdens of child rearing, the court held hired maternity to be outside the policy's scope. It found a fundamental difference between contracts for hired maternity entered into prior to conception and baby-selling agreements entered post-natally, since the birth mother, in the hired maternity context, was not pressed by such special burdens, and was "assisting" a "desperate" couple obtain a baby.[210]

The court termed reliance on the Kentucky law against baby selling a static preference for nature over the artifices of science and technology.[211] Citing an equivalent degree of "tampering with nature" in the state's AID statute,[212] the Court refused to interpret an express exemption from the legislative prohibition against baby selling granted to IVF arrangements involving ova donation as forestalling, *inclusio unius, exclusio alterius*, an implied exemption for hired maternity. Existing law, the court reasoned, ought to be so interpreted not to impinge on scientific or technological progress.[213]

In effect, the court held that, as individuals, a man and woman may contract for his use of her gestational capacity and for the termination of her parental rights in the resulting child. Implicitly, the court treated the AID exchange as a contractual equivalent covering the transfer of sperm and termination of parental rights.[214] The court justified extending common law contract principles to cover these arrangements under a policy favouring applications of science and technology, although it also recognized a countervailing policy favouring a gestational mother's post-natal freedom to affirm the parent-child relationship without reference to prenatal history, as will be seen in a further discussion of the case below. The case's most striking novelties were the validation of an exchange of money for the use of a woman's gestational capacity, the contractual alienation of her parental rights, and the brokerage of both aspects of the underlying exchange. The implied justification for this innovation is the value of individual autonomy, expressed through contract. The opinion sets out two significant conditions to the enforceability of hired maternity contracts, yet to be discussed, placing it in the moderate form of the individual autonomy model.

In *Johnson* v. *Calvert*,[215] the California Supreme Court responded to a case of hired "gestational" maternity arising from surrogate embryo transfer, with the intending parents being the resulting child's two genetic parents. Its response constitutes the most authoritative validation of hired maternity contracts by any American court. The court held that such contracts were not "on [their] . . . face, inconsistent with public policy".[216] It held such

76

contracts to be outside the consent requirements of the state's adoption law, since the two kinds of arrangements were dissimilar. While it held contractual allocations of parental rights and duties subject to statutory assignment of parental status, the court also held parental status assignable according to intent discerned in the contract, where the statute was silent. The California statute on parentage allowed the recognition of only one legal mother, but was silent on whether the gestational or the genetic mother was to receive that status. Under these circumstances, the court concluded that a contractual preference for the genetic mother should be enforced. Citing scholarly commentary favouring what has here been termed the individual autonomy model,[217] the court rejected the best interests of the child as the basis of parental status, reasoning that contractual intent better serves the purposes of stability, unitary custody, and arguably even the best interests of the child.

The court answered a constitutional objection to this override of the birth mother's claim of parental rights, by denying that, in the hired maternity context, the birth mother is analogous to parents traditionally given constitutional protection. It held that she had no parental status entitled to constitutional protection, having defined herself as a non-parent by contract. At least in cases of contracted gestational maternity, the court concluded that the non-genetic birth mother is "not exercising her own right to make procreative choices", but provides a "necessary and profoundly important service" enabling the exercise of that right by others. Although the facts of the case were limited to gestational hired maternity, the court's endorsement of hired maternity contracts was on its face neither restricted to non-genetic, gestational arrangements, nor limited to non-commercial agreements, or contracts voidable by the birth mother.

The court conceded that any statutory assignment of parental rights preempts contractual arrangement to the contrary. Its holding was correspondingly limited. The scope of the statute in the case ensured that the contractual assignment of parental status was subject to legal recognition only where a genetic and a gestational mother made opposing claims to a child. Individual autonomy, state conferral, and perhaps even natural endowment stand in tension in the opinion. The court's stated philosophy, however, gives clear precedence to individual autonomy. The other two values operate in service of this primary concern. The case represents the individual autonomy approach in moderate form.

In *McDonald* v. *McDonald*,[218] an appellate-level New York court had occasion to affirm an element of contractual intent in an allocation of parental rights, even though the enforceability of contract was not specifically at issue. In the case, a divorcing husband sought custody of his twin children on the ground that his wife was not the children's genetic and natural parent. The children had been gestated by the wife but conceived *in vitro* through third-party ova donation. The court rejected the challenge and declared the wife the legal mother of the children. It cited the reasoning of the California Supreme Court in *Johnson* v. *Calvert* as persuasive, holding that a non-genetic birth mother who commences gestation with an intention to rear the child is the child's natural mother, as a matter of law, and, as such, entitled to receive custody. Although the court did not develop the point, the spouses' intent was arguably cognizable because it arose in a contractual understanding implied between them, or as part of an express contractual understanding with the third-party ova donor.

In *Syrkowski* v. *Appleyard*,[219] the Michigan Supreme Court provided another, yet more tangential validation of hired maternity contracts, which should also be noted. In that case, the genetic father of a child born pursuant to a hired maternity contract sued the child's birth mother for a filiation order, under the state's paternity act.[220] The birth mother cooperated by admitting the allegations of the complaint and by joining in the father's request for relief.[221] Both the circuit court and the court of appeals had denied relief for an absence of subject matter jurisdiction, on the ground that the legislative intent of the Act did not extend to legally validating paternity in this context.[222] The court of appeals distinguished the support intended under the Act for children fortuitously born out of wedlock from the "monetary transaction" the court had before it.[223]

The state Supreme Court reversed and remanded, based on a finding that the paternity act's purpose was to obtain support from biological fathers for children born out of wedlock.[224] Since children conceived extramaritally to a woman without the consent of her husband are, within the meaning of the act, born "out of wedlock", the court held that the plaintiff had stated cause for relief under the statute, observing that "[a]ny other conclusion requires an impossibly restrictive and unnecessary interpretation of the statutory language".[225] The court limited itself to a technical interpretation of the statute's scope and refrained from taking a position on other remedies to which the plaintiff might be entitled.[226] Although not enforcing the contract as such, the court did not disturb the instrumental usefulness of the contract in obtaining recognition of parental status under the relevant Michigan statute. Its action can be interpreted as distinguishing genetic paternity, on the basis of natural endowment, from other features of hired maternity for recognition under the state's paternity act.[227] If so, the court's resolution of the case would, thus, accord with the natural endowment model in its moderate, informal social cooperation type, its tacit affirmation of the contract being merely an incidental feature.

(2) Cases Significantly Qualifying Enforcement

A number of cases, recognizing allowing hired maternity contracts as enforceable, qualify their enforcement to accord with public policies favouring informed post-natal consent by the birth mother or the best interests of the child, or militating against the commercialization or commodification of human relationships. *Surrogate Parenting Associates* v. *Commonwealth ex rel. Armstrong*,[228] discussed for its enforcement of the hired maternity contract above, is a leading example. The Kentucky court premised its approval of the contracts on two significant conditions. The first subjected the contract to the provisions of Kentucky law on the termination of maternal rights.[229] Under that law, consent to termination is voidable for five days after the birth of the child. The court, therefore, held contracts for hired maternity to be unilaterally voidable by the birth mother for the same period.[230] In this view, if the mother fails to disaffirm, the terms of the contract determine the rights and duties of the parties to the contract, that is, of the birth mother and genetic father. If she disaffirms, family law principles governing custody disputes between unmarried biological parents will apply.[231] Second, the court held that, even where the birth mother does not exercise her right to disaffirm, so that the terms of the contract retain their legal effect, the validation of the contract does not extend to the conferral of parental rights upon the wife of the genetic father. The court implied that doing otherwise would violate the state's anti-baby-selling statute.[232]

In moderating its affirmation of contract by giving the birth mother the power of avoidance through the term of pregnancy, the court followed a trend in recent contract doctrine stimulated by consumer protection concerns.[233] The power of avoidance serves to undercut the certainty of the genetic father's contractual expectations and, as a consequence, significantly undermines the possibility of a market in hired maternity. This compromise of the market, in practice, blurs the distinction between the market and informal, non-contractual social cooperation characterizing the moderate type of the natural endowment model.

Legal acknowledgement of the natural mother's right of avoidance helps to hold the waiver of her parental rights within a general framework belonging to the state for terminating parental rights—essentially the same framework the court acknowledges as determining any subsequent conferral of parental rights on the wife of the genetic father. In the scheme designed by the court, the state confers parental rights on the intended mother, presumably for the child's best interests, and monitors the waiver of the birth mother's rights as a matter of natural endowment. The Kentucky court's approach to the question of the alienation of gestational capacity and associated parental rights falls within the individual autonomy model, according to its moderate, consumer rights formulation, as already noted. Moderating values include both natural endowment and state prerogative. However, the court exaggerated the extent of continuity with the pre-existing law, unpersuasively analogizing hired maternity to voidable custody contracts.[234]

In *In re Adoption of Baby Girl L.J.*,[235] New York's Nassau County Surrogate's Court was asked to rule on an adoption petition by a genetic father and his spouse in connection with a hired maternity contract. The court approved the uncontested petition and ordered the adoption, holding, as had the Kentucky court, that hired maternity does not violate the state's baby-selling statute.[236] The court upheld contract provisions terminating maternal rights, transferring custody to the genetic father and his wife, giving a $10 000 fee to the birth mother, and providing for an attorney's fee.[237] It based its holding on a finding that scientific advances had outstripped the legislative intent of the anti-baby-selling statute.[238] Unlike its Kentucky counterpart, the New York court voiced "strong reservations about these arrangements both on moral and ethical grounds . . . ".[239] It justified the enforcement of the agreement, pending legislative enactment, strictly by reference to the best interests of the child and to strictures forbidding judicial legislation on matters beyond the scope of existing statutory law.[240]

The New York court, like the Kentucky court, qualified its approval of the contract by holding it voidable, not by the birth mother, although this may have been, in part, because the birth mother in the case did not contest the adoption,[241] but by the court itself in the course of acting on any adoption petition by the genetic father and his wife. In this view, avoidance would hinge on the child's best interest, and also on "any overreaching, unfair advantage, fraud, undue influence, or excessive payments" in violation of the adoption statutes.[242]

Subjecting the opinion to taxonomic classification may be questionable, because the court made clear that it meant no more than an interim justification for its holding pending legislative action on the topic. The state legislature subsequently enacted a law making hired maternity contracts unenforceable. Nonetheless, practically speaking, its holding fell within the same general scope as *Armstrong*. It upheld the commercial exchange of money for custody and the termination of parental rights on at least a voidable basis. By noting that the enforcement of the contract was contingent on the best interests of the affected child, the New York court called attention to an omission in the analysis of the Kentucky Supreme Court in *Armstrong*, and anticipated some of the reasoning of the New Jersey

80

Supreme Court in ultimately resolving *Baby M*. Thus, the case is ambiguous, accommodating individual autonomy, while not letting go of natural endowment.

(3) Cases Denying Enforceability

The New Jersey Supreme Court, in reversing Judge Sorkow's *Baby M* decision,[243] discussed above, provided the most authoritative American holding denying enforcement to a hired maternity contract. The court held a hired maternity contract void as against New Jersey's laws on baby selling and termination of parental rights.[244] It found the essence of the contract to be the transfer of the custody of the child and the termination of its natural mother's parental rights.[245] Any appearance to the contrary it held a subterfuge.[246] Together with the Michigan opinions discussed below, the New Jersey Supreme Court's opinion tipped the balance of judicial authority in the United States against even the conditional approval of commercial hired maternity contracts found in *Armstrong* and *Baby Girl L.J.*

Departing from the interpretation in *Armstrong*, the *Baby M* court held that the intent of the New Jersey statute against baby selling was not only to guarantee the validity of the birth mother's termination of her rights but also to ensure that custody conformed to the child's best interest.[247] The New Jersey court found that hired maternity contracts violate both purposes. The Kentucky court's reading of the law allowed it to affirm the exchange of money for custody and termination of parental rights on condition that the contract was voidable by the gestational mother. The New Jersey court's reading of the policy behind the statute did not permit this resolution. It held hired maternity contracts void, and not merely voidable, based on a finding that the law against baby selling prohibits the commercial exchange of money for custody, as contrary to the principle that custody should follow the child's best interest.[248] It also held the contract void because the New Jersey law regarding the termination of parental rights excluded any purely private disposition of that issue.[249]

In addition to the cited statutes, the court relied on five public policies to justify its holding: a policy against parents' privately assigning the custody of their children; a policy against enforcing a contract that separates a child from its natural parent; a policy against elevating the rights of the natural father over those of the natural mother; a policy against enforcing an arrangement in which truly informed consent could not have existed; and a policy against transferring child custody without regard to the best interests of the child.[250]

The court distinguished adoption from hired maternity by reference to the profit motive driving the hired maternity transaction.[251] It expressed concern that the dynamics of the transaction necessarily draws in commercial middlemen, and consequently that market forces will subject the supply of children to fluctuations determined by monetary incentives.[252] The court concluded that enforcing short-term market allocations of procreative resources would jeopardize the long-term well-being of all the parties, since profound personal consequences might not be apparent for years, even to the parties themselves.[253]

Against the backdrop of existing New Jersey law, the New Jersey Supreme Court opinion in *Baby M* falls within the ambit of the natural endowment model. The court acknowledged that the state legislature could opt to amend the law to reflect the individual autonomy model. But, the court implied, in dictum, that constitutional rights flowing from natural endowment would moderate, at least to some degree, any legislative election of individual autonomy.[254]

A lower court opinion from New York, *In the Matter of the Adoption of Paul*,[255] followed *Baby M*. The court, in that case, found that the state had a "well-established policy against trafficking in children" barring the termination of parental rights for value. It held hired maternity contracts for pay void. It also concluded that the birth mother's waiver of parental rights under the state's adoption law would be invalid where any de facto or informal payment occurred in connection with the void contract, since "intimidation [was] inherent in her contractual commitment to give up her child and the inducement of a $10 000 gain".[256] The court held that valid consent by the birth mother to the termination of her parental rights required the waiver of the $10 000 contract fee to ensure that her "surrender of her parental rights" was "truly voluntary and motivated exclusively by . . . [the child's] best interests".[257]

Several further opinions rely on legislative choice to hold hired maternity contracts, or provisions contained within them, unenforceable. Some of these cases develop arguments for the constitutionality of legislatively restricting the allocation of parental rights by contract. In *Doe* v. *Kelley*,[258] for example, the Michigan Court of Appeals upheld a statutory prohibition of commercial hired maternity contracts, rejecting the claim that they were an unconstitutional infringement on privacy. In the case, a couple wished to contract with a woman for the purpose of impregnating her with the husband's semen. The three brought joint suit for a declaratory judgement that Michigan's law against baby selling was unconstitutional, as applied to the proposed arrangement.[259] They argued that, as applied, the law constituted unwarranted governmental interference with the constitutional right of privacy in matters of reproductive choice.[260] The court noted that the law in question did not prohibit the extramarital conception intended, but only its pursuit on a contractual basis,[261] holding that privacy interests accorded constitutional protection do not extend to the contractual allocation of a child's legal status.[262] While conceding that informal social reallocations of procreative resources outside the traditional family may be constitutionally protected, it held that commercial exchanges of procreative resources are not. Subsequent to *Doe* v. *Kelley* and *Syrowski* v. *Appleyard*, Michigan enacted a statute specifically prohibiting commercial hired maternity arrangements. The constitutionality of the prohibition was upheld in *Doe* v. *Attorney General*.[263] In response to an argument that the statute impermissibly infringed upon a fundamental right of individual decision in matters of childbearing, the court held that, while the right may have been infringed, compelling state interests justified the infringement. Interests cited included: 1) a policy against the commodification of children; 2) a policy favouring the best interests of infants; and 3) a policy against the commercial exploitation of women. These cases upholding the legislative will reject the individual autonomy model in favour of natural endowment, when they concede the state's right to prohibit the commercial exchange of money for the custody of a child and for the waiver of parental rights.[264] Where they recognize non-commercial exchanges of procreative resources as possibly falling within the scope of constitutional protection, they tend towards the moderate, informal social cooperation type of natural endowment.

Other cases resolve disputes arising in hired maternity settings by reference to statutes in preference to existing contract, without detailed constitutional analysis. The case of *Andreas A.* v. *Judith N.*, for example, dealt with a New York filiation petition by both members of an intending couple in a case of "gestational surrogacy". The court in the case held that it could adjudicate paternity under New York's paternity law, while avoiding relying on the contract which was void under a recently enacted New York law. In contrast to *Johnson* v. *Calvert*, it refused to declare the wife the legal mother, notwithstanding her genetic contribution to the child.[265] The state paternity statute made no provision for conferring legal maternity on a woman other than the birth mother. The court held that the statute took precedence over the contract but because it did not specify maternal status under the circumstances, the court had no power to address the issue of the intending, genetic mother's legal status, stating "[t]he Legislature's silence cannot be construed as an imprimatur to the courts to legislate".[266]

In *In re Adoption of Matthew B.-M.*, a California case decided in advance of *Johnson* v. *Calvert*, the court refused to recognize the birth mother's withdrawal of consent to the child's adoption by the intending mother.[267] The birth mother was the child's genetic as well as gestational mother. The court specifically disclaimed the underlying hired maternity contract as the basis of its ruling, determining that, even if such contract were found to be against public policy, a fully performed illegal contract did not vitiate a subsequent formal waiver of parental rights. It held that the state's responsibility for the child's best interests required it to hold the birth mother's statutory waiver irrevocable and to order the adoption.

In re Marriage of Moschetta[268] held that a statute assigning parental rights overrides the hired maternity contract's disposition of parental rights and responsibilities. In the case, the California Court of Appeal distinguished the higher-court ruling of *Johnson* v. *Calvert* discussed above, holding that California's statute on waiver of parental rights preempted the contractual allocation of maternal rights under a hired maternity contract, in the case of "traditional" hired maternity, where the birth mother was the child's genetic as well as gestational mother. Even as it did so, however, it acknowledged that hired maternity differed from adoption of a child already conceived in that the child would never have been born had the intended parents known the birth mother would change her mind.

Several general conclusions emerge from a synthesis of American judicial decisions on hired maternity. Some courts have held that existing adoption laws regulating transfer of custody and termination of parental rights apply only obliquely to hired maternity arrangements, making such arrangements not unenforceable, but merely voidable. In one variant, the enforcement of the contract is conditioned on the post-natal consent of the biological mother. In another, it is conditioned on a post-natal judicial finding that the transfer of custody is in the child's best interests. No case extends the scope of contract beyond termination of the birth mother's parental rights or the transfer of custody to the genetic father, to confer parental rights on the genetically unrelated intended mother. At most, the cases appeal to the contract to justify according parental rights on a woman who is already at least a genetic or gestational mother. The most significant innovation in these cases is their validation, in some jurisdictions, of the exchange of monetary consideration for parental rights. Even more striking is the implication, in some opinions, that monetary compensation may be allowable for secondary brokering and channelling functions. A second, weightier line of cases holds that existing adoption laws or specially enacted laws on hired maternity prohibit the legal enforcement of hired maternity transactions, as against public policy. This barrier to enforcement does not ban hired maternity from proceeding on a non-binding and non-commercial basis. These cases grant the natural ties of the birth mother and genetic

84

father precedence not only over contract, but over the presumption of paternity arising from the birth mother's marriage.

In the aggregate, both lines of cases suggest possible further development of the United States Supreme Court's jurisprudence on sex, marriage, and the family. The decisions have been cautious about developing constitutional doctrine themselves, but several have at least framed the issues. A minority take the Supreme Court's privacy jurisprudence as support for extending the right of privacy in reproductive decisions to the protection of third-party reallocation of reproductive resources.[269] The scope of such protection might be held to extend to informal exchanges and even to commercial exchanges, as deemed necessary to a protected end. If such commercial exchanges are not protected as an aspect of privacy, an argument is available that the equal protection clause mandates them, wherever a legislature approves AID payments to sperm vendors.[270] This latter argument turns on whether gestation is a factual distinction sufficient to support separate legal classification.

By contrast, the majority of cases hold that the Constitution mandates the conclusion that the termination of parental consent in hired maternity cannot be final as a matter of contract, but only as a matter of formal waiver registered by the state. This second, better-reasoned argument rests on the Supreme Court's traditional recognition of the right of natural parents to rear, educate, and have the companionship of their children.[271] This alternative interpretation would seem to require that the enforcement of the contractual termination of parental rights be considered as state action, à la *Shelley* v. *Kraemer*.[272] The recognition of both reproductive privacy rights and parental rights of rearing and companionship are tempered, in this second view, by respect for compelling state interests in the welfare of the children conceived and in the institutions of marriage and family life, generally.[273]

b. Existing Statutory Enactments on Hired Maternity

Conflicting judicial responses to hired maternity demonstrate the need for a legislative response in the area; neither common law principles nor existing legislative frameworks adequately guide adjudication in hired maternity disputes.[274] By 1994 at least nineteen states, as stated above, had enacted relevant legislation.[275] Their approaches range from a fairly unrestricted validation to the criminalization of agreements. A closer examination of these enactments clarifies contract's role in the current statutory regulation of human procreation.

85

The Arkansas hired maternity law represents the earliest, and the highest water mark, in the statutory recognition of hired maternity contracts.[276] Arkansas provides that:

> a child born by means of artificial insemination to . . . a surrogate mother . . . shall be that of: (A) the biological father and the woman intended to be the mother if the biological father is married; or (B) the biological father only if unmarried; or (C) the woman intended to be the mother . . . when an anonymous donor's sperm was utilized for artificial insemination.[277]

This statute, in Walter Wadlington's words "not a model of either comprehensiveness or clarity", merits close analysis principally because it represents the extreme statutory affirmation of hired maternity.[278] Broadly, it allows contractual intent to decide the right to the parent-child relationship and to validate the acquisition by contract of procreative resources. It permits binding contractual reallocations of the procreative resources of ova and gestational capacity; confirms the allocation of maternal status chosen by the parties; and by implication allows the direct exchange of money for the termination of parental rights and custody of a child. In these respects, the Arkansas law extends the force of contract beyond that of any adjudicated hired maternity case. Even the most liberal jurisdictions have not judicially extended the scope of contract beyond the termination of the birth mother's maternal rights, to the affirmative contractual conferral of parental rights on a genetically unrelated "intended" mother. It goes beyond the typical AID framework in its validation of the contractual ordering of human procreation since AID statutes avoid openly suggesting that parental status is conferred by contract, even as they implicitly rely on contractual exchanges.

The statute's validation of contract is not unqualified. For example, it operates to confer legal maternity on an intended mother under the first clause by virtue of the genetic father's marriage,[279] reflecting an acknowledgement by the statute of continuing force of the marriage contract. Further, the statute integrates its validation of contractual intention with state AID provisions which are arguably founded on state conferral. Since the statute appears to validate the contractual assignment of legal maternity to an intended mother only where she is named at a time prior to conception, the statute does not validate making the baby disposable for further trade at birth.[280] The statute provides this much protection against commodifying children. The underlying premise of state conferral suggests that the state may still impose parens patriae policy restrictions on the particular provisions of hired maternity contracts.

The statute is largely redundant in its conferral of legal paternity on the genetic father. Existing law recognizes the paternity of the genetic father according to the traditional norm of biological fatherhood plus action establishing a de facto parent-child relationship.[281] Thus, the effect of the law is merely to validate exchanges assembling the adjunct procreative resources necessary to attain genetic fatherhood. The statute is silent as to the status of "intended" fathers under hired maternity arrangements who are not also genetic fathers.[282] The law may mean to restrict the availability of hired maternity to genetic fathers. If intended fathers not contributing genetically are entitled to legal paternity under Arkansas' statute, that entitlement may be rationalized by direct analogy to the state's grant of legal maternity to the intended mother under the contract in accord with the statute's clause (C) cited above. Or, it might be justified separately by a marital presumption in relation to the man's wife's claim under the same clause; in the latter case, his parental status would not depend on contract any more than does that of a genetic father claiming parental rights.[283] While it expressly employs contract in determining maternal rights, the law continues a minor stress on natural endowment by registering the birth to the birth mother. The law provides for a subsequent court ordered substitution of birth certificates to reflect the legal maternity of the intended mother.[284]

Notwithstanding these qualifications, the Arkansas law gives unparalleled scope to ordinary contract in the legal ordering of human reproduction. The operation of the statute is required formally to effect the assignment of parental rights, but the effect of the statute ordinarily appears to be the enforcement of the underlying contract with respect to all particular rights and duties involved in pregnancy management and transfer of child custody. Even the conferral of parental rights, formally occurring by statute, is automatic and requires no state certification of the parents as fit or of the conferral as being in the child's best interest. By validating a contract assigning parental rights and custody, the law eliminates any clear basis for cognizable public policy objections to particular details of the transaction.

In addition to its implicit allowance of the exchange of parental rights for money, the statute's notable innovation is the finality it imposes on the birth mother's obligation to yield custody and other rights in advance of any de facto abandonment of the child. The termination of the sperm donor's rights under Arkansas' AID provision may be interpreted as resting on a present waiver expressed through conduct that is subject to characterization as abandonment. By contrast, under the hired maternity contract, legally binding waiver occurs months before the actual relationship of nurturance concludes. Thus, contract preempts a claim with a double grounding in natural endowment: genetic relationship and gestational nurturance. The Arkansas statute is an instance of the individual autonomy model. Like the holding of the trial court in *Baby M*, it tends toward the strong, laissez faire type.

An alternative legislative response makes hired maternity contracts enforceable but avoidable by the birth mother. This approach was in effect under Kentucky's law against baby selling on an interim basis after *Surrogate Parenting Associates, Inc.* v. *Commonwealth ex rel. Armstrong*[285] but before legislative revision rendered hired maternity contracts void and unenforceable.[286] In this approach, the exchange of money for parental rights is sanctioned, as it is in Arkansas, but the parties must assume the risk that the birth mother will change her mind. Under such a scheme, parties undoubtedly would structure agreements to minimize unprotected reliance. For example, they might postpone payment until transfer of custody. They would also attempt to supply the birth mother with every legal and extralegal inducement not to exercise her right of rescission. Maternity brokers presumably would develop human management techniques reducing this risk.[287] Even so, some risk would be irreducible, since, for the term of the pregnancy, the ultimate allocation of custody and parental rights would remain uncertain. If the birth mother avoids the contract, the parties face an unpleasant custody battle. As in the *Baby M* case, the intended parents and the birth mother may be left in a lifelong relationship rather than the sharply limited, finite business transaction originally sought.[288]

The "enforceable, but voidable" option would impede the operation of contract, making it contingent on the birth mother's choice not to rescind. Both her right of rescission and the rules governing rights and duties in the event of its exercise are grounded in the value of natural endowment. However, the parties could presumably control the risk of rescission sufficiently to ensure a market and subordinate the importance of natural endowment in the typical case, so that the approach belongs taxonomically in the individual autonomy model. Market forces would be sufficiently dampened to place the approach within the moderate consumer rights, rather than strong laissez faire form.

As has been seen, cases such as *Doe* v. *Kelley*[289] and *Syrkowski* v. *Appleyard*[290] interpret existing state laws on private adoption and AID as defeating contractual intentions in hired maternity arrangements. Another legislative approach, facilitating the hired maternity contract but on a more tentative basis than Kentucky's in the interim after Armstrong, simply acts to remove hired maternity from the formal scope of existing laws. This is the approach taken in Iowa and West Virginia[291] where the hired maternity law provides that the effect of the states' baby selling statute does not reach hired maternity arrangements. These laws prevent the baby selling statute from disrupting hired maternity contracts, and simultaneously establish that hired maternity contracts may not be against public policy. A related technical accommodation of hired maternity is found in Wisconsin whose legislative reponse to hired maternity has been simply to provide that the "surrogate mother" is to be registered on the resulting child's birth certificate, pending different ultimate court order of parentage.[292] Without more, agreements providing for the exchange of money for the conception, gestation, and transfer of children would not seem to be denied enforceability in any of these three jurisdictions. The uncertainty their statutes leave respecting the scope of contract enforcement reflects both its provisional and unstable character and its tendency towards one or the other of the moderate forms of either the individual autonomy or natural endowment models.

Remaining legislative approaches invalidate the application of contract in the sphere of hired maternity, with greater and lesser firmness. The minimal invalidation adopted in Indiana, Louisiana and Nebraska simply declares hired maternity contracts void and unenforceable.[293] Unlike the interim approach in Kentucky, which lent social approval to hired maternity arrangements by declaring them enforceable even if voidable, the approach in Indiana, Louisiana and Nebraska withdraws social sanction by declaring the subject matter of the contract void as against public policy.[294] The law discourages hired maternity arrangements by communicating a negative societal assessment and by exposing both sides of the transaction to the heightened risk of uncompensated reliance. Under Kentucky's interim approach, only the intending couple assumed a risk. Here, both sides assume the risk that, after performing, they will face the other party's non-performance without legal remedy.

Void transactions may continue to be arranged with only so much abatement as is brought about by prices discounted to match the probability of non-performance. The frequency of transactions will depend on the willingness of women to serve as birth mothers at the lower prices intending parents are willing to pay, given the uncertain outcome. The readiness of parties to enter these contracts will also depend on the degree to which reliance costs can be avoided prior to notice of the other party's performance or non-performance. Unprotected reliance, whether the emotional investment on both sides, or the burdens and risks of the birth mother in pregnancy, can never be completely avoided in such transactions. A substantial curtailment of hired maternity arrangements can be expected in Indiana, Louisiana and Nebraska for this reason alone. Still, some exchanges of money for the reallocation of procreative resources and parental rights will continue to occur. Where the arrangement goes forward, the parties are likely to create every inducement for voluntary performance. They may resort to extralegal coercion.[295] The status of the transaction as legally void and unenforceable places the parties in a grey zone where resort to such means is more frequent and more effective.

Where hired maternity transactions occur, but one side withholds performance, party expectations are disappointed and significant uncompensated reliance accrues. The non-performing party may be unjustly enriched, and yet restitutionary relief is ordinarily not available.[296] Fraud may even have induced the uncompensated performance. The familial status of the participants in relation to any resulting child is ill-defined and must be determined according to traditional rules. Nebraska, at least, limits this last problem by specifying that the intended father has parental rights by reason of his biological relationship to the child, the voidness of the arrangement notwithstanding.[297] The costs of the Indiana-Louisiana-Nebraska approach include party uncertainty; residual, uncompensated emotional reliance; unpoliced fraud; and the consummation of some number of exchanges contravening an express public policy. These costs are incurred not just by the parties, but by society. In selecting their approach, Indiana, Louisiana and Nebraska clearly concluded that they had reason to suppose these costs lower than societal costs attending outright prohibition or, for that matter, those resulting from enforcing hired maternity contracts.[298] Taxonomically, their approach falls within the natural endowment model. It implicitly permits, while discouraging, informal exchanges, even on a monetary basis. It falls within the model's moderate, informal social cooperation type, while signalling that hired maternity is second best to the traditional family.

The incidental societal cost associated with the Indiana-Louisiana-Nebraska approach has led other states seeking to invalidate hired maternity contracts to select other routes for doing so. These states have chosen one of two remaining alternatives. Both alternatives make compensated hired maternity contracts void and unenforceable. One affirms and even bureaucratizes the informal, altruistic social cooperation that can be expected to fill some of the gap left by the non-enforcement of contract. In this sense, it endorses non-marital procreation where Indiana, Louisiana and Nebraska do not. The other alternative prohibits compensated hired maternity agreements and may back the prohibition with a sanction, while either simply remaining remote from any ensuing uncompensated "donated maternity" arrangements, or else actively discouraging even these through a statutory allocation of parental status. Florida, Nevada, New Hampshire, and Virginia have adopted the first alternative.[299] Arizona, District of Columbia, Kentucky, Michigan,

New York, North Dakota, Utah, and Washington have enacted the second.[300]

Beyond declaring commercial hired maternity exchanges void, Nevada and Florida sanction and channel informal, donative exchanges occurring by means of hired *gestational* maternity. Nevada enforces donative arrangements in the limited case of intended parents who are both also genetic parents. The Nevada statute limits consideration payable to the birth mother to "medical and necessary living expenses related to the birth of the child as specified in the contract".[301] Further, it limits eligibility to a couple in a valid marriage who contribute both the ovum and sperm through surrogate embryo transfer to a gestational hired mother. Within these limits, the law provides that "a person identified as an intended parent in [such] . . . a contract must be treated in law as a natural parent under all circumstances".[302]

A Florida statute makes similar provision for enforcing non-commercial exchanges in which the birth mother is the gestational mother, but not a genetic parent. Under the statute, contracts for gestational services with surrogate embryo transfer, unlike contracts for gestation after artificial insemination, are enforceable, if the following conditions are satisfied: 1) compensation is restricted to reasonable expenses directly relating to pregnancy, birth and aftercare; 2) at least one of the intended parents is a genetic parent; 3) the intended mother is incapable of gestation or the gestation poses a risk to her or her offspring's physical health; and 4) the gestational mother promises to take over the rights and responsibilities of parenthood if the intended parents are shown not to be the genetic parents.[303] The law provides for expedited affirmation of parental status according to the terms of the contract, upon the child's birth.

The Florida provision differs substantially from that of Nevada only in leaving room for enforcing arrangements relying on either third-party ova or sperm donation. Nevada and Florida's approaches to "gestational surrogacy" are arguably still grounded in natural endowment while departing from the traditional family to accommodate an element of individual autonomy. They subordinate gestational to genetic contribution to resolve conflicts that this opening to informal social cooperation creates. Their regimes resemble *In re Marriage of Moschetta*'s interpretation of *Johnson v. Calvert*, discussed earlier.

Florida introduces a more complex scheme of state oversight in the case of "traditional" or "full" hired maternity in which the birth mother contributes not only gestational but genetic parentage, as distinguished from the exclusively gestational arrangements just described. The Florida approach essentially absorbs that form of hired maternity in which the birth mother

91

contributes both ovum and gestation into the existing framework of private adoption, terming it "preplanned adoption".[304] It validates private coopera- tion reallocating procreative resources and provides a framework within which resulting reciprocal expectations can be structured.[305] At the same time, the arrangement envisioned under the statute cannot properly be considered contract. The law provides that any contract for hired maternity is void.[306] Consideration for the transfer of parental rights is prohibited.[307] The birth mother's fees and expenses may be paid, but they are not refundable and may not be conditioned on the birth of a healthy baby.[308] Each side has a statutory right to terminate the agreement at will.[309] The statute limits third-party finders or brokers.[310]

The transfer of parental rights, the expected consummation of the agree- ment, depends on non-avoidance by both sides and court approval. The statute stipulates that other appliable law will allocate rights and duties among the parties, according to biological relationship and the best interests of the child, in the event that the arrangement is not consummated. If the intended parents terminate their involvement, the statute specifies that the birth mother is the child's legal mother.[311] Regardless of whether the birth mother rescinds, the genetic father will have paternal rights and duties under law.[312] If the birth mother does rescind within seven days of birth, the intended couple has no right to an ongoing relationship with the child, except where a court grants it in compliance with other applicable law.[313]

Essentially, the Florida statute validates non-commercial arrangements for obtaining a reallocation of procreative resources, treating the transfer of rights from birth mother to intended mother as the arrangement's salient feature. The genetic father's parental right of relationship with the child is largely contingent on the post-natal waiver by the birth mother of her parental rights.

New Hampshire also provides for the governmental channelling of non- monetized exchanges,[314] calling for even closer governmental supervision than any found under the Florida statute. A hired maternity arrangement will be enforced in New Hampshire, only where the following criteria are met: 1) the parties are twenty-one years of age and have been certified as having undergone medical and non-medical evaluation and counselling;[315] 2) the contract is preauthorized by a court in advance of conception upon its findings that: a) the informed consent of the parties has been given, b) no prohibited or unconscionable term is involved,[316] c) the parties have been evaluated as "qualified" and d) the best interests of the intended child will be served; 3) the parties have registered their informed consent in writ- ing;[317] 4) conception is in the manner prescribed by the relevant governmen- tal agency;[318] 5) the birth mother has been certified medically acceptable as such;[319] 6) the intended mother is certified physically unable to bear a child without risk to her health or the health of the child;[320] 7) at least one of the intended parents is a genetic parent;[321] 8) the ovum comes from either the birth mother or the intended mother;[322] 9) the birth mother is healthy and already has experienced at least one pregnancy and live birth;[323] and 10) fees are limited to pregnancy-related expenses and losses.[324] The birth mother has seventy-two hours from birth—one week with extenuating circumstances—to avoid the agreement. Parental rights are assigned to the intended parents only if the birth mother does not change her mind in the time specified.[325] If she avoids the contract, parental rights vest in her, and in her husband if she is married.[326]

Virginia is a third state channelling non-monetized exchanges. It exerts a degree of control and supervision over the arrangements comparable to that of New Hampshire, its law being a modified version of the Uniform Status of Children of Assisted Conception Act, which will be separately discussed below.[327] The Virginia statute provides for judicial preauthorization conditioned on the following: 1) the responsible social services department must have reported home studies for the parties;[328] 2) the parties must meet the standards of fitness governing adoption;[329] 3) the parties must have given their informed consent;[330] 4) anticipated costs must be adequately provided for;[331] 5) the woman to carry the child must be married, must have experienced at least one live birth, and must be capable of gestation without unreasonable risk to her health or to that of the resulting child;[332] 6) all parties must have undergone physical and psychological examination and have reciprocal access to the results;[333] 7) the intended mother must be infertile, be unable to bear a child or be unable to do so without unreasonable risk to her own or the unborn child's physical or mental health;[334] 8) at least one of the intended parents must be foreseen as a genetic parent;[335] 9) the husband of the woman who is to bear the child must be party to the agreement;[336] 10) all parties must have received counselling; [337] and 11) the agreement may not be substantially detrimental to the interests of any affected person.[338]

Any party may terminate the agreement by giving written notice prior to conception, and the birth mother who is also the genetic mother has the option of avoiding the contract for 180 days from the presumed date of conception.[339] Where the contract is not avoided, the court will order the issuance of a new birth certificate naming the intended parents as the parents of the child, upon receipt of notice from the intended parents within seven days of birth that the child was born within 300 days of the presumed date of conception, together with proof that at least one intended parent is the child's genetic parent.[340] If a genetic relationship cannot be established

93

between the child and at least one intended parent or if the birth mother disaffirms within the period allowed, the birth mother and her husband are to be treated as the legal parents of the child.[341]

Where the parties to a hired maternity arrangement fail to obtain the court's prior approval, the contract will, nonetheless, be enforceable, once it is reformed to comply with the demands of the statute.[342] The penalty the intended parents encounter for not obtaining prior approval is that the birth mother who is the genetic mother has twenty-five days after birth rather than only 180 days from the presumed date of conception to decide not to go through with the agreement.[343] If the birth mother who is the genetic mother refuses to relinquish her parental rights, she and her husband are treated as the legal parents of the resulting child.[344] The statute is unduly complicated but it appears that, where the parties fail to obtain the court's prior approval of the contract, parental status is assigned as follows: the gestational mother is the legal mother unless the intended mother is the genetic mother or the birth mother relinquishes her parental rights within twenty-five days of birth, in which cases the intended mother is the legal mother; if either intended parent is a genetic parent, then the intended father is also the legal father unless the birth mother who is also the genetic mother refuses to relinquish her parental rights and her husband is a party to the agreement, in which case the birth mother's husband is the legal father; if neither intended parent is a genetic parent but the husband of the birth mother is a party to the agreement, then the husband of the birth mother is the legal father.[345]

Despite their concern with elements of natural endowment, the overall statutory responses to hired maternity in Florida, New Hampshire and Virginia are rooted in state conferral. Because they treat both genetic and gestational contributions as parameters within which individualized procreative reallocations must occur and remain preoccupied with clear and definite boundaries between family units and the security of the status of children conceived, even as they accommodate a greater diversity of procreative collaboration than is traditional, they might be thought to fall within the natural endowment model in its strong form, qualified to allow pluriform modes of family formation in place of the traditional family. But, unlike traditional practices of polygamy and polyandry, these laws do not allow the multiple participants in the procreative project to participate in the rearing of the child. Thus, they do not fit within the strong form of the natural endowment model which links reproduction and rearing functions. The formality of their provisions is self-evidently incompatible with the type of informal social cooperation. The depth of state involvement and inconsistencies in the way elements of natural endowment are treated calls for the conclusion that these statutes fall within the state conferral model, albeit in its moderate form.

An alternative means of responding to donative hired maternity in the wake of the prohibition of commercial exchanges is found in Arizona, District of Columbia, Kentucky, Michigan, New York, North Dakota, Utah, and Washington.[346] These jurisdictions make hired maternity contracts, implicitly or explicitly, void as against public policy. In addition, each takes one or more further steps to discourage the practice of hired maternity. The steps taken flow from the jurisdiction's particular legislative goals. Some jurisdictions appear to have the broad goal of eliminating all non-marital reallocations of procreative resources occurring through hired maternity in any form.[347] Others have the narrower goal of eliminating the exchange of money for gestational capacity and parental rights.[348] Others seek to prevent the exploitation of the gestational capacity of women suffering from mental or developmental disability or incapacity.[349]

All of these jurisdictions, except North Dakota, prohibit hired maternity transactions where they occur for compensation. The Michigan law has been clarified judicially as not pertaining to donative or non-commercial exchanges of procreative resources.[350] Michigan and Washington also prohibit inducing a woman to enter the contract as birth mother, where she suffers from any of the enumerated contractual incapacities.[351] Sanctions for violating the prohibition include a civil penalty in New York of $500 for a first-time offence by a non-broker participant, to criminal liability for a second-offence in New York or a first offence in other jurisdictions. Criminal offences range from a "class B" misdemeanour in Utah to a felony for brokerage in Michigan.[352] Some of these states adjust their penalties to punish direct participation in a commercial reallocation of procreative resources less severely than commercial brokerage or facilitation.[353]

Michigan and Washington further stipulate that, where parties attempt a for-profit exchange in violation of the statute, the statute, and not the contract, establishes parental rights and status. Under their statutes, the "best interests" of the child determine assignment of custody.[354] The gestational mother is given the procedural advantage of being allowed to "retain physical custody of the child" pending an adjudication to the contrary.[355]

The donative exchange of procreative resources is not necessarily ruled out in this group of states. Unlike Florida, New Hampshire, and Virginia, however, these states do not formally validate donative reallocations through a mechanism for channelling these exchanges or for allocating parental rights and duties arising from party expectation. Where Florida, New Hampshire, and Virginia give donative arrangements a measure of social approval, states like Michigan communicate at best tolerance of them, when

95

they express strong societal disapproval of monetary exchanges.[356] The resolute societal judgement their law communicates against commercial hired maternity creates a climate in which even donative exchanges are not likely to flourish. Michigan's law, for example, restricts hired maternity as far as it can, short of prohibiting it outright, an alternative difficult to enforce and possibly vulnerable to constitutional attack.[357] Taxonomically, these laws belong within the model of natural endowment in its strong form, favouring the traditional family.

A subgroup of these states, at least Arizona, New York, North Dakota, and Utah, have taken steps, in addition to, or in lieu of, prohibiting compensated hired maternity contracts. They statutorily assign maternal status so as to make even donative hired maternity arrangements futile, thereby discouraging attempts at non-marital third-party reallocation of procreative resources through the practice. All stipulate that the gestational mother in a hired maternity arrangement is the legal mother, apparently regardless of whether she provides the ovum. In this scheme, notwithstanding the contract provision, the intended mother's status is akin to that of the sperm donor under AID, even where she is the genetic mother.[358] The same states tend to designate the husband of the birth mother the father of the child, some conditionally or rebuttably, others unconditionally or irrebuttably.

Taxonomically, this final group of states also belongs within the strong form of the model of natural endowment, favouring the traditional family. It simultaneously discourages the quest of individual autonomy through paid exchanges and affirms gestational and genetic contributions as the basis for legal parenthood. For the sake of stability in nurturance, it promotes the traditional family by guaranteeing clear boundaries between family units, understood in a traditional manner, as oriented to gestation.

To capture the significance of the entire array of legislative developments, considered together, it is helpful to ask how those developments advance or alter existing trends in the judicial treatment of hired maternity. At the end of the spectrum most favourable to contract obligation, the Arkansas law extends the trend seen in the trial court's holding in *Baby M*. The statute goes further than did the opinion by conferring rights on the intended mother, and not just terminating the biological mother's parental rights, by reason of contractual intention, removing, thereby, a check implicit in the opinion. On its face, the statute may appear to give contract less untrammelled scope, since technically its allocation of parental rights depends on state conferral. Still, the statute in practice would do little to limit the effective range of contractual exchanges that may be entered into and legally enforced in the area. The statute, more so than even the opinion, commercializes human procreation. The contract principle, if it takes hold, can be expected to gradually transform the framework of law onto which it has been grafted.

Most American jurisdictions do not look to Arkansas to set trends in family law, and there is reason to characterize the state's law as not well considered. Consequently, there is little reason to suppose the Arkansas option will exercise particular influence. Another legislative option favouring contract in the area of hired maternity is the "enforceable but voidable" option found on an interim basis in Kentucky. This approach facilitates the commercial reallocation of procreative resources, and the reallocation of parental rights. It incorporates a double check on any resultant commercialization of human reproduction, by cancelling the contractual allocation of parental rights upon post-natal avoidance by the birth mother and by requiring adjudication of any claim by the genetic father's wife to assume a substituted parental role under law. Each check is based on natural endowment. Whether, in practice, the courts can find ways to enforce these checks, over and against the momentum of commercial allocations, is an open question. The approach would enable at least a moderate commercialization of procreation.

If a jurisdiction validates hired maternity contracts on any of these bases, it must cope with the problem of integrating its validation into a framework of law recognizing parental rights in other contexts. One approach is to preserve the traditional marital presumption of paternity for the sake of defining separate family units. This strategy plainly compromises the value of individual autonomy. At a minimum, the state must exempt hired maternity contracts from its baby selling law, as Iowa, for example, does. Such provisions for legitimating hired maternity contracts eliminate a certain contradiction in the law, at the risk of leaving in place, or even accelerating, fragmentation and disintegration in the broader structure of existing law on conjugal and procreative relations.

The majority of jurisdictions enacting substantive legislation on hired maternity has followed the trend of the New Jersey Supreme Court in *Baby M*. These jurisdictions treat contract obligation as void and unenforceable, with regard to both allocation of procreative resources and assignment of parental rights. A review of these enactments indicates that, where contract is excluded in this fashion, further questions remain. The legislature must decide how, if at all, to channel exchanges that proceed despite the absence of enforceability of contract. An initial question is whether to prohibit the de facto commercial exchange of procreative resources and parental rights. Such prohibition may be adopted to prevent substantial, uncompensated reliance costs and protect against extralegal forms of coercion and the harmful symbolism of transactions that offend basic societal notions of human dignity.

97

A second question is how parental rights are to be harmoniously allocated when parties proceed with hired maternity transactions, notwithstanding their unenforceability. Some states seek to channel these transactions, on a donative basis, especially where the intending parents are also the genetic parents, through judicial preauthorization and close state supervision. Others do not. With respect to the assignment of parental rights, one legislative solution assigns rights based on the parties' biological contribution to the conception, without regard to the existence of a contract. This biological basis for resolving disputes may be accompanied by a preference for the birth mother, with a corresponding termination of the genetic father's parental rights, as in the AID regime. It may even be accompanied by an assignment of paternal rights to another on the basis of birth mother's marital status. The addition of such rules assigns rights out of regard for the formal integrity of family units, discouraging efforts to obtain parental rights through the reallocation of procreative resources by making them futile.

C. The Role of Contract within the Leading Proposal for Statutory Reform of the Law of Procreation

In 1988 the National Conference of Commissioners on Uniform State Laws promulgated the Uniform Status of Children of Assisted Conception Act.[359] Previous promulgations by the Conference of Commissioners affecting the family, such as the Uniform Marriage and Divorce Act[360] and Uniform Parentage Act,[361] have been widely adopted, and the present effort can be expected to receive careful review whether or not it is ever widely adopted. The Uniform Status of Children of Assisted Conception Act attempts to supply a unified framework for consistent attribution of parental rights regardless of reproductive technology or arrangement. The last step in the present analysis of contract's role under the contemporary law of procreation examines the place of contract in this legislative proposal. It is the final condition for a definitive statement of the question currently before lawmakers as they address contract's role in ordering procreation.

The Uniform Status of Children of Assisted Conception Act purports to clarify the status of children born through technologically assisted conception.[362] However, a closer reading of the statute discloses that the scope of the Act does not include the status of children whose conception has been artificially assisted, but the status of children whose conception has resulted from the reallocation of procreative resources. The Act distinguishes the regulation of activity associated with reproductive technology and excludes it from its coverage.[363] The status of children conceived with technological assistance within a marital relationship, such as through homologous artificial insemination or *in vitro* fertilization, does not fall within the scope of the Act.[364] At the same time, the definition of technological assistance includes simple, manual techniques such as self-administered artificial insemination by donor.[365] The Act encompasses only conceptions which rely on third-party contributions of procreative resources and occur by means other than coitus.

Although it builds on the statutory scheme already devised for AID, the Act goes beyond the typical AID framework in several ways. First, it includes both ovum and sperm donation.[366] Second, it eliminates the requirement of supervision by a physician.[367] Third, it applies to unmarried as well as married women.[368] Fourth, it more clearly validates the idea that the relationship of the parties will be vendor and buyer.[369] Finally, the Act deems the seller of the gamete a non-parent.[370] This last effect underscores the Act's radical reformation of the AID framework, which treats the parties "as if" they were parent and not parent respectively. Under the statute, to acquire gametes is to acquire parental rights.[371] This approach creates certainty regarding legal parenthood. The Act empowers individual autonomy and contract, but only as incidents to state conferral, and, in doing so, resolves the remaining ambiguity under AID law and the Arkansas hired maternity provision.

Under the Act, the transfer of gametes for monetary consideration necessarily becomes a subject of contract in the ordinary sense of a commercial bargain. The vendor may sue the recipient for payment if it is not voluntarily tendered. The fee for ova would be expected to be higher than for sperm, given the greater investment of time and the invasiveness of the donation procedure.[372] Fees for both sperm and eggs would vary with the marketability of the genotype and health of the vendor. It remains to be determined whether liability for warranty under the Uniform Commercial Code would apply.[373]

The Act imposes significant conditions on the contractual transfer of procreative resources in only one area, the sale of gestational capacity.[374] Enforceable exchanges involving such transfers are allowed only under the Act's proposed Alternative A. This alternative restricts enforcement to contracts supervised, both in formation and performance, by the state.[375] The role of the state under this alternative is evidence that the wide range given to contract under the Act is actually subordinate to state conferral.

Alternative A, the Act's centerpiece as originally drafted, validates the contractual reallocation of gestational capacity,[376] as long as stated conditions are satisfied. Under it, gestational capacity can be exchanged for money, and the cancellation or transfer of maternal rights occurs by operation of law. Broadly, its conditions, resembling those of the Virginia hired maternity statute, which was with significant revision modelled on it,

99

include court approval of the contract at formation and the lapse of a period for reconsideration by the gestational mother early in the pregnancy. In order to obtain approval by the court, the intending couple must be married;[377] they must present a medically verifiable ground for not having their own pregnancy;[378] the gestational mother and her husband, if any, must give written consent;[379] the gestational mother must already have experienced a delivery, and her health may not be unreasonably threatened by the pregnancy;[380] before approving the proposed contract, the court must find that both the intending couple and the gestational mother and her husband, if any, meet the jurisdiction's standards of fitness for adoptive parents;[381] and, it also must determine that the arrangement is not detrimental to the interests of any party.[382] Various rules also are included to guarantee each party full information and adequate representation.[383] The child in prospect must be represented by a guardian ad litem.[384]

In the scheme envisioned by Alternative A, the freedom of contract is not conferred equally on all potential parties; the government decides what restrictions will apply and to whom. The Act gives a woman with full reproductive capacity the greatest power in contract: she can sell her ova;[385] she can buy ova and sperm and acquire exclusive parental rights to the resulting child;[386] and she can sell her gestational capacity, with a limited right of avoidance.[387] If she is married, her husband is subject to paternal duties, since his consent to paternal duty is presumed, on the basis of fact of the marriage.[388] The fertile married man has the next greatest power to engage in contractual transactions regarding the full complement of procreative resources. He can sell his sperm, and he can buy sperm and ova.[389] If his wife agrees to be implanted, he acquires parental rights by virtue of the marriage, and risks only her abortion decision.[390] He may "rent" the gestational capacity of an unmarried woman, assuring himself at least shared parental rights in her child.[391] The woman incapable of gestation, whether single or married, has the least contractual power. She cannot acquire reliable control over gestation through either marriage or contract. She can sell her ova and acquire ova and sperm, but the promised use of another woman's gestational capacity by her is not strictly enforceable.[392] The differential power that the Act extends to parties wishing to commercially engage procreative resources flows from the continuing special treatment even this Act accords the gestational bond. If artificial wombs became available,[393] the differential power to contract would be equalized.

Respect for natural endowment may appear to explain the limitations on contract under Alternative A. The gestational bond is singled out and recognized as overriding claims to parental rights based in contract. Within the framework created by Alternative A, the biological mother may terminate the arrangement within 180 days of the last insemination [394] and, if she is married, thereby, with her husband acquire exclusive rights to rear the child in question.[395] The preference accorded to the gestational mother prevails over a claim registered by the intended mother, even where the intended mother is also the donor of the egg and thus the child's genetic mother.[396] The comment to this provision justifies the disappointment of the intended parents' expectation by reference to the risk of unfulfilled expectation generally pervading the procreative enterprise. The gestational mother's change of heart, in this view, is no different from any other cause resulting in a failure to bring a child to term.[397]

The avoidance right of the gestational mother, however, should be understood as grounded in individual autonomy in a form other than bargain, rather than in natural endowment. Alternative A does not treat the bond of nurturance between the mother and foetus as worthy of any intrinsic respect. In fact, the law treats the reassignment of parental rights as irrevocable 180 days after conception even as the gestational bond of nurturance between the mother and foetus is becoming increasingly intense and socially apparent. From that point, irrevocable contract obligation is placed in direct collision with any emotional and nurturing sense of obligation felt by the birth mother. The justification for the 180-day voidability provision lies, then, for the drafters, not in the meaning of natural endowment, but rather in an analogy to the woman's abortion right.[398] If the woman has the right to assert her autonomy by terminating the pregnancy until the end of the second trimester, they reason that her autonomy should also be permitted expression through cancellation of the agreement within the same amount of time.

The drafters' concern for individual autonomy moderates a more fundamental reliance on state conferral as a basis for assigning rights and duties. The drafters justify their substitution of state conferral for the law's current preference for natural endowment on two levels. The immediate justification is the predictability provided by a scheme based on state conferral, which the drafters claim best serves the interests of children conceived through the reallocation of procreative resources. They assume that reallocations will occur and, unless a clear allocation of parental status is dictated by the state, the interests of the resulting children will be prejudiced.[399] In fact, the concern of the drafters appears to be at least as much with the stable ordering of property transfers, through gift and inheritance based on relationship, as it is with the best interests of the children "of assisted conception".[400]

The more far-reaching justification provided by the drafters is reminiscent of that adopted by the Kentucky Supreme Court in *Surrogate Parenting*

Associates v. *Commonwealth ex rel. Armstrong.*[401] The drafters assume
that the law's role, in an area such as the new reproductive technologies, is
to facilitate technological "progress".[402] Remarkably, the drafting committee expressed this choice in quasi-religious categories in the draft prefatory
note presented to the National Conference of Commissioners on Uniform
State Laws for approval. The prefatory note named as the law's goal the
facilitation of the "miracle" of science to solve the problem of infertility
"that literally be-devils our society".[403] The use of this language signals
a fundamental, if not necessarily well reasoned, value choice.

D. The Role of Contract in Ordering Procreation: The State of the Legal Question

The regime of legal ordering centred on the marriage contract has always
been accompanied by alternative rules for ordering the parent-child
relationship where birth occurs out of wedlock. Ordinary contract rules,
however, have been prohibited from operating either within the zone of the
marital contract or within the ambit of natural parent-child relationships. The
purpose of the barrier has been to avoid the "commodification" of children
or human sexual expression. An existing legal trend is the retreat of the
marriage contract regime before both status based on natural endowment and
individual autonomy expressed through informal social cooperation. This
trend represents movement along the older axis of tension operative in the
law. Legal developments in the new reproductive technologies can be
understood as largely falling along this same axis of historic tension.

The general response to the new reproductive technologies under existing
law allows procreative reallocation to occur. But it restricts the transfer of
parental rights to cases involving present waiver or the present assumption
of a nurturing and rearing role that becomes available through genetics,
marital relationship, or a child's present need. Under this approach, the
transfer of the rearing role may leave room for some residual continuing
exercise of parental rights in the genetic or gestational transferor. The
approach also concedes an ongoing role to the marital contract in ordering
basic family relationships, if only by operation of continuing presumptions
of paternity in at least some settings.

However, the law of artificial insemination by donor may form a notable
exception.[404] If the fees involved cover the donor's costs, and if the
severance of paternal rights flows from present waiver or abandonment,
rather than sale or governmental cancellation, then the legal framework
corresponds to the moderate natural endowment approach. On the other
hand, if fees are seen as a monetary exchange, the donor is seen as a

vendor, and paternal rights are viewed as transferred by implied-in-fact contract, then the AID statutes represent a new approach, grounded in individual autonomy. Moreover, the ambiguity of artificial insemination legislation is open to another interpretation. The allocation of parental rights in the scheme may be seen as a matter of state conferral. AID law can be interpreted as leading towards a substitution of state conferral for natural endowment as the grounds for parental rights. The Uniform Status of Children of Assisted Conception Act represents just such an interpretation.

Even more than artificial insemination by donor, hired maternity represents a decisive moment of choice confronting the law's response to human reproduction. The weight of relevant case law and statutory responses excludes the enforcement of contracts and, to some degree, the exchange of money for maternal rights. On the other hand, the prohibition of extramarital, third-party procreation generally has not been proposed. The law's emerging response places hired maternity within the traditional tension existing within the scope of natural endowment as a ground of parental rights. Some case law and statutory responses chart a different direction. Not only does this alternative response allow the enforcement of monetary exchanges for the parental rights of genetic donors, it foresees the state's application of force to sever the mother-child bond in de facto existence at birth. The basis proposed for the change is an unstable combination of individual autonomy and state conferral, with eventual dominance by this latter value.

The need for consistent principles to guide the recognition of parental rights has been recognized by many, on the basis of one or another vision of social stability. At one end of the spectrum, proposals have been made to clarify and apply received principles grounded in natural endowment. At the other end, at least one proposal, the Uniform Status of Children of Assisted Conception Act, especially in the form including Alternative A, proposes a sweeping reorientation of the law of parental rights formulated in terms of state conferral. Some commentators have proposed the third alternative of individual autonomy as a core principle permitting the consistent ordering of parental rights. Any role accorded contract in ordering the reallocation of procreative resources and parental rights will take its precise form from the underlying option that the legal system ultimately elects.

103

Endnotes

1. UNIF. STATUS ACT, *supra* note 6 Intro.
2. One far-reaching social change is the extent to which human reproduction has come to occur outside the marital relationship. *See U.S. Study Finds One in Five Births Out of Wedlock*, N.Y. Times, Sept. 29, 1985, at 65, col. 1.
3. See S. GREEN & J. LONG, *supra* note 55 Ch. 1, at 97 (discussing the evolution of the definition of marriage as society evolved); Reiss, *The Universality of the Family: A Conceptual Analysis*, in MARRIAGE AND THE FAMILY 53 (1969) (cross-cultural comparison of the functions of family). The present legal ordering of marriage has been called "anachronistic and inappropriate". L. WEITZMAN, THE MARRIAGE CONTRACT 135 (1981). Legal concepts emerge from the "linguistic and imaginative characterization of behavior which is to a large extent unconscious" engaged in by legislators. M. GLENDON, *supra* note 189 Ch. 1, at 5. Social scientists view the world more realistically. As a result, common words like "family" and "marriage" have very different subtexts, depending on who is using them. *See id.*
4. Legally, marriage can be viewed as status, form of property, type of trust, jurisdictional entity, or microsovereignty, as well as contract. W. O'DONNELL & D. JONES, *supra* note 140 Ch. 1, at 1.
5. Traditionally, inalienability rules have prohibited contracts which would limit freedom of marital consent as with contracts in restraint of marriage or marriage brokerage agreements; encourage divorce, as in certain kinds of antenuptial agreements; make enforceable agreements between parties to a sexual relationship; or make special enforceable commitments between marriage partners. *See* J. LAWSON, *supra* note 8 Ch. 1, §§ 318-20, 366-68. Marital relations were viewed as a species of public trust beyond the "legal" scope of contract. *See* 15 S. WILLISTON, *supra* note 9 Ch. 1, § 1741 (explaining that contract law does not control marriage). More recently, the tendency is to view marriage as one public policy limitation among others, for example, the policy against restrictions on restraint of trade. *See* E. FARNSWORTH, *supra* note 4 Ch. 1, § 5.4. Notwithstanding the voidness of marriage brokerage contracts, unenforceable marriage brokerage apparently flourishes, at least in one context. *Would You Order a Mate Through The Mail?* Wash. Post Parade Mag., Aug. 7, 1988, at 14, col. 1 (discussing international brokerage services for American men seeking Asian wives).
6. For case law stressing this conception, see United States v. Yazell, 382 U.S. 341, 359 (1966); Ryan v. Ryan, 277 So. 2d 266, 268-69 (Fla. 1973); Ponder v. Graham, 4 Fla. 23, 44-46 (1851); *accord* Maynard v. Hill, 125 U.S. 190, 205-06 (1888). Under American law, marriage has been acknowledged to be "a civil contract, an institution, a domestic relation and a sacrament". 1 C. VERNIER, AMERICAN FAMILY LAWS 45 (1931).
7. *See* Clark, *The New Marriage*, 12 WILLAMETTE L.J. 441, 450-51 (1976) (discussing the evolution and recent judicial treatment of marriage); Weisbrod, *Family, Church and State: An Essay On Constitutionalism and Religious Authority*, 26 J. FAM. L. 741 (1987-88) (analyzing church-state interactions on family issues). Weitzman criticizes the received law of marriage as inappropriately grounded in the "Judeo-Christian ideal". L. WEITZMAN, *supra* note 3 Ch. 2, at 204. There can be no question that the institution has lost some of its operative significance as a matter of sociology. *See* S. GREEN & J. LONG, *supra* note 55 Ch. 1, at 99 (discussing the erosion of traditional views of marriage).

8. Weber distinguished "status contracts", which, through "straightforward magical acts or at least acts having a magical significance", brought about a political, personal, or familial relation between parties and a "purposive contract" of the market type. M. WEBER, LAW IN ECONOMY AND SOCIETY, in THE ECONOMICS OF CONTRACT LAW, *supra* note 14 Ch. 1, at 105-6.

The status, as opposed to contractual, aspect of marriage has been stressed since the nineteenth century. *See* Engdahl, *Proposal for a Benign Revolution In Marriage Law and Marriage Conflicts Law*, 55 IOWA L. REV. 56, 57 (1969). Among the characteristics of "status contracts" are the absence of a right of rescission or a right to change fundamental terms by subsequent agreement, the change such contracts effect on societal status, and the common law merger of legal identity. The status contract of marriage is not a contract for purposes of the fourteenth amendment prohibition of the impairment of contract. 1 C. VERNIER, *supra* note 6 Ch. 2, at 51. Incapacity under such contracts is also measured differently than it is under the regime of ordinary contract. *See id.* (comparing marriage under common law to the law of ordinary contract).

9. *See, e.g.*, J. JACKSON, THE FOUNDATION AND ANNULMENT OF MARRIAGE 275 (1969) (lack of consent will be "sufficient to rescind an ordinary commercial contract", it is not necessarily sufficient to annul a marriage). Long before the modern period, however, the marriage contract coexisted with commercial exchanges that were given legal recognition in some form and was compared to them by contemporaries. *But see* W. WEYRAUCH & S. KATZ, *supra* note 189 Ch. 1, at 1-2 (noting that the marriage contract is similar to other "long-term contracts" such as employment, partnership, cotenancy, or business for profit).

10. *See supra* text accompanying notes 23-8 Ch. 1.

11. The reform movement involved developing new laws and legal institutions, but also normalizing and channelling social practice so that it began more consistently to reflect Christian ideals. H. BERMAN, LAW AND REVOLUTION 85-119, 530 (1983). George Duby traces the setting of social practice, during this same period, into a consensus that monogamy was proper. G. DUBY, THE KNIGHT THE LADY AND THE PRIEST: THE MAKING OF MODERN MARRIAGE IN MEDIEVAL FRANCE (1983).

12. G. DUBY, *supra* note 11 Ch. 2, at 227-31.

13. "During the twelfth century ecclesiastical courts acquired complete jurisdiction over [marriage]." H. POTTER, *supra* note 13 Ch. 1, at 218. For the significance of canon law to the development of English legal institutions, see C. DUGGAN, *The Reception of Canon Law in England in the Later-Twelfth Century*, in CANON LAW IN MEDIEVAL ENGLAND XI (1982).

14. H. BERMAN, *supra* note 11 Ch. 2, at 230. A looser concept of an exchange of consent giving rise to a union of lives gave way to a more highly juridicized notion of an exchange of consent resulting in a continuing bond of contractual obligation. *See generally* T. MACKIN, WHAT IS MARRIAGE? 186-89 (1982) (outlining the history of this trend through the writings of theologians). Within the canon law of the Roman Church, the conceptualization of marriage as a juridical contractual bond became more exclusive and pronounced in the centuries following the Council of Trent. The Church attempted to gain firmer discipline in its practice following the Reformation. As a consequence, the contractual bond was increasingly treated as the essence of marriage. Discussion of marriage during and after the Second Vatican Council has centered on finding substitutes for the conceptualization of marriage as contract. *See* Basset, *The Marriage of Christians—Valid Contract, Valid Sacrament?*, in THE BOND OF MARRIAGE 117, 133-45 (W. Bassett ed. 1968).

15. H. BERMAN, *supra* note 11 Ch. 2, at 174, 201, 530; T. MACKIN, *supra* note 14 Ch. 2, at 20-22.

16. T. MACKIN, *supra* note 14 Ch. 2, at 20-22.

105

17. Basset, *supra* note 14 Ch. 2. Similarly, canonists were concerned by marriages occurring within prohibited degrees of consanguinity. *See* G. DUBY, *supra* note 11 Ch. 2, at 189-91 (citing the annulment of the marriage of Louis VII of France and Eleanor of Aquitaine who were related within the fourth degree of consanguinity).

18. Divorce was not prohibited in either the Code or a code on divorce designated Novel 22. M. GLENDON, *supra* note 189 Ch. 1, at 17; Noonan, *Novel 22*, in THE BOND OF MARRIAGE, *supra* note 14 Ch. 2.

19. *See* Kelly, *Clandestine Marriage and Chaucer's "Troilus"*, 4 VIATOR 435, 437-43 (1973).

20. H. BERMAN, *supra* note 11 Ch. 2, at 230.

21. On concern with preservation of familial property interests, see G. DUBY, MEDIEVAL MARRIAGE (1978). Twelfth-century canon law was more liberal than civil law in recognizing legitimacy, acknowledging as legitimate children whose parents married subsequent to their birth. Although the ecclesiastical courts generally had jurisdiction over questions of legitimacy, the civil courts, under the Statute of Merton, refused to recognize the retroactive legitimating force of marriage, because of its effect on property rights. 1 F. POLLOCK & F. MAITLAND, THE HISTORY OF ENGLAND BEFORE THE TIME OF EDWARD I 127 (2d ed. 1923).

22. It is commonly held that the medieval position on illegitimacy led to the denial of parental support to the child born out of wedlock, and that parental support was only statutorily mandated under the Elizabethan Poor Law of 1576. This perception appears to be incorrect. The common law doctrine of *filius nullius* appears originally to have meant only that the common law courts had no jurisdiction to enforce parental support as a matter of law. Jurisdiction belonged to ecclesiastical courts which enforced such support as a matter of natural equity with the contempt sanction of excommunication. Helmholz, *Support Orders, Church Courts, and the Rule of Filius Nullius: A Reassessment of the Common Law*, 63 VA. L. REV. 431 (1977). Bastardy, the practical consequence of which was disqualification from inheritance, was primarily litigated in the common law courts. Helmholz, *Bastardy Litigation in Medieval England*, 13 AM. J. LEG. HIST. 360, 367-82 (1969).

23. This view of marriage is illustrated by the phrase: *Nuptiae autem sive matrimonium est viri et mulieris conjunctio, individuam consuetudinem vitae contines*. (Marriage, or matrimony, is a joining together of a man and woman, carrying with it a mode of life in which they are inseparable.) J. INST. 1.9.29 (T. Sandars trans. 1941). The model of Roman marriage incorporated by Justinian was the *matrimonium liberum* based on the free consent of the spouses and which had come to prevail in the Roman society of late antiquity. Earlier forms of Roman marriage had been conceived in terms of the passing of the wife from the hand (*manus*) of her father to that of her husband. These included *conferreatio*, based in a patrician religious ritual; *coemptio*, a fictitious sale of the bride; and *usus*, a kind of chattel right in the bride arising from uninterrupted possession for one year. Johnston, *The Roman Family*, in MARRIAGE AND THE FAMILY, *supra* note 3 Ch. 2, 78-80.

24. H. BERMAN, *supra* note 11 Ch. 2, at 75, 168; 2 W. HOLDSWORTH, A HISTORY OF ENGLISH LAW 87-89 (1903); T. MACKIN, *supra* note 14 Ch. 2, at 147-8.

25. T. MACKIN, *supra* note 14 Ch. 2, at 161-4.

26. *Id.* at 164-67.

27. Although Pope Alexander III (1159-81) took the first definitive step in resolving the dispute, he sided with Lombard only after a period of indecision. Alexander's judgment was subsequently reaffirmed by Pope Urban II (1185-87) and Pope Innocent III (1189-1216). T. MACKIN, *supra* note 14 Ch. 2, at 168-70.

28. *See* W. GOODSELL, A HISTORY OF MARRIAGE AND THE FAMILY 221-31 (1934); S. GREEN & J. LONG, *supra* note 55 Ch. 1, at 193. Even today, a finding of consent is essential to determining that a common law marriage exists. *See* Boswell v. Boswell, 497 So. 2d 479 (Ala. 1986).

29. *See* H. CLARK, *supra* note 23 Intro., § 6.2. California, for example, only allows a husband to challenge his paternity of his wife's child within two years of the date of birth. After that period, the state enforces child support based on an irrebuttable presumption of paternity. CAL. FAM. CODE ANN. § 7541 (Deering 1994).

30. *Id*. § 2.3.

31. *Id*. § 2.1.

32. *See* S. GREEN & J. LONG, *supra* note 55 Ch. 1, at 85 ("[T]hese laws marked the end of valid marriages by simple contract").

33. Luther and others had criticized the Catholic Church for tolerating the abuse of clandestine marriages. The Council of Trent in the decree *Tametsi* (*Decretum de Reformation Matrimonii*) (1563) established that thereafter marital consent could be validly expressed only in the presence of a priest and two or three witnesses. T. MACKIN, *supra* note 14 Ch. 2, at 196-7. Parallel regulations were adopted within a relatively short time by continental Protestants. *See* M. GLENDON, *supra* note 189 Ch. 1, at 29.

34. *See* H. CLARK, *supra* note 23 Intro., § 2.1.

35. *Id*. § 2.3.

36. Roughly thirty-seven states have decided, either by statute or case law, to cease recognizing common law marriage. *Id*. § 2.4.

37. *See* Meister v. Moore, 96 U.S. 76, 78-79 (1878) (unless expressly barred by statute, common law marriages are valid).

38. *See* W. GOODSELL, *supra* note 28 Ch. 2, at 266-70.

39. The first step was taken by Lord Hardwicke's Act, which required that nearly all marriages be solemnized by the Church of England. The Marriage Act of 1876 abolishing the requirement of solemnization implied that the regulation of marriage was a secular power. *See id*. at 333-34, 438-39. *Cf*. F. POTOTSCHNIG, STAATLICH-KIRCHLICHE EHEGESETZGEBUNG IM 19. JAHRHUNDERT 55-61 (1974) (discussing the efforts of the Hapsburg monarchy to assert control over marriage in place of the Catholic Church during the nineteenth century).

40. The state acknowledges the religious significance of marriage to the extent that solemnization by religious leaders is authorized by statute. However, while solemnization is not a requirement for a marriage contract to be valid, a license from the state is required in all American jurisdictions. *See* H. CLARK, *supra* note 23 Intro., § 2.3.

41. The classical border between the sphere of marriage and the scope of commercial contract was formed in large part by restraints on any sort of obligation that might have compromised the freedom of marital consent, a privileged choice. *See* J. LAWSON, *supra* note 8 Ch. 1, § 319-21.

42. *See infra* text accompanying notes 4-28 Ch. 1.

43. The standard treatise on marriage, prior to relatively recent developments in Supreme Court jurisprudence on marriage, emphasized that marriage was not a simple contract because: it could not be rescinded, inability to perform did not release one from it, performance could never be completed, assent to it was based on a different age of capacity, it could not be rescinded for failure of consideration, it did not give rise to a suit for damages for non-fulfilment of duties, duties under it were not derived from terms but from law, by legislation the state may annul it at pleasure, and all of its other elements were derived from

status not contract. KEEZER ON THE LAW OF MARRIAGE AND DIVORCE § 1, at 6 (J. Morland 3d ed. 1946) [hereinafter KEEZER].

Marriage is not a contract within the sense of the contract clause of the Constitution. *See* Gleason v. Gleason, 26 N.Y.2d 28, 42, 256 N.E.2d 513, 520, 308 N.Y.S.2d 347, 356 (1970). Recent conceptual confusion in family law adds to the difficulty in distinguishing the marriage contract from ordinary contract. Some conclude that there has been "[a]n accelerated movement from status to contract . . . discernible in the realm of family relations", so that even making the distinction becomes less meaningful. Weyrauch, *supra* note 1 Ch. 1, at 417.

44. The agreement is enforced against third-party interference through actions for adultery, alienation of affections, and loss of consortium. W. O'DONNELL & D. JONES, *supra* note 140 Ch. 1, at 3.

45. Goetz & Scott, *Principles of Relational Contracts*, 67 VA. L. REV. 1089 (1981). Marriage is now compared to partnerships, franchises, and servicing agreements. *See* L. WEITZMAN, *supra* note 3 Ch. 2, at 243-44 (arguing that the marriage relationship is similar to a long-term business contract and, therefore, acquires the same legal characteristics); W. WEYRAUCH & S. KATZ, *supra* note 189 Ch. 1, at 1-5 (comparing marriage to partnership); Weyrauch, *supra* note 1 Ch. 1, at 421 ("[M]arriage is beginning to acquire many of the characteristics of a pooling of resources and becomes co-ownership in present and future property similar to a business venture".).

46. The usual enforcement device in business is a suit for an accounting. For an application to marriage, *see In re* Estate of Broadie, 208 Kan. 621, 625, 493 P.2d 289, 293 (1972); Holcroft v. Dickenson, Carter 233, 74 Eng. Rep. 933 (1672); 1 C. VERNIER, *supra* note 6 Ch. 2, at 23; W. WEYRAUCH & S. KATZ, *supra* note 218, at 4. On divorce, see Posner v. Posner, 233 So. 2d at 384 (Fla. 1970), *aff'd*, 257 So. 2d 530 (Fla. 1972); Unander v. Unander, 265 Or. 102, 506 P.2d 719 (1973); Stanard v. Bolin, 88 Wash. 2d 614, 565 P.2d 94 (1977); RESTATEMENT (SECOND) OF CONTRACTS §§ 178, 192 (1979). Recently, the distinctive property implications of marital status and family relationship have become much less important. *See* M. GLENDON, THE NEW FAMILY AND THE NEW PROPERTY (1981).

47. *See, e.g.*, Posner v. Posner, 233 So. 2d 381 (Fla. 1970), *aff'd*, 257 So. 2d 530 (Fla. 1972). At least four states have enacted section 3 of the Uniform Premarital Agreement Act, giving scope to the recognition of contract. UNIF. PREMARITAL AGREEMENT ACT § 3, 9B U.L.A. 373 (1987). On the trend generally, see Bruch, *Of Work, Family Wealth, and Equality*, 17 FAM. L.Q. 99 (1983); W. WEYRAUCH & S. KATZ, *supra* note 189 Ch. 1, at 43-44. The practice seems to be to uphold contractual resolution of property and inheritance rights as long as certain standards of fairness and disclosure are met. S. GREEN & J. LONG, *supra* note 55 Ch. 1, § 1.27, at 68, § 2.01, at 102.

48. Such suits have been excluded in twenty-two jurisdictions under so-called Heart Balm Acts. *E.g.*, CAL. CIV. CODE § 43.5(d) (West 1982); COLO. REV. STAT. § 13-20-202 to -203 (1987); N.J. STAT. ANN. § 2A:23-1 (West 1987).

49. This is especially true where fault is taken into account in dividing property to assigning post-dissolution support obligations. *See, e.g.*, IDAHO CODE § 32-705 (Supp. 1994) (right to maintenance premised on showing of fault). To some degree, the risk of unfavourable discretionary awards relating to property division and alimony can be controlled by antenuptial agreement. W. WEYRAUCH & S. KATZ, *supra* note 189 Ch. 1, at 99.

50. Even in recent Supreme Court jurisprudence, marriage is described as "hopefully enduring". Griswold v. Connecticut, 381 U.S. 479, 486 (1965).

51. By 1985 every state provided for no-fault divorce. *See* W. O'DONNELL & D. JONES, *supra* note 140 Ch. 1, at 133 (noting that South Dakota became the last state to adopt no-fault divorce).

52. *See* Glendon, *Marriage and the State: The Withering Away of Marriage*, 62 VA. L. REV. 663, 704-6 (1976). This practice also has been called "successive polygamy", *Id.* at 672-73, and "serial monogamy", L. WEITZMAN, *supra* note 3 Ch. 2, at 104-204.

53. *See* M. GLENDON, *supra* note 1 Intro., at 63-111. If the obligation were strictly "at will", it would be illusory and not technically contractual. However, even the notice and waiting requirements of no-fault divorce statutes lend a sufficient future orientation to marriage to satisfy the criteria of contract. A right to the no-fault dissolution of marriage is analogous not only to commercial contracts subject to termination clauses but also to the right to "efficient breach" which is implicitly countenanced by the law of commercial contract. Kornhauser, *An Introduction to the Economic Analysis of Contract Remedies*, 57 U. COLO. L. REV. 683, 692-95 (1986) (discussing the concept of efficient breach).

54. *See* Blumberg, *Cohabitation Without Marriage: A Different Perspective* 28 UCLA L. REV. 1125 (1981) (discussing claims of unmarried cohabitants to benefits and rights normally considered incidents of marriage); Weyrauch, *supra* note 1 Ch. 1 (examining the contractual implications of formal and informal family relationships).

55. Weyrauch, *supra* note 1 Ch. 1, at 428 ("[A]greements are more likely to be honored if they use the language of property").

56. *See* Merritt, *Changing Marital Rights and Duties by Contract: Legal Obstacles in North Carolina*, 13 WAKE FOREST L. REV. 85 (1977).

57. *E.g.*, Marvin v. Marvin, 18 Cal. 3d 660, 684-85, 557 P.2d 106, 122-23, 134 Cal. Rptr. 815, 831-32 (1976); Latham v. Latham, 274 Or. 421, 547 P.2d 144 (1976). *Contra* Hewitt v. Hewitt, 77 Ill. 2d 49, 394 N.E.2d 1204 (1979) (holding that the property of unmarried cohabitants may not be contractually devised). In addition to contractual obligations, courts have used the rules of property to enforce the reasonable expectations of the parties. *E.g.*, Carlson v. Olson, 256 N.W.2d 249 (Minn. 1977); Beal v. Beal, 282 Or. 115, 577 P.2d 507 (1978). One commentator has concluded that "[s]ince common law judges are traditionally property oriented, sexual cohabitation becomes less objectionable if it is presented in terms borrowed from the law of property rather than from the law of personal service contracts". Weyrauch, *supra* note 1 Ch. 1, at 428; *see* Note, *Domestic Partnership: A Proposal for Dividing the Property of Unmarried Friends*, 12 WILLAMETTE L.J. 453, 475 (1976).

58. *See, e.g.*, Hewitt v. Hewitt, 77 Ill. 2d 49, 394 N.E.2d 1204 (1979) (retaining the traditional approach).

59. H. CLARK, *supra* note 23 Intro., §§ 1.1, 1.2.

60. *See* L. WEITZMAN, *supra* note 3 Ch. 2, at 168; *see also* Orr v. Orr, 440 U.S. 268 (1979) (striking down gender-based alimony); Carlson v. Carlson, 75 Ariz. 308, 256 P.2d 249 (1953) (allowing wife to refuse husband's choice of domicile).

61. The best known advocate of this movement is Lenore Weitzman. *See* L. WEITZMAN, *supra* note 3 Ch. 2, at 219-250 (1981); Weitzman, *Legal Regulation of Marriage: Tradition and Change*, 62 CALIF. L. REV. 1169 (1974). Weitzman expresses the opinion that business contracts presuppose relations of "mutual goodwill, cooperation and even affection in coping with the inevitable problems that arise in an ongoing enterprise", and concludes "that the dichotomy between business morality and personal morality is no longer clearcut. In fact, the developing standards for business contracts suggest the increasing appropriateness of the contractual model for marriage". L. WEITZMAN, *supra* note 3 Ch. 2, at 244. Farnsworth also concludes that "[r]ecent changes in the attitude toward marriage have been reflected in a greater willingness to grant parties the same freedom of contract in this area that they enjoy in other areas, as long as the agreement is a fair one in the circumstances". E. FARNSWORTH, *supra* note 4 Ch. 1, § 5.4.

62. *See* 15 S. WILLISTON, *supra* note 9 Ch. 1, § 1745.

63. This issue is distinct from whether prostitution should be criminalized. *See generally* J. DECKER, PROSTITUTION: REGULATION AND CONTROL (1979) (discussing the rationales for legalizing prostitution).

64. *See, e.g.*, Marvin v. Marvin, 18 Cal. 3d 660, 684, 557 P.2d 106, 122, 134 Cal. Rptr. 815, 831 (1976) (a contract between unmarried partners is unenforceable only to the degree that it is expressly based upon the immoral consideration of meretricious sexual services). One interpretation is that the law continues to consider marriage the only legally cognizable forum for sexual expression, but that policy considerations growing out of problems in enforceability have led to a relaxation of constraints. *See* Hafen, *supra* note 103 Ch. 1, at 567.

65. The Conjunction of Man and Wife, is the Law of Nature; and the Consent of the
  Mind is regarded in Contracts, because the Mind only can lawfully give Consent:
  But to Consummation of Marriage, Copulation is requisite, and by the Parties being
  in Bed Together, the Law Presumes it. There are Signs of Consent to Contracts of
  Marriage, which are effectual in Law, as the Woman thereby tacitly agrees to the
  Propositions of the Man.

G. JACOB, THE STUDENT'S COMPANION: OR THE REASON OF THE LAWS OF ENGLAND 123 (1725 & photo. reprint 1978).

66. Non-interference by the state in the marital relationship meant that the parties were, effectively, entitled to the "self-help" of taking sex over the protest or resistance of the partner. The victim, in such cases, could not obtain state assistance under either tort or criminal law. *See* Note, *To Have and to Hold: The Marital Rape Exemption and the Fourteenth Amendment*, 99 HARV. L. REV. 1255 (1986). Concern for the individual rights of the partners, particularly the wife, has appropriately led to the rejection of this view. *See* C. MACKINNON, FEMINISM UNMODIFIED: DISCOURSES ON LIFE AND LAW (1987) (noting this trend but arguing that more progress is needed).

67. The rights and duties of the parties to the marriage are owed not in terms of vested interests, but rather flow from a relationship of fealty, which in many ways is similar to feudal notions of personal allegiance as the source of rights and duties between members of medieval society. *See* H. BERMAN, *supra* note 11 Ch. 2, at 306 (discussing the reciprocal pledges of faith or fealty between vassal and lord as "the equivalent—almost—of a marriage"). Notwithstanding developments in the Supreme Court jurisprudence of marriage, the fealty character of marriage is still recognized by the Court. *See, e.g.*, Griswold v. Connecticut, 381 U.S. 479, 486 (1965) (marriage deemed "a bilateral loyalty" and "a coming together for better or for worse, hopefully enduring, and intimate to the degree of being sacred"). For those ideologically versed in individualism, the question is how marital and parental fealty is to be distinguished from involuntary servitude flowing from a contract of irrevocable personal employment. *See* Note, *supra* note 8 Intro., at 1938 (parent-child and spousal relationships bear "a striking similarity to slavery").

68. The rights of consortium, support, alimony, distributive share, dower, inheritance, the legitimacy of children, the benefits of workers' compensation, social security, pension systems, exemptions, widow's allowance, and special state and federal tax treatment all flow from marital status. *See* S. GREEN & J. LONG, *supra* note 55 Ch. 1, at 1-10; W. O'DONNELL & D. JONES, *supra* note 140 Ch. 1, at 182. Disability and unemployment benefits, eligibility for child custody and adoption, and access to markets in homes and apartments, mortgages, insurance, and credit have also been cited as advantages. L. WEITZMAN, *supra* note 3 Ch. 2, at 217-18.

Status-based regulation places the contract of marriage outside the scope of the commerce clause of the U.S. Constitution. *See supra* note 43 Ch. 2. "Without a prior judicial imprimatur, individuals may freely enter into and rescind commercial contracts, for example, but we are unaware of any jurisdiction where private citizens may covenant for or dissolve marriages without state approval". Boddie v. Connecticut, 401 U.S. 371, 376 (1971).

As status consequences of marriage become somewhat uncertain, a substitute status has been built on cohabitation. *See* Caudill, *Legal Recognition of Unmarried Cohabitation: A Proposal to Update and Reconsider Common Law Marriage*, 49 TENN. L. REV. 537, 540 (1982) (arguing that the state has identical interests in legal marriage and unmarried cohabitive relationships, so the same legal burdens and protections should apply). A controversial current example is San Francisco's ordinance recognizing the status of cohabitant lovers. *See* S. GREEN & J. LONG, *supra* note 55 Ch. 1, at 166. Along the same lines, cities beginning with Berkeley, Los Angeles, Santa Cruz, San Francisco and West Hollywood, California; Madison, Wisconsin; and Takoma Park, Maryland have passed ordinances recognizing homosexuals' domestic partners. *Gay Couples Seek Legal Recognition*, NAT'L L.J., July 31, 1989, at 24, col. 4. As of 1993, about 130 local jurisdictions had given some legal recogniztion to homosexual relationships. WASH. POST, April 18, 1993, at A1, col. 4.

69. The relationship of law to conventional social norms is a controversial issue. Bowers v. Hardwick, 478 U.S. 186 (1986) (Blackmun, J., dissenting) (criticizing the majority's use of the historical condemnation of sodomy to uphold the constitutionality of Georgia's criminalization of sodomy).

70. *See, e.g.*, Kilgrow v. Kilgrow, 268 Ala. 475, 479-80, 107 So. 2d 885, 889 (1958) (refusing to enforce agreement regarding child's religious education); Cord v. Neuhoff, 94 Nev. 21, 573 P.2d 1170 (1978) (refusing to enforce agreement limiting husband's duty to support wife). RESTATEMENT (SECOND) OF PROPERTY § 190 comment a (1981) gives two reasons for the restriction: public interest in the marital relationship and workable standards for adjudication in the context of such an intimate relationship. For a statement of the classic balance between the scope of family relation and contract, see W. CLARK, HANDBOOK OF THE LAW OF CONTRACTS § 164 (3d ed. 1914).

71. On coverture and estates in the entirety with rights of courtesy and dower, see 2 F. POLLOCK & F. MAITLAND, *supra* note 21 Ch. 2, at 403; W. STORY, A TREATISE ON THE LAW OF CONTRACTS NOT UNDER SEAL § 83 (2d ed. 1847).

72. A woman committing most sorts of crimes in her husband's presence had the defense that she was acting under his constructive coercion. L. HOLCOMBE, WIVES AND PROPERTY: REFORM OF THE MARRIED WOMEN'S PROPERTY LAW IN NINETEENTH CENTURY ENGLAND 30 (1983).

73. H. CLARK, *supra* note 23 Intro , § 7.1.

74. *See, e.g.*, Chiesa v. Rowe, 486 F. Supp. 236 (W.D. Mich 1980) (right to claim loss of consortium); Vogel v. Pan Am. World Airways, Inc., 450 F. Supp. 224 (S.D.N.Y. 1978) (right of wrongful death claim). The trend began with the passage of a Mississippi statute in 1839. KEEZER, *supra* note 43 Ch. 2, § 14 (citing Miss. Laws of 1839, ch. 46).

75. *E.g.*, spousal immunity from testifying. *See* Trammel v. United States, 445 U.S. 40 (1980).

76. *See supra* note 68 Ch.2.

77. *See* Wisconsin v. Yoder, 406 U.S. 205 (1972) (parents' right to provide children with religious training); Pierce v. Society of Sisters, 268 U.S. 510, 535 (1925) (parents' right to send children to parochial school); Meyer v. Nebraska, 262 U.S. 390, 399-400 (1923) (parents' right to have children taught in German). *See generally* McCarthy, *The Confused Constitutional, Status and Meaning of Parental Rights*, 22 GA. L. REV. 975 (1988) (noting that the parent child relationship involves fundamental rights).

78. Contract inaugurates marriage, but what exists thereafter is a relationship. Maynard v. Hill, 125 U.S. 190, 211 (1888).

79. The state's interest also may extend to the welfare of the adult partners, particularly of women who are dependent. *See* Jacob, *Another Look at No-Fault Divorce and the Post-Divorce Finances of Women*, 23 LAW & SOC'Y REV. 95, 113 (1989) (no-fault divorce has not changed the economic effects of divorce on women, according to empirical study); Kay, *Equality and Difference: A Perspective on No-Fault Divorce and Its Aftermath*, 56 U. CIN. L. REV. 1 (1987) (traditional allocation of child-rearing duties perpetuates dependence of women, even under no-fault divorce).

80. *See* Krause, *Artificial Conception: Legislative Approaches*, 19 FAM. L.Q. 185, 192 (1985) ("[S]ociety [has an] undisputed interest . . . and even duty to safeguard the circumstances in which children are born and reared. That very interest is the essential basis of all regulation of marriage and family law".)

81. "Marriage . . . [which has] more to do with the morals and civilization of a people than any other institution, has always been subject to the control of the legislature". Maynard v. Hill, 125 U.S. 190, 205 (1888); *see also* Trimble v. Gordon, 430 U.S. 762, 769 (1977) (remarking on "the family unit, perhaps the most fundamental social institution of our society"); Poe v. Ullman, 367 U.S. 497, 551-52 (1961) (Harlan, J., dissenting) ("[T]he integrity of . . . [family] life is something so fundamental" that it is constitutionally protected.). *But see* People v. Onofre, 51 N.Y.2d 476, 488, 415 N.E.2d 936, 940, 434 N.Y.S.2d 947, 951 (1980) (constitutional right of privacy protects "indulgence in acts of sexual intimacy by unmarried persons"), *cert. denied*, 451 U.S. 987 (1981); Commonwealth v. Bonadio, 490 Pa. 91, 415 A.2d 47 (1980) (no rational basis for regulating voluntary sexual acts between unmarried persons). One explanation for this difference of opinion is that the state is becoming less concerned with the relationship per se, and more concerned with "aspects of marriage formation that affect society in general . . ". Glendon, *supra* note 52 Ch. 2, at 683.

82. Allowing suits for alienation of affection and criminal conversation and the right of "self help" in statutes excusing the homicide of spousal paramours are indications of state policy against adultery. *See* 1 C. VERNIER, *supra* note 6 Ch. 2, at 16.

83. Bellotti v. Baird, 443 U.S. 622 (1979) (noting that, unlike a minor's right to have an abortion, the right to marry is postponed but still preserved by age of majority statutes). Roscoe Pound noted of marriage regulations:

> These are on the one hand a social interest in the maintenance of the family
> as a social institution and on the other hand a social interest in the protection
> of dependent persons, in securing to all individuals a moral and social life and
> in the rearing and training of sound and well-bred citizens for the future.

Pound, *Individual Interests in the Domestic Relations*, 14 MICH. L. REV. 177, 182 (1916). There is a traditional notion that marital partners are charged by society with an *officium* to produce children. T. MACKIN, *supra* note 14 Ch. 2, at 146.

84. *See* Reynolds v. United States, 98 U.S. 145 (1878) (holding laws prohibiting polygamy are a permissible limit on religious practice); Baker v. Nelson, 291 Minn. 310, 191 N.W.2d 185 (1971) (upholding constitutionality of a law prohibiting same-sex marriages), *appeal dismissed*, 409 U.S. 810 (1972); M.T. v. J.T., 140 N.J. Super. 77, 355 A.2d 204 (1976) (transsexual marriage upheld because marriage included a man and woman). *But see* Note, *Polygamy and the Right to Marry: New Life for an Old Life Style*, 11 MEM. ST. U.L. REV. 303, 305 (1981) (arguing that polygamy laws should be revised); Note, *The Legality of Homosexual Marriage*, 82 YALE L.J. 573 (1973) [hereinafter Note, *Homosexual Marriage*] (arguing that laws prohibiting homosexual marriages may be unconstitutional in states that adopt the equal rights amendment as state law).

85. However, a state incest provision has been struck down, as applied to genetically unrelated persons related merely by adoption. Israel v. Allen, 195 Colo. 263, 577 P.2d 762 (1978).

86. *See* W. WEYRAUCH & S. KATZ, *supra* note 189 Ch. 1, at 357; *see also* Note, *The Right of the Mentally Disabled to Marry*, 15 J. FAM. L. 463 (1976-77).

87. 381 U.S. 479 (1965).

88. *Id.* at 486; *see also* Carey v. Population Servs. Int'l, 431 U.S. 678 (1977) (holding a ban on the commercial distribution of nonmedical contraceptives an unconstitutional invasion of family autonomy); Roe v. Wade, 410 U.S. 113 (1973) (holding that the state must have a compelling interest to interfere with a woman's right to terminate her pregnancy); *cf.* Stanley v. Georgia, 394 U.S. 557 (1969) (holding that individuals have a right to possess obscene materials in their homes). *See generally* K. REDDEN, FEDERAL REGULATION OF FAMILY LAW (1982) (discussing the development of the right to privacy as the basis for the right of access to and use of contraceptives); L. TRIBE, AMERICAN CONSTITUTIONAL LAW 1337-62, 1400-09, 1414-20 (1988) (surveying and analysing the development of the right to privacy in the areas of contraception, abortion, association, and family); Burt, *The Constitution of the Family*, 1979 SUP. CT. REV. 329, 391-95 (outlining the relationship between the right to privacy and family integrity claims). For a description of state law trends in this area, see *supra* text accompanying notes 57-60 Ch. 2; see also M. GLENDON, *supra* note 189 Ch. 1, at 2 (noting an international trend of "progressive withdrawal of official regulation of marriage formation, dissolution, and the conduct of family life . . . ".).

89. *See generally* Hafen, *supra* note 103 Ch. 1 (tracing the Court's treatment of the right of sexual privacy and the "formal family").

90. Zablocki v. Redhail, 434 U.S. 374 (1978) (states may not prohibit persons who are currently not meeting existing child support obligations from marrying); Loving v Virginia, 388 U.S. 1 (1967) (holding that the state's power to regulate marriage is not unlimited and recognizing marriage as a fundamental right). *But see* Califano v. Jobst, 434 U.S. 47 (1977) (ineligibility for social security dependent's benefits upheld as constitutional under application of rational basis test).

91. *See, e.g.*, People v. Onofre, 51 N.Y.2d 476. 415 N.E.2d 936, 434 N.Y.S.2d 947 (1980) (holding unconstitutional under the equal protection clause a state law prohibiting consensual sodomy), *cert. denied*, 451 U.S. 987 (1981). *See generally* Wilkinson & White, *Constitutional Protection for Personal Lifestyles*, 62 CORNELL L. REV. 563. 569 (1977) (discussing the need to balance protection of personal lifestyle rights and maintenance of sufficient conformity to encourage responsibility and respect for the law); Note, *Developments in the Law—the Constitution and the Family*, 93 HARV. L. REV. 1156 (1980) (discussing rights associated with marriage, procreation, and the family).

92. *See* Bowers v. Hardwick, 478 U.S. 186 (1986) (upholding a state law forbidding homosexual sodomy); Lovisi v. Slayton, 539 F.2d 349 (4th Cir.), *cert. denied*, 429 U.S. 977 (1976) (upholding a Virginia law prohibiting consensual sodomy as applied to married couples who permit others to watch or engage in the proscribed conduct); Doe v. Commonwealth's Attorney, 403 F. Supp. 1199 (E.D. Va. 1975) (upholding Virginia's law prohibiting sodomy as it applies to homosexuals), *aff'd*, 425 U.S. 901 (1976). More surprising is the decision in Hollenbaugh v. Carnegie Free Library, 436 F. Supp. 1328 (W.D. Pa 1977), *aff'd*, 578 F.2d 1374 (3d Cir. 1978), *cert. denied*, 439 U.S. 1052 (1978), wherein the plaintiffs, employees of the defendant library, were fired for openly cohabiting while one of them was married. The district court held that the library's actions violated neither the plaintiffs' right to equal protection nor to privacy. *Id.* at 1332-1334. Even the Supreme Court in *Roe v. Wade* eschews a broad right "to do with one's body as one pleases". 410 U.S. at 154. *See generally* Katz, *Majoritarian Morality and Parental Rights*, 52 ALB. L.

REV. 405 (1988) (arguing that the Supreme Court has followed divergent paths in recognizing privacy rights in the area of reproduction and parenting, while refusing to similarly recognize sexual privacy rights); Schneider, *State Interest Analysis in Fourteenth Amendment "Privacy" Law: An Essay on the Constitutionalization of Social Issues*, 51 LAW & CONTEMP. PROBS. 79 (1988) (criticizing the Supreme Court's treatment of sexual expression issues and advocating that such issues are not amenable to constitutionalization at all).

93. *See* Thornburgh v. American College of Obstetricians & Gynecologists, 476 U.S. 747, 772 (1986); Carey v. Population Servs. Int'l, 431 U.S. 678, 685 (1977); Eisenstadt v. Baird, 405 U.S. 438, 453 (1972). American law more than any in Western Europe has come to embody the idea that the termination of marriage and pregnancy is a matter of individual right. M. GLENDON, *supra* note 1 Intro., at 113.

94. Planned Parenthood v. Danforth, 428 U.S. 52, 71 (1976). The State does have an interest in ensuring that appropriate information is conveyed to the mother. Akron v. Akron Center for Reproductive Health, Inc., 462 U.S. 416, 445 (1982). At some point, the mother's right is eclipsed by the state's compelling interest in protecting potential life. Webster v. Reproductive Health Servs., 492 U.S. 490 (1989).

95. The federal courts have not addressed the issue. In a highly publicized state case dealing with the disposition of extracorporeal embryos, the Tennessee Supreme Court held that the individual preferences of the two parents are to be balanced, with a presumption favouring the parent who wishes to veto implantation. *Davis v. Davis*, 842 S.W.2d 588, 604 (1989), *cert. denied*, 113 S. Ct. 1259 (1992). In so holding, the court reversed a trial court determination that seven *in vitro* embryos were human beings and that the wife should be allowed to pursue implantation based on the best interests of the embryos. *Id.* at 594.

96. *See infra* notes 110-11 Ch. 2 and accompanying text. *See generally* Comment, *Equal Protection for Illegitimate Children: A Consistent Rule Emerges*, 1980 B.Y.U. L. REV. 142 (concluding that Supreme Court jurisprudence on equal protection of illegitimate children distinguishes between regulations that serve administrative purposes and those that merely express moral conditions of promiscuity).

97. *See* Lalli v. Lalli, 439 U.S. 259 (1978); Trimble v. Gordon, 430 U.S. 762, 769 (1977); New Jersey Welfare Rights Org. v. Cahill, 411 U.S. 619 (1973); Gomez v. Perez, 409 U.S. 535 (1973); Glona v. American Guar. & Liab. Ins. Co., 391 U.S. 73 (1968). *But see* Mathews v. Lucas, 427 U.S. 495 (1976) (upholding differential treatment of an illegitimate child in providing social security death benefits); Weber v. Aetna Cas. & Sur. Co.. 406 U.S. 164, 184 (1972) (Rehnquist, J., dissenting) (classification not impermissible per se).

98. There is a "world-wide pattern of approximating the status of the child born outside marriage to that of the child born within marriage . . . . The legal institution [of marriage] is being drained of some of its content by the increasing number and social acceptance of births outside legal marriage". Glendon, *supra* note 52 Ch. 2, at 714-15 (footnotes omitted).

99. *See* Stanley v. Illinois, 405 U.S. 645 (1972) (state violated procedural due process by terminating unwed father's parental rights without a hearing where father lived with children and supported them).

100. *See* Caban v. Mohammed, 441 U.S. 380, 389 (1979) (where "unwed father may have a relationship with his children fully comparable to that of the mother", statute granting unwed mother, but not father, a veto over adoption violates the equal protection clause); *see also* Lehr v. Robertson, 463 U.S. 248 (1983) (where unwed father had not established any familial relationship with child, state not obligated to extend him the right to veto adoption); Quilloin v. Walcott, 434 U.S. 246, 256 (1978) (where unwed father has never exercised actual or legal custody of child, his interests are distinguishable from a separated or divorced father's).

101. *See supra* note 111 Ch. 2.

102. The human leukocyte alloantigen (HLA) test is highly reliable. S. GREEN & J. LONG, *supra* note 55 Ch. 1, at 278. Contrast the maxim, *Mater est quam gestatio demonstrat*. (She who is the mother shows this by carrying the child.)

103. For a discussion of legal claims on behalf of unwed mothers who seek exclusive parental rights, see Bartlett, *Re-Expressing Parenthood*, 98 YALE L.J 293, 306-15 (1988); *see also* Ikemoto, *Providing Protection for Collaborative, Noncoital Reproduction: Surrogate Motherhood and Other New Procreative Technologies, and the Right of Intimate Association*, 40 RUTGERS L. REV. 1273, 1286-90 (1988); Karst, *The Freedom of Intimate Association*, 89 YALE L.J. 624 (1980) (suggesting the outlines and constitutional origins of these rights). *See generally* L. TRIBE, *supra* note 88 Ch. 2, at 1337-62 (analyzing the *Griswold* line of cases); Bartlett, *Rethinking Parenthood as an Exclusive Status: The Need for Legal Alternatives When the Premise of the Nuclear Family Has Failed*, 70 VA. L. REV. 879, 912-27 (1984) (discussing the rights of unwed fathers); Hafen, *supra* note 103 Ch. 1 (arguing that modern Supreme Court cases uphold the family in spite of their individualistic rhetoric); Note, *Reproductive Technology and the Procreation Rights of the Unmarried*, 98 HARV. L. REV. 669 (1985).

104. However, the legal recognition or the status of illegitimacy is not unconstitutional per se. Mathews v. Lucas, 427 U.S. 495, 506 (1976); Jimenez v. Weinberger, 417 U.S. 628, 632-33 (1974).

105. The critical legal studies school would view this as a positive development. *See* Unger, *The Critical Legal Studies Movement*, 96 HARV. L. REV. 561 (1983) (criticizing governmental intervention in personal relations underlying equal protection). However, others are not as sanguine: "one can only imagine what would happen from a jurisprudential perspective if marriage and minority status were to fall by the wayside in the quest for individual fairness". Hafen, *supra* note 103 Ch. 1, at 489.

106. *See* Planned Parenthood v. Danforth, 428 U.S. 52, 71 (1976) (giving greater weight to the wife's interest in deciding whether to terminate pregnancy because she is more directly affected). An alternative solution would be to dictate that whichever individual had played the most multifaceted role in reproduction would prevail in any conflict. W. O'DONNELL & D. JONES, *supra* note 140 Ch. 1, at 236.

107. Fineman, *Law and Changing Patterns of Behavior: Sanctions on Non-Marital Cohabitation*, 1981 WIS. L. REV. 275 (urging the adoption of liberal laws regarding cohabitative arrangements). *But see* Coombs, *Shared Privacy and the Fourteenth Amendment, or the Rights of Relationships*, 75 CALIF. L. REV. 1593, 1593 (1987) (arguing that people usually do not contemplate the legal repercussions of intimate relationships).

108. *See* 1 C. VERNIER, *supra* note 6 Ch. 2, at 170-72 (state regulation of marriage "has a fundamental physiological basis, the propagation of the human family . . ".).

109. *Id.*; Hafen, *supra* note 103 Ch. 1, at 465 n.6 ("No state would knowingly issue a marriage license to a homosexual couple").

110. *See* 4 C. VERNIER, *supra* note 6 Ch. 2, at 149 (discussing differences in parental rights between mothers and fathers of illegitimate children).

111. Because of the punitive impact of this system of inducement on children, the Supreme Court of the United States has found it unconstitutional. *See* Gomez v. Perez, 409 U.S. 535 (1973); *see* 1 C. VERNIER, *supra* note 6 Ch. 2, at 149. Illegitimate Children are deemed legitimate as a matter of law in several states. *See, e.g.*, ARIZ. REV. STAT. ANN. § 8-601 (1989); OKLA. STAT. tit. 10, § 1.2 (1987); OR. REV. STAT. § 109.060 (1993).

112. Hafen, *supra* note 103 Ch. 1.

113. *See* Carey v. Population Servs. Int'l, 431 U.S. 678 (1977) (holding minors have a right of access to contraceptives); Planned Parenthood v. Danforth, 428 U.S. 52 (1976) (holding husband cannot be given a veto over wife's decision to terminate pregnancy); Eisenstadt v. Baird, 405 U.S. 438 (1972) (holding access to contraceptives must be the same for married and unmarried individuals).

114. *See* W. O'DONNELL & D. JONES, *supra* note 140 Ch. 1, at 213 (arguing test for eligibility to have children should be stability rather than marriage). Even a preference for marriage as a measure of stability conceivably could be deemed impermissible. *See* Roberts v. United States Jaycees, 468 U.S. 609 (1984) (marriage is a strong example of a relationship protected by freedom of association, but not the only one); *supra* note 81 Ch. 2 and accompanying text.

115. *See supra* note 131 Ch. 1 and accompanying text.

116. For example, impotence is a recognized ground for annulment. S. GREEN & J. LONG, *supra* note 55 Ch. 1, at 44-46.

117. *See supra* note 75 Ch. 2 and accompanying text.

118. H. CLARK, *supra* note 23 Intro., § 2.12.

119. *See* 4 C. VERNIER, *supra* note 6 Ch. 2, at 149 (viewing rules on illegitimacy as an attempt to discourage illicit intercourse).

120. In one view, the natural father's rights to relate to his child are contingent on his willingness to marry the child's mother. Stanley v. Illinois, 405 U.S. 645, 664 (1972) (Burger, C.J., dissenting). The traditional English common law rule, never fully adopted in America, gave the "father an almost unlimited right to the custody, control and earnings" of his natural children. 4 C. VERNIER, *supra* note 6 Ch. 2, at 4.

121. *E.g.*, Michael H. v. Gerald D., 491 U.S. 110 (1989) (1989) (not a constitutional violation to prefer the legal husband over the natural father in assigning parental rights); OR. REV. STAT. § 109.070(1) (1989) (creating a presumption that husband is the father of children born to wife during marriage).

122. *See* Santosky v. Kramer, 455 U.S. 745 (1982) (state must demonstrate parental unfitness to terminate custody); Caban v. Mohammed, 441 U.S. 380 (1979) (father's marital status insufficient to deny parent-child relationship). The Family Support Act premises parent-child duties less on the parental marriage relationship, and more directly on biological relationship. The Family Support Act of 1988, Pub. L. No. 100-485, 102 Stat. 2343 (1990).

123. In English common law, the father was the sole guardian. *See* W. WEYRAUCH & S. KATZ, *supra* note 189 Ch. 1, at 496; 4 C. VERNIER, *supra* note 6 Ch. 2, at 4. This principle was gradually replaced in American courts by the "tender years" doctrine, which gives primary custody of small children to the mother. *See, e.g.*, Washburn v. Washburn, 49 Cal. App. 2d 581. 122 P.2d 96 (1942) (all other matters being equal, the mother gains custody). Now, three-fourths of the American states give equal recognition to both parents in granting custody. W. O'DONNELL & D. JONES, *supra* note 140 Ch. 1, at 160. Unwed mothers ordinarily have the right of custody. *See, e.g.*, Jones v. Smith, 278 So. 2d 339 (Fla. Dist. Ct. App. 1973), *cert. denied*, 415 U.S. 958 (1974).

124. When a child is born within a relationship formalized by marriage, the state presumes the paternity of the mother's husband. Thus, in an indirect sense, his marital contract may be a basis for acquiring parental rights over a biologically unrelated child. However, the state makes that decision for public policy reasons; the couple does not decide the question. *See* notes 78-86 Ch. 2 and accompanying text.

125. Along the same lines, English and Australian committee reports stipulate that married couples or couples in long-term relationships should have priority in obtaining infertility services. Knoppers & Sloss, *supra* note 70 Ch. 1, at 678 (citing the WARNOCK REP., *supra* note 21 Intro., and the WALLER REP., *supra* note 21 Intro.).

126. Such assignments are not enforceable even with respect to claims pertaining to the children of the marriage. *See* Hess v. Hess, 115 Or. 595, 599, 239 P. 124, 125 (1925) (A divorce decree does not affect "the rights of the child and the duties of the parents toward the child. This proposition is so elementary that it hardly requires the citation of authorities in its support"); RESTATEMENT (SECOND) OF CONTRACTS § 191 comment a, illustration 1 (1979) (separation agreements providing for custody of child enforceable only if in child's best interest); Mnookin & Kornhauser, *Bargaining in the Shadow of the Law: The Case of Divorce*, 88 YALE L. J. 950, 958 (1979) (arguing that courts may and should enforce parental custody agreements and only intervene if the best interests of the child are not reflected in the agreement).

127. The court may treat the transfer of custody under a contract as final, if so doing is in the child's best interest. RESTATEMENT (SECOND) OF CONTRACTS § 191 comment a, illustration 2 (1979) (stating that custody contracts are "unenforceable", except where outcome happens to further the best interests of the child). The "parental rights doctrine" creates a presumption in favour of returning custody to the natural parent if that will further the child's best interests and the parent so desires. Cook v. Cobb, 271 S.C. 136, 245 S.E.2d 612 (1978). For a critique of the doctrine, *see* McGough & Shindell, *Coming of Age: The Best Interests of the Child Standard in Parent-Third Party Custody Disputes*, 27 EMORY L.J. 209 (1978).

128. *See generally* Hershkowitz, *Due Process and the Termination of Parental Rights*, 19 FAM. L.Q 245 (1985) (discussing limits to the state's ability to terminate parental rights).

129. The rule is nothing other than an application of the "best interests of the child" doctrine. It ratifies the contract allocation of custody, where doing so reinforces what has become the child's primary bond of stability. *See* Reimche v. First Nat'l Bank, 512 F.2d 187 (9th Cir. 1975) (adoption by natural father through agreement valid); *In re* Shirk's Estate, 186 Kan. 311, 350 P.2d 1 (1960) (contract not illegal where parent allowed grandparent to adopt her child in exchange for a promise to leave her property); Clark v. Clark, 122 Md. 114, 89 A. 405 (1913) (mother held to have entered binding agreement with child's grandfather); Enders v. Enders, 164 Pa. 266, 30 A. 129 (1894) (grandfather held to have binding contract with son's wife), The question, in the present context, is whether the rule should be different where the conflict emerges while the child is still in the embryonic or fetal stage. Some propose that property concepts be interposed in this context. *See infra* note 257 Ch. 3 and accompanying text.

130. *See generally* H. CLARK, *supra* note 23 Intro., § 20.4 (describing consent requirements for voluntary termination of parental rights through adoption).

131. *See, e.g.*, Jenks v. Brown, 250 Ala. 534, 35 So. 2d 359 (1948) (recognizing that the child's welfare is the primary consideration in custody disputes and considering the marital status of each parent as one factor in the decision).

132. Zainaldin, *The Emergence of a Modern American Family Law: Child Custody, Adoptions, and the Courts, 1796-1851*, 73 NW. U.L. REV. 1038 (1979).

133. *See* H. WITMER, E. HERZOG, E. WEINSTEIN & M. SULLIVAN, INDEPENDENT ADOPTIONS (1963).

134. *See In re* Baby M, 109 N.J. 396, 537 A.2d 1227 (1988).

135. H. CLARK, *supra* note 23 Intro., § 20.4.

136. Private adoption, like all forms of adoption, is not provided for under common law. 4 C. VERNIER, *supra* note 6 Ch. 2, at 10-12. Adoption has been used to obtain legally enforceable status rights in lieu of contract. *E.g., In re* Adoption of Adult Anonymous, 106 Misc. 2d 792, 800, 435 N.Y.S.2d 527, 531 (1981). However, adoption does not entail the termination of parental rights by contract. *See* UNIF. ADOPTION ACT § 7, 9 U.L.A. 39 (1988).

137. *See* Note, *The Constitutional Rights of Natural Parents Under New York's Adoption Statutes*, 12 N.Y.U. REV. L. & SOC. CHANGE 617, 619 (1983-84) ("[O]nce the natural parent executes the consent to adoption, the parental rights may be terminated immediately and irrevocably".).

138. N. BAKER, BABY SELLING: THE SCANDAL OF BLACK MARKET ADOPTION (1978); Note, *Black-Market Adoptions*, 22 CATH. LAW. 48, 50 (1976).

139. Landes & Posner, *supra* note 166 Ch. 1, at 338.

140. *See supra* text accompanying notes 132-37 Ch. 2.

141. *See* Note, *supra* note 20 Intro., at 9.

142. *But cf.* Smith v. Organization of Foster Families for Equality and Reform, 431 U.S. 816, 823-28 (1976) (foster care placement not rigorously scrutinized by state).

143. According to Ronald Dworkin, associational relationships generate obligations "through a series of charities and events", not one act of commitment. R. DWORKIN, LAW'S EMPIRE 197 (1986).

144. Supreme Court jurisprudence can still be understood as resting on respect for natural endowment. *See* Hafen, *supra* note 103 Ch. 1, at 491-92.

145. "The experience with AID should be instructive for those interested in legal regulation of the other new reproductive technologies". Healy, *supra* note 5 Intro., at 139-40.

146. *See* Annas & Elias, *supra* note 12 Intro., at 149.

147. The donation of gametes through AID has become a residual basis of parental rights. The gestational role of the "surrogate" becomes such a basis. *See supra* notes 138-45 Ch. 1 and accompanying text.

148. AID was first performed by a physician without the knowledge or consent of his anaesthetized patients. Gena Corea argues that this practice constituted a form of procreative "rape". G. COREA, *supra* note 156 Ch. 1; *see also* Robertson, *Technology and Motherhood: Legal and Ethical Issues in Human Egg Donation*, 39 CASE W. RES. L. REV. 1, 2 (1988-89) (discussing egg donation, a less accepted, more difficult method of treating infertility than AID); Note, *The Need for Statutes Regulating Artificial Insemination by Donors*, 46 OHIO ST. L.J. 1055, 1057 (1985) [hereinafter Note, *Need for Statutes*] (asserting that the widespread and growing use of AID has given rise to the need for regulation of the legal problems facing AID-conceived children, donors, doctors and patients), Note, *Artificial Insemination: A Legislative Remedy*, 3 W. ST. U.L. REV. 48, 50 (1975) [hereinafter Note, *Artificial Insemination*] (discussing the need for comprehensive legislation to regulate the performance and administration of AID).

149. Note, *Need for Statutes*, *supra* note 148 Ch. 2, at 1056. *See generally* W. FINEGOLD, ARTIFICIAL INSEMINATION 5-7 (1964) (giving a brief history of the use of artificial insemination); Special Project, *Legal Rights and Issues Surrounding Conception, Pregnancy, and Birth*, 39 VAND. L. REV. 597, 673-78 (1986) (discussing the background and legal authority behind AID).

150. *See, e.g.*, Curie-Cohen, Luttrell & Shapiro, *Current Practice of Artificial Insemination by Donor in the United States*, 300 NEW ENG. J. MED. 585, 588 (1979); Vetri, *supra* note 126 Ch. 1, at 507 (noting that a 1984 estimate put the number of births resulting from AID at 20,000).

151. *See* Beck, *A Critical Look at the Legal, Ethical, and Technical Aspects of Artificial Insemination*, 27 FERTILITY & STERILITY 1 (1976) (discussing the contract-like procedures involved prior to AID insemination that serve as the basis for asserting paternity rights). *See generally* Comment, *Artificial Insemination and the Law*, 1982 B.Y.U. L. REV. 935, 950-52 (AID contracts implicate various constitutional interests, such as privacy, as well as the best interests of the child).

152. This argument has met with mixed success. *Compare* People v. Sorensen, 68 Cal. 2d 280, 284, 437 P.2d 495, 498, 66 Cal. Rptr. 7, 10 (1968) (holding rejecting contentions that AID is adultery and resulting child is illegitimate) *and* MacLennan v. MacLennan, 1958 Sess. Cas. 105, 113 (Scot.) (finding AID is not adultery even without the husband's consent) *with* Doornbos v. Doornbos, No. 545.14981 (Super. Ct. Cook County, Ill., Dec. 13, 1954), *appeal denied*, 12 Ill. App. 2d 473, 139 N.E.2d 844 (1956) (determing AID is adultery when the donor is a third party regardless of consent); Orford v. Orford, 49 O.L.R. 15, 20 (1921) (AID is a form of adultery and alimony can be denied on this basis).

153. *See, e.g.*, People v. Sorensen, 68 Cal. 2d 280, 289, 437 P.2d 495, 501, 66 Cal. Rptr. 7, 13 (1968) (father-child relationship established by father having taken on responsibility for AID child); Gursky v. Gursky, 39 Misc. 2d 1083, 1088, 242 N.Y.S.2d 406, 411 (1963) (upholding illegitimacy but ordering support on the basis of implied contract to support).

154. *See, e.g.*, People v. Sorensen, 68 Cal. 2d 280, 289, 437 P.2d 495, 501, 66 Cal. Rptr. 7, 13 (1968); Strnad v. Strnad, 190 Misc. 786, 787, 78 N.Y.S.2d 390, 392 (N.Y. Sup. Ct. 1948) (holding child legitimate where mother's husband consented to AID procedure).

155. Judicial review of AID remains isolated and sporadic and has contributed little to the development of this branch of law. Healey, *supra* note 5 Intro., at 206.

156. GA. CODE ANN. § 19-7-21 (1991). This law has been criticized from the feminist perspective as protecting male anonymity. It has also been argued that donor anonymity ignores the real interests of the child. *See* Note, *Artificial Insemination*, *supra* note 148 Ch. 2, at 59.

157. UNIF. PARENTAGE ACT, 9B U.L.A. 287 (1987).

158. The following state statutes relate to artificial insemination: ALA. CODE § 26-17-21 (1992); ALASKA STAT. § 25.20.045 (1991); ARIZ. REV. STAT. ANN. § 12-2451 (Supp. 1994); ARK. STAT. ANN. § 9-10-201 (1993); CAL. FAM. CODE § 7613 (Deering 1994); COLO. REV. STAT. § 19-6-106 (1986); CONN. GEN. STAT. § 45a-771f (1993); FLA. STAT. § 742.11 (1994); GA. CODE ANN. § 19-7-21 (1991); IDAHO CODE § 39-5405 (1993); ILL. STAT. ch.40, para. 1-3 (Smith-Hurd 1993); KAN. STAT. ANN. § 23-129 (1988); LA. CIV. CODE ANN. art. 188 (West 1993) MD. EST. & TRUSTS CODE § 1-206(b) (1991); MASS. GEN. L. ch.46, § 4B (West 1994); MICH. COMP. LAWS § 700.111 (1980); MINN. STAT. § 257.56 (1992); MO. STAT. ANN. §210.824 (Vernon 1994) MONT. CODE ANN. § 40-6-106 (1991); NEV. REV. STAT. § 126.061 (1993); N.H. REV. STAT. ANN. §.168:B-3II (1994); N.J. STAT. ANN. § 9:17-44 (1993); N.M. STATE ANN. § 40-11-6 (1994); N.Y. DOM. REL. LAW § 73 (McKinney 1988); N.C. GEN. STAT. § 49A-1 (1984); OHIO REV. CODE ANN. § 3111.37 (Anderson 1989); OKLA. STAT. tit. 10, § 552 (1987); OR. REV. STAT. § 109.243 (1993); TENN. CODE ANN. § 68-3-306 (1992); TEX. FAM. CODE ANN. § 12.03 (Vernon Supp. 1995); VA. CODE ANN. § 20-158A (1994); WASH. REV. CODE § 26.26.050 (1986); WIS. STAT. ANN. § 891.40 (Supp. 1994); WYO. STAT. § 14-2-103 (1994). Calls for universal AID legislation are still heard. *See* Note, *Artificial Insemination Donor Rights in Situations Involving Unmarried Recipients*, 26 J. FAM. L. 793 (1987-88); Note, *Need for Statutes*, *supra* note 148 Ch. 2, at 1076.

159. UNIF. PARENTAGE ACT, *supra* note 81, Ch. 1.

160. *Id.*

161. *Id.* § 5(b). One court has held that the Uniform Parentage Act, as enacted, leaves residual parental status in the sperm donor, so that a subsequent adoption proceeding is necesary legally to terminate the sperm donor's parental rights. *Welborn v. Doe*, 10 Va. App. 631, 635, 394 S.E.2d 732, 734 (1990).

162. "With respect to . . . artificial insemination with donor sperm (AID), the search for legal answers during the past two decades has produced a substantial body of law. Yet, . . . many gaps remain". Healey, *supra* note 5 Intro., at 139.

163. "Virtually all statutes acknowledge the legitimacy of a child conceived by AID following the informed consent of the mother and her husband". *Id*. at 141.

164. UNIF. PARENTAGE ACT, *supra* note 81 Ch. 1, § 4.

165. *Cf.* Kershner v. Kershner, 244 A.D. 34, 278 N.Y.S. 501 (1935) (holding husband's duty to support his wife may not be contractually terminated), *aff'd*, 269 N.Y. 655, 200 N.E. 43 (1936).

166. *See supra* notes 30-37 Ch. 2 and accompanying text.

167. *See supra* note 65 Ch. 2 and accompanying text.

168. *See, e.g.*, OR. REV. STAT. § 677.365 (1993); Vetri, *supra* note 126 Ch. 1, at 512 (discussing the relationship between the mother's marital status and the requirement of consent).

169. *E.g.*, COLO. REV. STAT. § 19-6-106(2) (1986). Artificial insemination by donor for single women parallels the recent trend affirming single-parent adoption, although there is at least one significant difference between the two developments. An existing child's need, which may otherwise go unmet, serves to justify the former.

170. *But see* Stanley v. Illinois, 405 U.S. 645 (1972) (holding that states must provide a natural father with a hearing and an opportunity to be heard before terminating his parental rights). *See supra* notes 99-102 Ch. 2 and accompanying text.

171. UNIF. PARENTAGE ACT, *supra* note 81 Ch. 1.

172. *See supra* notes 152-63 Ch. 2 and accompanying text.

173. Radin, *supra* note 28 Intro., at 1925-36.

174. *See* Jhordan C. v. Mary K., 179 Cal. App. 3d 386, 224 Cal. Rptr. 530 (1986) (holding that sperm donor who provides semen directly to mother rather than through physician is not precluded from bringing a paternity action). *But see In re* R.C., Minor Child, 775 P.2d 27 (Colo. 1989) (determining that absent a signed release of parental rights the intent of the adult parties is dispositive, and that the parties' agreement is admissible).

175. *See* Jhordan C. v. Mary K., 179 Cal. App. 3d 386, 224 Cal. Rptr. 530 (1986) (holding that unmarried recipient and donor with whom she was personally acquainted by their conduct preserved donor's status as the child's father); C.M. v C.C., 152 N.J. Super. 160, 377 A.2d 821 (1977) (known donor's consent and active participation in the insemination procedure evidenced an intent to assume the responsibilities of parenthood). *See generally* Shaman, *Legal Aspects of Artificial Insemination*, 18 J. FAM. L. 331, 343 (1980-81) (discussing artificial insemination donors as parents).

176. Shaman, *supra* note 175 Ch. 2, at 344. In a representative case, an alleged agreement between the unmarried mother and father of child conceived by artificial insemination that the father would waive his parental rights was held unenforceable, where the parties had not complied with statutory waiver requirements. *In re* Thomas S. v. Robin Y., 209 A.D. 2d 298, 618 N.Y.S. 2d 356, (N.Y. App. Div. 1994).

177. UNIF. PARENTAGE ACT, *supra* note 81 Ch. 1. Thus, recognition of paternity has been denied, where the statute is satisfied, even though the sperm donor has subsequently developed a continuous caring relationship with, and extended ongoing financial support to the child. Leckie v. Voorhies, 128 Or. App. 289, 292, 875 P.2d 521, 523 (1994). However several states have enacted statutes which expressly provide that, pursuant to a consensual arrangement between the woman and the donor, the donor may be recognized as the father with concomitant rights and responsibilities. N.J. STAT. ANN. § 9:17-44(b) (West 1993); WASH. REV. CODE § 26.26.050 (1986). New Mexico and Wisconsin also allow an AID contract to allocate rights to the donor. OFFICE OF TECHNOLOGY ASSESSMENT, *supra* note 21 Intro., at 278.

178. *See generally* E. FARNSWORTH, *supra* note 4 Ch. 1, § 5.4, at 341-47 (discussing freedom or contract in marital and cohabitational relationships).

179. OFFICE OF TECHNOLOGY ASSESSMENT, *supra* note 21 Intro., at 240.

180. *See* Curie-Cohen, Luttrell & Shapiro, *supra* note 150 Ch. 2, at 586-87 (describing routine steps involved in the artificial insemination process).

181. *See* RESTATEMENT (SECOND) OF CONTRACTS § 73 (1979) (in order to assert a legal claim, performance or forbearance must have been bargained for and given in exchange of a promise).

182. UNIF. PARENTAGE ACT, *supra* note 81 Ch. 1.

183. *Id.*

184. *Id.* Alternatively, the allocation of parental rights and duties may be enforced as a matter of estoppel. *Levin v. Levin*, 626 N.E.2d 527 (Ind. Ct. App. 1993).

185. Hired maternity contracts often provide for such anonymity. *See* OFFICE OF TECHNOLOGY ASSESSMENT, *supra* note 21 Intro., at 275. Children born under such arrangements may argue for the same rights to know the facts of their origin as adoptees. S. GREEN & J. LONG, *supra* note 55 Ch. 1, at 246.

186. For a discussion of how societies make choices to allocate resources, see G. CALABRESI & P. BOBBIT, TRAGIC CHOICES (1978). Some evidence of the contractual interpretation can be seen in the courts' emphasis on private intention when legally justifying posthumous AI, *Hecht v. Superior Ct.*, 16 Cal. App. 4th 836, 20 Cal. Rptr. 2d 275 (1993), or when imposing paternity even where the technicalities of the AID statute are not complied with, *K.B. v. N.B.*, 811 S.W. 2d 634 (Tex. Ct. Appeals 1991), *cert. denied*, 112 S. Ct. 1963 (1992). There is reason to suppose, however, that recognition of eligibility to enter such contracts might be limited to those offering genetic or gestational contributions or at least associated with a genetic or gestational parent through a legal marriage. *Curiale v. Reagan*, 222 Cal. App. 3d 1597, 272 Cal. Rptr. 520 (1990) (refusing to enforce a contract assigning parental rights to the birth mother's lesbian mother).

187. *See supra* notes 30-37 Ch. 2 and accompanying text.

188. Some feminists have claimed a right of "self-insemination". Hanmer, *Transforming Consciousness; Women and the New Reproductive Technologies*, in Man-Made Women, *supra* note 156 Ch. 1, at 95; Kritchevsky, *The Unmarried Woman's Right to Artificial Insemination: A Call for an Expanded Definition of Family*, 4 HARV. WOMEN'S L.J. 1, 18-19 (1981). This argument was rejected by the court in Jhordan C. v. Mary K., 179 Cal. App. 3d 386, 224 Cal. Rptr. 530 (1986). There has been judicial recognition that impregnation through intercourse is incompatible with legal acknowledgement of a contractual understanding of nonpaternity. *Estes v. Albers*, 504 N.W.2d 607, 608 (S.D. 1993).

189. *See* M. Field, *supra* note 20 Intro., at 5 (discussing the growing use of hired maternity arrangements), NEW YORK STATE TASK FORCE REPORT, *supra* note 192 Ch. 1, at 7 (hired maternity has become an alternative to the declining number of babies available for adoption). A typical contract provides for $10 000 plus expenses, $3000 - 7000 for brokers, plus psychologist, and $5000 for an attorney, with between $30 000 and $50 000 total cost. OFFICE OF TECHNOLOGY ASSESSMENT, *supra* note 21 Intro., at 275-6.

An extensive literature on the subject has developed. *See, e.g.*, Cohen, *Surrogate Mothers: Whose Baby Is It?* 10 AM. J.L. & MED. 243 (1985) (discussing the increase in hired maternity and associated legal implications while proposing that such contracts be revocable prior to birth and that no payment other than expenses be exchanged); Coleman, *Surrogate Motherhood: Analysis of the Problems and Suggestions for Solutions*, 50 TENN. L. REV. 71, 72 (1982) (discussing how the increase in hired maternity has created constitutional, contractual, and parental legal problems and concluding that this practice falls under the right of privacy); Eaton, *supra* note 21 Intro., at 689 (discussing procedures and analyzing and comparing measures taken in the United States to those in Great Britain, Australia, and Canada); Jackson, *Baby M and the Question of Parenthood*, 76 GEO. L.J. 1811 (1988) (suggesting a new outlook on parenthood and visitation rights for the gestational mother in hired maternity cases); Krimmel, *The Case Against the Commercialization of Childbearing*, 24 WILLAMETTE L. REV. 1035, 1036 (1988) (discussing the increase in hired maternity and arguing that it exploits the mother and child and should be prohibited); O'Brien, *Commercial Conceptions: A Breeding Ground For Surrogacy*, 65 N.C.L. REV. 127, 142 (1986) (contrasting the sale of semen with the sale of infants to show that hired maternity exploits the natural mother); Note, *Surrogate Motherhood: The Outer Limits of Protected Conduct*, 4 DET. C.L. REV. 1131, 1133 (1981) (discussing the increase in hired maternity and the need for Michigan courts to reconcile the parents' right to privacy with the state's right to control the conduct of its citizens); Note, *supra* note 190 Ch. 1, at 1289 (proposing a solution to the problems resulting from baby selling and adoption laws, paternity and artificial insemination regulations, and opposition to hired maternity arrangements); Note, *supra* note 8 Intro., at 1941-49 (discussing the failure of paternalism as a ground for deciding whether the gestational mother's right to abort is inalienable); Note, *Surrogate Motherhood: Contractual Issues and Remedies Under Legislative Proposals*, 23 WASHBURN L.J. 601 (1984) (showing the increase in hired maternity as reflected by new legislation addressing problems not adequately dealt with by existing statutes); Note, *Development in the Law: Surrogate Parenthood Contracts After Baby "M"*, 24 WILLAMETTE L. REV. 1053 (1988) (discussing hired maternity procedures and subsequent legal developments resulting from these contracts).

Dr Richard Levin of Surrogate Parenting Associates, Inc. claims to have "performed what became the world's first publicly proclaimed case of contractual surrogate parenting" in 1979. *Surrogacy Arrangements Act of 1987: Hearing Before the Subcomm. on Transportation, Tourism, and Hazardous Materials of the House Comm. on Energy and Commerce on H.R. 2433*, 100th Cong., 1st Sess. 112 (1987) (statement of Dr. Richard Levin, a physician specializing in reproductive endocrinology and infertility) [hereinafter *Hearing on Surrogacy Arrangements Act*].

190. The "surrogate" mother has also been termed "gestational hostess" or "uterine hostess". Hollinger, *supra* note 6 Intro., at 873. The misleading character of the term "surrogacy" has been widely commented upon. *See, e.g.*, Means, *supra* note 16 Intro., at 445 n.1 (noting that more accurately, "surrogate mother" means the adoptive, not the natural, mother). The term "surrogate mother" indicates that the "surrogate" is a substitute for the mother. In fact, the woman who gestates the child is universally considered to be the child's mother. *See, e.g.*, WEBSTER'S THIRD NEW INTERNATIONAL DICTIONARY 1474 (1986) (defining mother as "a woman who has given birth to a child . . . "). For this reason the term "surrogate motherhood" is inappropriate.

191. "From 1,000 to 1,400 surrogacy arrangements have been made in the country to date, with 800 to 1,000 babies born under them . . . ". Evans, *Surrogate Mothers Could Keep Babies*, Wash. Post, Dec. 21, 1988, at B1, col. 3; NEW YORK STATE TASK FORCE REPORT, *supra* note 192 Ch. 1, at 25.

192. *See In re* Baby M, 109 N.J. 396, 537 A.2d 1277 (1988); *see also* Annas, *Baby M: Babies (and Justice) for Sale*, HASTINGS CENTER REP., June 1987, at 13; Jackson, *supra* note 189 Ch. 2.

193. *See* Annas, *The Baby Broker Boom*, HASTINGS CENTER REP., June 1986, at 30, 31 (condemning 1986 court decisions enforcing hired maternity arrangements on the basis that "commercial surrogacy promotes the exploitation of women and infertile couples, and the dehumanization of infants"); Krimmel, *supra* note 128 Ch. 1, at 35 (suggesting parenting should not be separated from the decision to have a child). *See generally* Pollit, *supra* note 105 Ch. 1 (criticizing pro-surrogacy attitudes and arguments).

194. Stark, *A Womb of One's Own*, 19 PSYCH. TODAY 11 (1985).

195. Wadlington, *United States: The Continuing Debate About Surrogate Parenthood*, 27 J. FAM. L. 321 (1988-89).

196. *See infra* notes 199-273 Ch. 2 and accompanying text. In Great Britain, the courts have issued a number of decisions on hired maternity including *A. v. C.* 1 Fam. 445 (1985); *Re P* 2 Fam. 421 (1987); *Re Adoption Application* 2 Fam. 291 (1987); and *Re W* 1 Fam. 385 (1991).

197. *See infra* notes 274-358 Ch. 2 and accompanying text. *See also* Wadlington, *Contracts to Bear a Child: The Mixed Legislative Signals*, 29 IDAHO L. REV. 383 (1992/93). In Great Britain, hired maternity has been the subject of action by Parliament. Surrogacy Arrangements Act, 1985, ch. 49 (Eng.); Human Fertilization and Embryology Act, 1990, ch. 57 (Eng.).

198. *See, e.g.*, OFFICE OF TECHNOLOGY ASSESSMENT, *supra* note 21 Intro., at 203; NEW YORK STATE TASK FORCE, *supra* note 192 Ch. 1, at 97-106 (finding potential complications in hired maternity arrangements); WALLER REP., *supra* note 21 Intro.; (finding such arrangements completely unacceptable); COMITÉ CONSULTATIF NATIONAL, *supra* note 21 Intro. (holding the practice "unacceptable").

199. 217 N.J. Super. 313, 525 A.2d 1128 (N.J. Super. Ct. Ch. Div. 1987), *aff'd in part & rev'd in part*, 109 N.J. 396, 537 A.2d 1227 (1988).

200. *Id.* at 326, 525 A.2d at 1134.

201. *Id.* at 325, 400-01, 525 A.2d at 1133, 1171-72.

202. *Id.* at 388-89, 525 A.2d at 1166.

203. *Id.*

204. *Id.*

205. *Id.* at 375, 525 A.2d at 1159.

206. *Id.*

207. 704 S.W.2d 209 (Ky. 1986).

208. *Id.* at 211-12.

209. 704 S.W.2d at 212-13 (applying KY. REV. STAT. ANN. § 199.590 (Baldwin 1985) (amended 1988)). The revised Kentucky statute prohibits contracts that "compensate a woman for her artificial insemination". KY. REV. STAT. ANN. § 199.590 (Michie/Bobbs-Merrill Supp. 1994). For laws against baby-selling in other jurisdictions, see ARIZ. REV. STAT. ANN. § 8-114 (SUPP. 1994); CAL. PENAL CODE § 273 (West Supp. 1994); COLO. REV. STAT. § 19-5-213 (Supp. 1994); DEL. CODE tit. 13, § 928 (Supp. 1992); FLA. STAT. § 63.212 (Supp. 1994); GA. CODE ANN. § 19-8-24 (1991); IDAHO CODE § 18-1511, 18-1512. 18-1512(A) (1987 & Supp. 1994); ILL. REV. STAT. ch. 40 para. 1526, 1701, 1702 (1989); IND. CODE ANN. § 35-46-1-9 (Burns 1994); IOWA CODE § 600.9(2) (1981); MD. FAM. LAW CODE ANN. § 5-327 (Supp. 1994); MASS. GEN. LAWS ch. 210, § 11A (1987); MICH. COMP. LAWS § 710.54 (1993); NEV. ANN. REV. STAT. § 127.290 (Supp. 1993); N.J. STAT. ANN. § 9:3-54 (West Supp. 1993); N.Y. SOC. SERV. LAW § 374 (McKinney 1992); N.C. GEN. STAT. § 48-37 (1991); OHIO REV. CODE ANN. § 3107.10 (Anderson 1989); S.D. CODIFIED LAWS ANN. § 25-6-4.2 (1992); TENN. CODE ANN. § 36-1-134 (1991); UTAH CODE ANN. § 76-7-203 (Supp. 1994); WIS. STAT. ANN. § 948.24 (West Supp. 1994). Some type of restriction on the sale of embryos or fetuses, the intermediate case between AID and hired maternity, exist in a number of jurisdictions. *E.g.*, ARK. STAT. ANN. § 20-17-802 (1987); OHIO REV. CODE ANN. § 2919.14 (Anderson 1993); OKLA. STAT. tit. 63 § 1-735(A) (Supp. 1990); TENN. CODE ANN. § 39-15-208 (1991); UTAH CODE ANN. § 76-7-311 (1990).

210. 704 S.W.2d at 211-12.

211. *Id.* at 212.

212. *Id.*

213. *Id.* The state's position, however, is supported by the fact that, without compensation, few such arrangements are entered. The true restriction on technological development comes from the economy, not the law. N. Keane & D. Breo, THE SURROGATE MOTHER 311 (1981).

214. *Id.* at 212 n.3.

215. 851 P.2d 776 (1993).

216. A subsequent California Court of Appeal decision interpreted *Johnson v. Calvert* narrowly as not specifically holding hired maternity contracts enforceable in California. The court distinguished the intent expressed through contract that is relevant to applying the statute on parentage, from contractual intent that is itself enforceable. *In re Marriage of Moschetta*, 25 Cal. App. 4th 1218, 1231, 30 Cal. Rptr. 2d 893, 900 (1994).

217. *E.g.*, Schultz, *Reproductive Technology and Intent-Based Parentage: An Opportunity for Gender Neutrality*. 1990 WIS. REV. 297-398.

218. 196 A.D.2d 7, 12, 608 N.Y.S.2d 477, 480 (1994).

219. 122 Mich. App. 506, 333 N.W.2d 90 (1983), *rev'd*, 420 Mich. 367, 362 N.W.2d 211 (1985).

220. MICH. COMP. LAWS § 333.2824 (1979).

221. *Syrkowski v. Appleyard*, 122 Mich. App. at 506, 507, 333 N.W.2d at 90, 91.

222. *Id.*

223. *Id.* at 506, 509-10, 333 N.W.2d at 90, 93-94.

224. *Syrkowski v. Appleyard*, 420 Mich. at 375, 362 N.W.2d at 214.

225. *Id.* at 375, 362 N.W.2d at 214.

226. *Id.* at 374-75, 362 N.W.2d at 213.

227. *Id.* at 375, 362 N.W.2d at 214.

228. 704 S.W.2d 209 (Ky. 1986).

229. *Id.* at 212-13.

230. *Id.* The holding was followed in an opinion by the Washington Attorney General. 1989 Wash. AG LEXIS No. 4 (Feb. 17, 1989).

231. 704 S.W.2d at 212.

232. *Id.* at 212-13 (citing KY. REV. STAT. ANN. § 199.590(2) (Baldwin 1985) (amended 1988)).

233. *See* E. FARNSWORTH, *supra* note 4 Ch. 1, § 4.29.

234. 704 S.W.2d at 213.

235. 132 Misc. 2d 972, 505 N.Y.S.2d 813 (N.Y. Sur. Ct. 1986).

236. *Id.* at 974, 978, 505 N.Y.S.2d at 815, 818. *But see, In re* Adoption of Paul, 146 Misc. 2d 379, 550 N.Y.S.2d 815 (N.Y. Fam. Ct. 1990) (holding hired maternity contracts void because they are illegal).

237. 132 Misc. 2d at 977-79, 505 N.Y.S.2d at 817-18.

238. *Id.* at 978, 505 N.Y.S.2d at 817-18.

239. *Id.* at 978, 505 N.Y.S.2d at 817.

240. *Id.* at 978, 505 N.Y.S.2d at 818. The court forwarded copies of the decision to the appropriate legislative committees, with a request for review and guidance.

241. *Id.* at 973, 505 N.Y.S.2d at 814.

242. *Id.* at 977-78, 505 N.Y.S.2d at 818; *cf., In re* R.K.S., 112 DAILY WASH. L. REP. 1117, 1120 (D.C. Super. Ct. Fam. Div. April 13, 1984) (requiring an extensive pre-adoption investigation that focuses on the "surrogate mother service" agency and on the legal sufficiency of the gestational mother's consent to the adoption).

243. *In re* Baby M, 109 N.J. 396, 537 A.2d 1227 (1988). The holding was followed by the Oregon Attorney General. 1989 Ore. AG LEXIS 26 (April 19, 1989). In general, the scholarly response to the opinion has been favorable. "A majority of 11 law professors across the country surveyed by the [*New Jersey Law Journal*] believe that the state supreme court's

decision in the Baby M case follows sound legal tenets". *Baby M Decision Wins Solid Marks*, N.J.L.J., Feb. 18, 1988, at 1, col. 4. *But see* Posner, *supra* note 7 Intro., at 29 (terming opinion "nothing short of an intellectual disaster").

244. *In re* Baby M, 109 N.J. 396, 442-44, 537 A.2d 1227, 1250-51 (1988). This decision is supported by the weight of governmental opinion world-wide. *See supra* note 198 Ch. 2. *But see* Note, *supra* note 20 Intro., at 24 (stating "[F]ears that justify the baby-broker legislation do not justify the prohibition of money changing hands in a surrogate transaction[.]").

245. 109 N.J. at 422, 537 A.2d at 1240.

246. *Id.*

247. *Id.* at 425, 537 A.2d at 1242.

248. *Id.* at 441-44, 537 A.2d at 1250.

249. *Id.* at 444, 537 A.2d at 1251.

250. *Id.* at 434-38, 537 A.2d at 1246-8.

251. *Id.* at 438-39, 537 A.2d at 1248-9.

252. *Id.* at 439, 537 A.2d at 1249.

253. *Id.* at 438-41, 537 A.2d at 1248-50.

254. *Id.* at 441-42, 537 A.2d at 1250.

255. 146 Misc.2d 379, 550 N.Y.S.2d 815 (1990).

256. *Id.* at 385, 550 N.Y.S.2d at 819.

257. *Id.*

258. 106 Mich. App. 169, 307 N.W.2d 438 (1981), *cert. denied*, 459 U.S. 1183 (1983).

259. MICH. COMP. LAWS § 710.54 (1979).

260. 106 Mich. App. at 172-73, 307 N.W.2d at 440.

261. *Id.* at 174, 307 N.W.2d at 441.

262. *Id.*

263. 194 Mich. App. 432, 437, 487 N.W.2d 484, 486 (1992).

264. 106 Mich. App. 169, 307 N.W.2d 438 (1981), *cert. denied*, 459 U.S. 1183 (1983).

265. 156 Misc.2d 65, 71, 591 N.Y.S.2d 946, 950 (1992).

266. *Id.*

267. 232 Cal. App. 3d 1239, 1255, 284 Cal. Rptr. 18, 24 (1991), *cert. denied* 112 S. Ct. 1685 (1992).

268. 25 Cal. App. 4th 1218, 1222, 30 Cal. Rptr. 2d 893, 895 (1994).

269. *See* M. FIELD, *supra* note 20 Intro., at 46-74 (concluding that given the uncertain social climate surrounding hired maternity, constitutional approach to the issue will provide little benefit); S. Green & J. Long, *supra* note 55 Ch. 1, at 251-52 (discussing cases asserting a right to privacy in regard to hired maternity contracts); Robertson, *supra* note 8 Intro., at 957-67 (arguing that procreative liberty protects the freedom to contract for collaborative reproductive transactions with gestational mothers); Stark, *Constitutional Analysis of the Baby M Decision*, 11 HARV. WOMEN'S L.J. 19 (1988) (arguing that hired maternity contracts are constitutional); Note, *supra* note 21 (asserting that the right of privacy protects a married couple's decision to have children through hired maternity). *See generally* Attanasio, *The Constitutionality of Regulating Human Genetic Engineering: Where Procreative Liberty and Equal Opportunity Collide*, 53 U. CHI. L. REV. 1274 (1986) (exploring the constitutional and public policy concerns regarding regulation of "positive genetic engineering").

270. S. GREEN & J. LONG, *supra* note 55 Ch. 1, at 253.

271. *See* Lassiter v. Department of Social Servs., 452 U.S. 18, 31 (1981) (parents' interest in preserving the parent-child relationship is "an extremely important one"); Pierce v. Society of Sisters, 268 U.S. 510, 535 (1925) (states do not have the authority to require instruction in public school only); Meyer v. Nebraska, 262 U.S. 390, 401 (1923) (parents have a right and natural duty to educate their children); *see also* McCarthy, *supra* note 77 Ch.2 (idenifying complications that arise when parents are in conflict with the state over children); Stark, *supra* note 269 Ch. 2 (discussing the trial court's opinion in *Baby M*).

For a general discussion of waiver of constitutional rights, see Brady v. United States, 397 U.S. 742, 748 (1970) (holding waiver must be a voluntary and informed act reflecting the circumstances and likely consequences); Shapiro, *Courts, Legislatures, and Paternalism*, 74 VA. L. REV. 519, 572-75 (1988) (suggesting flat prohibition on the waiver of personal rights is improperly paternalistic). Regarding waiver of parental rights, *see* Note, *supra* note 103 Ch. 2 (discussing out-of-court waivers of parental rights in adoptions). A more fundamental constitutional attack views hired maternity arrangements as a violation of the thirteenth amendment. *See* Means, *supra* note 16 Intro., at 478 (arguing that the agreement entails the sale of a child and, where specifically enforced, the rental of a woman).

272. 334 U.S. 1 (1948). This decision represents the culmination of a series of successful attacks on the public-private distinction. *See* Horwitz, *The History of the Public/Private Distinction*, 130 U. PA. L. REV. 1423, 1426 (1982) (discussing the evolution of attacks on the public-private distinction culminating in *Shelley*); *see also In re* Baby M, 109 N.J. 396, 451 n.15, 537 A.2d 1227, 1255 n.15 (1988) (discussing the application of *Shelley*).

273. Even if autonomy is given full recognition, at some point its recognition must be balanced against a countervailing concern for community. *See* Minow, *We, the Family: Constitutional Rights and American Families*, 74 J. AM. HIST. 959 (1987) (discussing limits in the use of "family" rhetoric to resolve disputes).

274. *See* Andrews, *The Aftermath of Baby M: Proposed State Laws on Surrogate Motherhood*, HASTINGS CENTER REP., Oct./Nov. 1987, at 31 (discussing state legislative reaction to hired maternity arrangements); Dunne & Serio, *Surrogate Parenting After Baby M: The Ball Moves to the Legislature's Court*, 4 TOURO L. REV. 161 (1988) (arguing that legislative regulation of hired maternity would provide an otherwise unavailable benefit to infertile couples); Note, *supra* note 190 Ch. 1, at 1284 n.5 (calling for a comprehensive statute governing hired maternity arrangements); Comment, *Womb For Rent: A Call for Pennsylvania Legislation Legalizing and Regulating Surrogate Parenting Agreements*, 90 DICK. L. REV. 227, 246 (1985) (urging enactment of comprehensive legislation focusing on the best interests of the child).

275. *See infra* notes 276-358 Ch. 2.

276. ARK. STAT. ANN. § 9-10-201 (1993).

277. *Id.* § 9-10-201(c)(1).

278. Wadlington, *supra* note 197 Ch. 2, at 402.

279. ARK. STAT. ANN. §9-10-201(c)(1) (1993). Whether technology is liberating or not is an appropriate question. Shulamith Firestone apparently viewed test-tube reproduction as a way to liberate women. S. FIRESTONE, THE DIALECTIC OF SEX (1970).

280. ARK. STAT. ANN. § 9-10-201(c)(1) (1993).

281. Stanley v. Illinois, 405 U.S. 645, 657-58 (1972).

282. ARK. STAT. ANN. § 9-10-201.

283. *Id.* § 9-10-201(a).

284. *Id.* § 9-10-201(c)(2).

285. 704 S.W.2d 209, 213 (Ky. 1986).

286. KY. REV. STAT. ANN. § 199.590(3) (Michie/Bobbs-Merrill 1994).

287. Compare N. KEANE & D. BREO, *supra* note 213 Ch. 2 (suggesting a facilitating procedure in which the surrogate mother and adopting parents are provided the information necessary to make independent decisions).

288. *In re* Baby M, 109 N.J. 396, 163-68, 537 A.2d 1227, 1261-64 (1988).

289. 106 Mich. App. 169, 307 N.W.2d 438 (1981), *cert. denied*, 459 U.S. 1183 (1983) (holding statute precludes payment of consideration in conjunction with use of the state's adoption procedures).

290. 420 Mich. 367, 362 N.W.2d 211 (1985).

291. IOWA CODE ANN. § 710.11 (1993); W. VA. CODE § 68-4-16 (Supp. 1994).

292. WIS. STAT. § 69.14(1)(h) (Supp. 1994).

293. IND. CODE ANN. § 31-8-2-1 (Burns Supp. 1994); LA. REV. STAT. ANN. § 9:2713(A) (West 1991); NEB. REV. STAT. § 25-21,200 (1989).

294. LA. CIV. CODE ANN. § 9:2713(A) (West 1990); NEB. REV. STAT. § 25-21,200 (1989) (preempting the contract by giving parental rights to the biological father in all cases.)

295. For example, Alejandra Munoz was induced to come to the United States illegally and enter a hired maternity arrangement through the misrepresentations of the intending couple. She was involuntarily confined to their home for the duration of her pregnancy. Hearing on *Surrogacy Arrangements Act, supra* note 189 Ch. 2, at 37 (statement of Alejandra Munoz). The majority of hired maternity arrangements proceed without judicial involvement. OFFICE OF TECHNOLOGY ASSESSMENT, *supra* note 21, at 268.

296. E. FARNSWORTH, *supra* note 4 Ch. 1, § 5.9. Uncertainty regarding outcomes, together with the potential for loss of reliance, serves as a deterrent to the arrangement. OFFICE OF TECHNOLOGY ASSESSMENT, *supra* note 21 Intro., at 268 ("The absence of governmental guidelines becomes an active barrier to the successful conclusion of the arrangement".).

297. NEB. REV. STAT. § 25-21.200(1) (1989).

298. The primary cost involved is the violation of the principle of respect for persons that underlies the rule of law generally. As such, it would be a principled ground for refusing the legal enforcement of such arrangements, without regard to further consequences At the same time, outright prohibition or criminalization might generate unacceptable indirect costs to the general welfare.

299. FLA. STAT. § 63.212(1)(d) (Supp. 1994); N.H. REV. STAT. ANN. §§ 168-B:1-B:30 (1994); VA. CODE ANN. § 20-156 165 (1994).

300. ARIZ. REV. STAT. ANN. §§ 25-218 (1991); D.C. CODE ANN. §16-401-02 (Supp. 1994); KY. REV. STAT. ANN. §199.590(4) (Baldwin Supp. 1994); MICH. COMP. LAWS § 710.69 (1979); N.Y. DOM. REL. LAW §§121-24 (McKinney Supp. 1994); N.D. CENT. CODE §14-18-05 (1991); UTAH CODE ANN. §76-7-204 (Supp. 1994); WASH. REV. CODE §26.26.210 - 260 (Supp. 1994). North Dakota's approach is a variant which discourages donated and unenforeable-compensated arrangements alike, through its rule allocating parental rights without actually prohibiting compensated arrangements.

301. NEV. REV. STAT. § 10.126.045 (Supp. 1993). Nevada also exempts hired maternity arrangements from its law against baby selling. *Id.* § 127.287(5).

302. *Id.* § 126.045(2).

303. FLA. STAT. § 43.742.14 (Supp. 1994).

304. FLA. STAT. § 63.212(1)(i) (Supp. 1994). This solution also has been proposed by commentators. *E.g.*, Cohen, *supra* note 189 Ch. 2, at 247-48.

305. This solution seeks to avoid the costs of the approach taken by Louisiana, Indiana, and Nebraska. *See supra* text accompanying note 298 Ch. 2. It also affirms altruistic arrangements as a positive societal good.

306. FLA. STAT. § 63.212(1)(i) (Supp. 1994).

307. *Id.*

308. *Id.* §§ 63.212(1)(i), (3)(a).

309. *Id.* § 63.212(2)(i).

310. *Id.* § 63.212(3),(4).

311. *Id.* § 63.212(2)(c).

312. *Id.* § 63.212(2)(d).

313. *Id.* § 63.212(2)(e).

314. N.H. REV. STAT. ANN. §§ 168-B:1-21 (1994).

315. Id. §§ 168-B-16I(a) and B:17I.

316. *Id.* § 168-B:23.

317. *Id.* § 168-B:16I(c).

318. *Id.* § 168-B:16II.

319. *Id.* § 168-B:16III.

320. *Id.* § 168-B:17II.

321. *Id.* § 168-B:17III.

322. *Id.* § 168-B:17IV.

323. *Id.* § 168-B17V.

324. N.H. REV. STAT. ANN. § 168-B:25V (1994).

325. *Id.* § 168-B:25IV.

326. *Id.* § 168-B:26.

327. VA. CODE ANN. § 20-156 (1994). *See infra* notes 359-403 Ch. 2 and accompanying text.

328. *Id.* § 20-160B(2).

329. *Id.* § 20-160B(3).

330. *Id.* § 20-160B.(4).

331. *Id.* § 20-160B(5).

332. *Id.* § 20-160B(6).

333. *Id.* § 20-160B(7).

334. *Id.* § 20-160b(8).

335. *Id.* § 20-160B(9).

336. *Id.* § 20-160B(10).

337. *Id.* § 20-160B(11).

338. *Id.* § 20-160B(12).

339. *Id.* § 20-161.

340. *Id.* § 20-160D.

341. *Id.* §§ 20-160D, -158D.

342. *Id.* § 20-162A.

343. *Id.* § 20-162A(3).

344. *Id.* § 20-158E(2).

345. *Id.* §§ 20-158E(1)-(3).

346. *See supra* note 80 Ch. 2.

347. *E.g.*, UTAH CODE ANN. § 76.7.204 (Supp. 1994).

348. *E.g.*, MICH. COMP. LAWS §§ 722.859(1), 3(a) (Supp. 1992).

349. MICH. COMP. LAWS § 722.857(1). This statute was sustained in the face of a court challenge. *See* Holusha, *Michigan Surrogacy Law Upheld*, Chicago Daily Bull., Sept. 20, 1988, at 3, col. 5.

350. *See* Holusha, *supra* note 349 Ch. 2. As such, even this strict law does not amount to more than what Margaret Radin refers to as "market-inalienability". It does not prohibit alienation, but only a form of mercantile exchange that is deemed "commodified". Radin, *supra* note 28 Intro., at 1853-5.

351. MICH. COMP. LAWS § 722.851-63 (Supp. 1992); WASH. REV. CODE § 26.26.230 (Supp. 1994).

352. N.Y. DOM. REL. LAW §14-123 (McKinney Supp. 1994); KY. REV. STAT. ANN. § 199.590(3) (Baldwin 1990); MICH. COMP. LAWS §§ 722.855, 722.859 (1979); UTAH CODE ANN. §76-7-204 (Supp. 1994).

353. MICH. COMP. LAWS § 722.859(2)-(3).

354. Id. § 722.861; WASH. REV. CODE ANN. § 26.26.260 (West Supp. 1994).

355. MICH. COMP. LAWS § 700.111.

356. KY. REV. STAT. ANN. § 199.590(3); MICH. COMP. LAWS § 722.851.

357. The New Jersey Supreme Court has been criticized for taking a similar viewpoint and implying that surrogate arrangements are more than unenforceable, and in fact criminal under the baby selling laws. Burt, *Court Stumbles by Raising Specter of Criminality—Barren Couples to Resort to "Back Alleys"*, N.J.L.J., Feb. 18, 1988, at 27, col. 1. In assessing the wisdom of criminalizing hired maternity contracts, the costs associated with such an action must be balanced against the social costs imposed by the enforcement of hired maternity contracts.

358. Id. § 700.681.

359. UNIF. STATUS ACT, *supra* note 6 Intro.; For alternative proposals, see *Model Surrogacy Act*, *supra* note 5 Intro.; NEW YORK STATE TASK FORCE, *supra* note 192 Ch. 1, at A-1 - A-5. The former proposal was considered and rejected by the ABA House of Delegates in February 1989. The House of Delegates voted instead to endorse the Uniform Status Act. *Wrestling with Surrogate Motherhood*, Wash. Post, Feb. 12, 1989, at A3, col. 3-6. As of 1994, the Uniform Status Act has been adopted in two states only: North Dakota, modified to make hired maternity contracts unenforceable, with parentage remaining with the birth mother, N.D. CENT. CODE § 14-18-01 to 07 (1991), and Virginia, with a variety of modifications, VA. CODE ANN. §§ 20-156 to 165 (1994).

360. 9A U.L.A. 147 (1973).

361. UNIF. PARENTAGE ACT, *supra* note 81 Ch. 1, at 287

362. UNIF. STATUS ACT, *supra* note 6 Intro., § 1 prefatory note and comments.

363. Id. § 1 comment.

364. Id. § 1(i)-(ii), § 1 comment.

365. Id. § 1(1)(i)-(ii).

366. Id. § 1(2).

367. Id. § 1 comment.

368. Id. § 3.

369. Id. § 9(a)

370. "A donor is not the parent of a child conceived through assisted conception". Id. § 4(a)

371. "A child whose status as a child is declared or negated by this [Act] is the child only of his or her parents as determined under this [Act]". Id. § 10.

372. See C. GROBSTEIN, *supra* note 2 Intro., at 21-23 (explaining the practical difficulties of ova retrieval).

373. U.C.C. §§ 2-314, -315 (1989).

374. UNIF. STATUS ACT, *supra* note 6 Intro., §§ 5-9 ("Alternative A" at 158-65, "Alternative B" at 165).

375. Id. § 5(b).

376. Bird, *On Baby M, Uniform Law Commission Splits*, N.J.L.J., Sept. 8, 1988, at 5, col. 1. Alternative B was added "over the objections of the 11-member committee that drafted the measure". The spokesman for the Uniform Law Commissioners said that "in his 15 years with the group, he has never seen an issue stir so much commotion among the commissioners as surrogate-parent contracts". Id.

377. UNIF. STATUS ACT, *supra* note 6 Intro., § 1(3). Under both alternatives, parties may reallocate gestational capacity in violation of the Act. Such extrastatutory transfers entail the same social costs resulting from uncertainty as those enumerated in connection with the Indiana, Nebraska and Louisiana statutes. Several legal consequences also follow from attempts to contract with the gestational mother without state supervision. The natural mother has no legally-enforceable right to her fee. The intending parents cannot count on the natural mother's waiver of her maternal rights. As long as the intending couple deal with an unmarried woman or a married woman whose husband has not consented to the arrangement, they enjoy legal recognition of the intending father's natural paternity. *Id.* § 5; UNIF. PARENTAGE ACT, *supra* note 81 Ch. 1, § 6. If the natural mother yields custody, the intending couple acquires this also, notwithstanding the extrastatutory nature of the arrangement. On the other hand, the intending parents apparently may formalize their rearing rights within a step-parent adoption proceeding under other relevant state law.

378. UNIF. STATUS ACT, *supra* note 6 Intro., § 6(b)(2).

379. *Id.* § 5(a).

380. *Id.* § 6(b)(6).

381. *Id.* § 6(b)(4).

382. *Id.* § 6(b)(10).

383. *Id.* §§ 6(b)(5), (b)(7), (b)(8), (C).

384. *Id.* § 6(a).

385. *Id.* § 1(2).

386. *Id.* § 1(1), § 2.

387. *Id.* § 7(b).

388. The burden is on the husband to sue and prove lack of consent within two years of learning of the child's birth. *Id.* § 3.

389. *Id.* § 1.

390. *Id.* §§ 1-3; *see* Planned Parenthood v. Danforth, 428 U.S. 52, 69 (1975); Roe v. Wade, 410 U.S. 113, 153 (1973).

391. UNIF. STATUS ACT, *supra* note 6 Intro., §§ 5, 8(b); UNIF. PARENTAGE ACT, *supra* note 81 Ch. 1, § 6.

392. UNIF. STATUS ACT, *supra* note 6 Intro., §§ 1, 2, 7(b).

393. C. GROBSTEIN, *supra* note 2 Intro., at 46-48.

394. UNIF. STATUS ACT, *supra* note 6 Intro., § 7(b).

395. *Id.* § 8(a)(2).

396. *Id.* § 2.

397. *Id.* prefatory note, § 7 comment.

398. *See* Wikler, *supra* note 156 Ch. 1, at 1046.

399. UNIF. STATUS ACT, *supra* note 6 Intro., prefatory note and comments.

400. *Id.* § 11.

401. 704 S.W.2d 209 (Ky. 1986).

402. UNIF. STATUS ACT, *supra* note 6 Intro., prefatory note.

403. First Draft of Prefatory Note and Comments, National Conference of Commissioners on Uniform State Laws (July 29-Aug. 5, 1988).

404. Despite the rapid evolution of legislation and case law, there remain many unanswered questions. *See* Healey, *supra* note 5 Intro., at 141-42 (noting the extent to which AID laws have not yet touched on traditional family law areas).

III. NORMATIVE EVALUATION OF CONTRACT AS A MEANS OF LEGAL ORDERING FOR HUMAN REPRODUCTION

A. The Basic Societal Choice Posed by Current Developments in Human Reproduction

To settle the legal ordering of human procreation, eventually the law will opt for one or another of the alternatives arrayed taxonomically early in this book. Decisions about the correct resolution of particular controversies regarding technologically assisted reproduction, then, will depend, in large part, on which alternative is chosen. A normative analysis of those taxonomic models applying contract, in one or another form, to the ordering of human procreation will be undertaken here.

An adequate evaluation of the alternative models cannot be undertaken from the starting point of the several concrete questions the law faces in the area of technologically assisted human reproduction. The more general question before the legal system must be synthesized and generically stated, since the value of available alternatives is best judged in relation to the generic question they are required to resolve. This question is in the mode of a basic choice arising within the concrete, historical existence of society.[1] This societal choice offers the appropriate point of departure for a normative evaluation of the use of contract in response to developments in human reproduction.

Clifford Grobstein persuasively argues that society should not allow a preoccupation with the widening reproductive projects that technological developments in genetics and human reproductive biology make possible to distract it from its responsibility for the consequences of those developments for human culture and, ultimately, for the biological resiliency of the human race.[2] He demonstrates that science and technology open the vista of a radical reordering of social, cultural, and biological patterns associated with human reproduction.[3] While such changes begin with individual choices, they may end by socially, culturally, and biologically transforming the human species. Neither science nor technology offer guidance as to the wisdom of the transformations they enable. Grobstein concludes that choices in the area require reference to values mediated by society.[4]

131

The scale of the transformation Grobstein depicts underscores the importance of the choice posed. Technology already allows the separation of reproduction from sexual intercourse and the separation of genetic from gestational motherhood. Eventually, it may permit the separation of reproduction from human gestation altogether. The transformative possibilities of technology extend well beyond.[5] Asexual human reproduction by a single parent may become possible as well as polysexual reproduction, giving a child six, seven, or eight genetic parents.[6] Reproduction may take on the characteristics of engineering, seeking not only the elimination of genetic flaws, but also the production of traits previously unknown.[7]

At the physiological level, basic procreative functions integral to biological and socio-behavioural definitions of maleness and femaleness may shift to the laboratory or otherwise be dissociated from their original anatomical settings.[8] Genetic endowment may be received by the offspring from a parent of just one sex or from a variety of individuals of one or both sexes.[9] Psychologically, such changes alter the pathmarks that provide personal and societal orientation and define relationships between the generations: all of this without yet considering changes which eugenic engineering might cause in the human genome.[10]

To the extent they occur, these changes will have major social and cultural consequences. They would alter shared patterns of meaning around which personal and intergenerational relationships are established.[11] As the locus of decision about reproduction shifts from a human pair under natural conditions to the individual assisted by technology, the potential arises for the unprecedented dominance of a minority in the establishment of the genetic endowment of the next generation. This could occur either if certain individuals came vastly to exceed others in the number of their genetic offspring or if the genetic engineering protocols suggested by a few came to be followed by the many. The result would transform basic social and political structures. More fundamentally, it could bring about a dramatic compromise of the resiliency of the human gene pool in ways compromising the capacity for human survival.[12]

According to Grobstein, the basic challenge confronting society is the need for a reasoned choice based on societal values concerning the direction human reproduction should take, given the removal by science and technology of limits once imposed by nature.[13] Grobstein shows that emerging technologies will not have an impact only at the margin but necessarily will resonate at the core of the social structure.[14] He is equally persuasive in rebutting the assumption that an appropriate and coherent societal direction can be achieved by considering each technology on an ad hoc basis.[15]

Scientific progress has made human reproduction a domain within which outcomes are determined not by "chance but by purpose".[16] It expands horizons of choice with respect to both reproductive ends and means.[17] The control which it offers begins with ever more refined knowledge concerning the physiology of human reproduction and proceeds to increasingly dramatic technological intervention in the natural reproductive process. The scientific process which yields this increase in technological possibilities, however, is not capable of resolving the crisis in societal values and practices that such options generate.[18] The advent of technologically assisted reproduction requires a philosophy and values capable of guiding societal decision making.

If concerns relating the advisability of fragmenting procreation into roles more diverse than those traditionally assumed by a single reproductive pair and relating to eugenics are set aside,[19] an important dimension of this societal challenge ineluctably remains:[20] the legal ordering of the basic human relationships implicated in the new reproductive technologies. These technologies create new persons and simultaneously generate uncertainty about who will have parental rights and duties with respect to them. The law may not responsibly regulate these technologies as if they comprised one more discrete societal activity, for they place at issue the societal values that will determine the structure of legal relationships between parents and children. The new reproductive technologies call for a coherent rationale for the values guiding the recognition of parental status. They necessitate a justification of legal norms governing disputes among adult participants.

B. A Normative Evaluation of Contract as a Principle Governing the Basic Human Relationships Implicated by the New Reproductive Technologies

The assessment of the contract-based responses to current developments in human reproduction requires an examination of four separate but converging considerations. These include: 1) state conferral, individual autonomy, and natural endowment as grounds of parental rights; 2) the enforcement of promises to reallocate procreative resources and parental rights; 3) restrictions on the alienability of procreative resources and parental rights; and 4) the proper balance among politics, personal life, and the market as spheres of societal activity. An exploration of these issues will permit a multifaceted normative evaluation of the models of legal response employing contract to answer developments in human reproductive technology.

133

1. State Conferral, Individual Autonomy, and Natural Endowment as Grounds of Parental Rights

The taxonomy elaborated earlier in this volume distinguished legal approaches to the new reproductive technologies according to whether they assigned parental rights based on state conferral, individual autonomy, or natural endowment. The normative consideration here is the proper ground of parental rights. If individual autonomy is the preferred value, contract is directly validated as a form for ordering the new technologies. If state conferral provides the preferred value, then contract receives a less absolute validation. If the preferred value is natural endowment, contract is essentially excluded.[21]

In a positivist understanding of the law, state conferral is, in one sense, the basis of all legal rights including both parental rights and the right generally to buy and sell resources.[22] Positivism is usually joined with some secondary principle that provides normative direction for state conferrals.[23] This principle might, for instance, be the utilitarian idea that the greatest good should be done for the greatest number.[24] It might be nothing more than the conviction that whatever the majority happens to prefer should be enacted as law. It might be some other ideal selected by the state. The state conferral model described here includes any form of positivist justification which does not directly subject state conferral to a normative direction derived from individual autonomy or natural endowment.[25]

The American constitutional tradition poses a fundamental difficulty for proposals that would make state conferral the basis of parental rights.[26] Within the American constitutional framework, parental rights serve as a fundamental constraint on the ability of the government to allocate benefits, burdens, rights, and duties.[27] Therefore, such rights implicitly rest on some ground that is distinguishable from state conferral. Current Supreme Court jurisprudence is founded on an unstable combination of natural endowment and individual autonomy.[28] Whether they are understood to be a function of natural endowment or individual autonomy, constitutionally recognized rights related to parenthood impose limits on the allocations the state may make in pursuit of its objectives.[29]

Proposals for ordering parental rights based on state conferral are accorded serious consideration despite their dissonance with constitutional tradition. One reason is that, in individual cases, reproductive projects introduce considerable uncertainty concerning the fate of the children conceived.[30] Another is the systemic uncertainty technologically assisted reproduction introduces into the static societal ordering required by property and other elements of social life.[31] Finally, the technological character of the new means of reproduction and the novelty of the forms of conduct involved imply that the law should be under no greater constraint when assigning rights and duties in this area than it is when regulating new technology generally.[32]

The appeal of the state conferral option lies in the predictability and order it would bring to a field cast into disarray by a contest for direction taking place between the values of natural endowment and individual autonomy. While traditional family law is grounded in natural endowment, the options made available by the new technologies seem to further the exercise of individual autonomy. Attempts to integrate recognition of individual autonomy into the existing framework based on natural endowment tend to disintegrate in the individual case and to disrupt the orderly assignment of status within society.[33] By contrast, the subordination of individual autonomy into a general framework of state conferral allows unequivocal resolution of individual conflicts and a consistent static ordering of society wherever static ordering is unavoidable.[34]

The new reproductive technologies themselves are viewed as a scientific achievement which ought to be publicly facilitated. This aspect of the state conferral option is not often noted, yet tends to mask the inconsistency between this option and American constitutional tradition. The predictability of basic societal status, which state conferral provides, serves to facilitate the more extensive application and development of the new technologies.[35] In their present form, arguments for the state conferral option are limited to a generalized principle that technological development should be encouraged and that the fruits of technology should be made available to individuals. Proponents of the new reproductive technologies, however, assert the right to control the traits of one's children in a quest for the perfect child.[36] The great danger of the state conferral model is that, while it begins by rejecting natural endowment in order to further individual use of these technologies, it may end by adopting the "quest for the perfect child" as a normative goal of the state.[37]

If the "best interests of children" is the banner under which this approach is generally advocated, the traditional role of the state in caring for neglected children under its parens patriae power is ordinarily the authority advanced in its support.[38] The state's parens patriae power is exercised in loco parentis; that is, only where necessary to fill a role defined by natural parenthood. Thus, the move to redefine parenthood as a right conferred or delegated by the state reverses the order of justification in the existing scheme. The existing parens patriae power of the state is not sufficient to justify use of the state conferral model to assign parental rights.

135

Still, as an abstract matter, the question of whether the state conferral of parental rights can be justified as being in the "best interests" of children is worth exploring. However, this question must be distinguished from the one arising in a custody battle under the "best interests" rule.[39] The best interests involved belong not to some determinate group of children, but rather to unborn generations of children.[40] It is in the best interests of children, in this abstract sense, to encourage immediate and irrevocable bonding between every child and at least one adult.[41] Any system of rules which, in assigning parental rights, disrupts parent-child bonding in infancy is flawed significantly. The enforcement of a contractual allocation of custody is not a sufficient guarantee against this flaw.[42]

Nonetheless, use of the "best interests" argument to validate state conferral suffers from two major defects. First, enhancing the chances of successful bonding is only one of several necessary values relevant to a child's best interests.[43] The "best interests" argument advanced in favour of state conferral fails to consider these other relevant values. Second, alternatives exist for achieving predictability in bonding during infancy. These alternatives focus on finding an ordering principle that will permit a consistent integration of natural endowment and individual autonomy in the assignment of parental rights, thereby avoiding the need to resort to state conferral as the general ordering principle.[44]

The plausibility of state conferral as the means of resolving the confusion created in the legal recognition of family relationships by the new reproductive technologies thus dissolves on closer examination. The arguments advanced to support it correctly point to problems that require resolution, but they do not justify the proposed solution either in a general sense or in reference to the American constitutional tradition. By eliminating natural endowment for the ostensible purpose of furthering the individual appropriation of technology, the option also eliminates natural endowment as a basis for rights that constrain the state. Even versions of the option that include contract as a prominent feature pose an unacceptable risk of statism or collectivism.[45]

Individual autonomy is the alternative to state conferral proposed by some to ground parental rights in the context of the new reproductive technologies. Recent trends in American constitutional law tend to reformulate reproductive and marital rights in terms of individual autonomy.[46] John Robertson, a prolific writer on law and the new reproductive technologies, argues in favour of employing contract principles to order the basic human relationships implicated by the new technologies from this starting point.[47] He asserts that progress in civil liberties generally has been a matter of giving increasing recognition to the individual's right to control his or her fecundity. He suggests that this negative right be matched with a positive right to pursue the production of a "perfect child" when, with whom, and by what means one chooses.[48] He asserts that this is the meaning of the right of autonomy in the area of human reproduction.

Robertson views the right to exchange procreative resources and parental rights for money and the right to obtain the legal enforcement of these exchanges as necessary corollaries to the positive right to procreate.[49] He argues that commercial reallocations ought to be legally enforced as a "fundamental right".[50] As such, contracts for the reallocation of procreative resources and parental rights deserve a special enforceability exceeding that which can be claimed by other business exchanges.[51] He explains that those who collaborate in procreation without intending to become parents should be deemed to be engaged in a complementary expression of autonomy.[52] He holds that they are fulfilling a right to experience whatever limited aspect of participation in procreation they desire. The market's effect in differentiating these specialized roles is, for Robertson, an additional benefit.[53]

As justification for this strong endorsement of procreative autonomy expressed through contract allocation, the author cites a progressive trend in developments over the past century.[54] He relies on the notion of inherent progress to justify the leap from existing precedents to a positive right to procreate, and the further leap to a positive right to obtain state enforcement of contractual promises in this context.[55] A secondary justification which Robertson raises for both extensions of existing law is the unfairness of limiting persons to the procreative resources which natural endowment alone provides. Such a limitation arbitrarily restricts the autonomy of individuals dissatisfied with their natural procreative endowment.[56]

For Robertson, the value of individual autonomy arises from the distinctive, innate significance of individual choices to undertake procreative projects, whether in quest of the perfect child or of some subjective experience in the procreative process.[57] Only in this setting does individual autonomy rise to the level of a fundamental right that may not be subordinated to state interests that are not compelling.[58]

Because he views reproductive contracts as separate from and more important than ordinary contract, Robertson advocates a variation on the marriage contract rather than inclusion of procreation within ordinary contract.[59] The decisive difference for Robertson is that the privileged choice objectifies and depersonalizes reproduction rather than placing it within a long-term personal relationship confined to pooling natural reproductive endowments. A significant consequence of this difference is that it lends generative arrangements two distinct legal and social forms: those persons who participate as "intenders" of children (buyers of procreative resources and parental rights) and those persons who participate in a passing, depersonalized experience, usually for money (sellers of procreative resources and parental rights).[60] Like the marriage contract, both kinds of agreements are distinguishable from ordinary market relationships. The distinction remaining between them, however, is of great conceptual importance and presages far-reaching changes in societal structure.

Others propose a more generalized understanding of individual autonomy as a normative basis for reallocating procreative resources and parental rights through contract. Rather than emphasizing the distinctiveness of procreation as a sphere within which individual autonomy is expressed, they begin with the premise of the equality of all preferences. Individual autonomy requires that the widest latitude be granted to exchanges which add to the aggregate satisfaction of individual preferences.[61] In this view, contracts for the reallocation of procreative resources and parental rights ought to be treated as a species of ordinary contract. The grounds that would support restricting such contracts are neither wider nor narrower than those for ordinary contract generally.[62]

Until now, the natural distribution of genes and procreative capacity has offset the disparities in wealth attendant upon a market economy. Both kinds of individual autonomy rationales seen here call for replacing natural allocation with market allocation. This, in turn, tends to redistribute resources and rights, like all other commodities available on the market, according to financial wealth.[63] Insofar as many individuals alienate resources and rights from a natural surplus, autonomy advocates assert that buyers gain and sellers do not lose the enjoyment of the end result: the acquisition of a rearing relationship with a child.[64] Alternatively, individuals who alienate resources and rights which they do not replace for themselves choose money in exchange for parenthood. Thus, social roles are redistributed as a form of wealth. Both types of individual autonomy arguments advocate a redistribution of reproductive wealth.

According to both, procreative resources and the parental rights to which they give rise should flow to those parties who have the intention or will to exploit them.[65] It is curious here that a distributive justice argument works, explicitly in some commentaries, in tandem with the value of individual autonomy embodied in the market exchange.[66] Distributive justice is typically advanced as a reason for imposing constraints on the market. Here, the value of the market is thought to advance the value of distributive justice.[67] The explanation readily presents itself. When a natural resource is made alienable, alienability initially serves greatly to increase the distribution of the resource. Only after the distribution reaches a market-based equilibrium can distributive justice become a side constraint on market alienation. Distributive justice is defined, for example, in the Rawlsian sense as equal distribution, except where it can be shown that the unequal distribution is nevertheless preferable even to those who receive the least; that is, the unequal distribution makes everyone better off.[68]

Both forms of the individual autonomy justification for employing contract argue that natural procreative resources ought to be redistributed and that the enforcement of contractual exchanges is one method for accomplishing this redistribution. Under the more general approach, the ideal distribution is simply the one the market would provide.[69] The narrower approach, which makes procreation a fundamental right, views market distribution as simply an instrument to some other ultimate redistribution.[70] Both perspectives, however, assert that natural procreative resources and parental rights ought to be appropriated and reallocated by individual autonomy and for the ultimate disposal of individual autonomy.[71]

Schemes that rest the allocation of parental rights upon the value of individual autonomy contradict the very value they claim to advance. The expectation that the parties seek to secure by contract is a change in legal relation directly affecting the identity of a third party, the child. Every child has a natural concern to know his or her origins, genetically and biological-ly.[72] The parties, by their agreement, deny the child the right to decide autonomously whether and how to develop that "natural" relationship".[73] This denial forecloses the autonomous development within a particular horizon of intrinsic human meaning for a lifetime. Further, these perspec-tives fail to comprehend that the contractual capacity of the parties themselves has come into existence only after an extensive period spent as unemancipated minors. During the period prior to emancipation, the adult custodian must contract for the child and is subject to a fiduciary duty to act on the child's behalf.[74] In the individual autonomy model, the adult contracts to trade away parental rights belonging to the very child over whom he has or, in the ordinary course of events would come to have, a fiduciary duty based on a relationship of dependency.[75]

The meaningful exercise of individual autonomy presupposes, moreover, that the individual has native preferences to express. The autonomous actor takes shape, in part, during the formative period of childhood and adoles-cence prior to the emergence of contractual capacity. Additionally, this emergence is a contemporaneous, existential matter, occurring through the experience of familial and social relationships which are zones relatively free of legal enforcement of bargains. The defective anthropology of the

139

individual autonomy model is apparent in this failure to recognize that individual autonomy grows from prior relationships of nurturance and simultaneous relationships of personal concern.[76] Because it ignores these two elements of mutual dependency between individual autonomy and natural endowment, the individual autonomy model is the *reductio ad absurdum* of Sir Henry Maine's thesis on the character of progressive societies.[77] To the same extent, it loses its validating link to the Lockean notion of social contract.[78]

While the application of contract to those human relationships implicated by the new reproductive technologies will diminish the constraints that respect for natural endowment currently places on individual autonomy, it is a mistake to suppose that the result will be unfettered individual autonomy. The contractual relationships in question may loosen the traditional structures of kinship, but will be recontextualized within a social structure that market forces create.[79] In the consumer rights type of the model, they will be further contextualized within professional and governmental bureaucracies.[80] Both contexts limit freedom of contract as an exercise of individual autonomy. The contours of these delimiting structures will tend to become the object of governmental action, rather than private cooperative planning, as has been the experience with ordinary contract during the century that followed the classical definition of freedom of contract.[81]

To the extent that individual autonomy recognizes natural endowment as the basis of parental rights in the ordinary case, it undermines the security of assigning parental rights based on contract. Rights of natural endowment that are placed in abeyance may always be revived and reasserted against exceptional rights based on individual autonomy.[82] The consequence is a predictable tendency within the individual autonomy model to drift into subordination to the state conferral model of assigning parental rights. In the longer run, it is questionable whether the individual autonomy model, if implemented, would further the value of personal autonomy as it has been understood within the American constitutional tradition.

The American constitutional system accords natural endowment an irreducible role in the legal allocation of parental rights, which flows from the breakdown of experience and meaning of individual autonomy at the boundaries of human life. Owing to the continual stream of births and deaths, human identity is intrinsically intergenerational.[83] Voluntary contractual exchanges cannot take care of business between generations; hence the need for the law of wills and estates.[84] Each generation is dependent, at its outset, on the previous, and, at its conclusion, on the succeeding. It is impossible for the new generation to contract for care and nurturance from the previous one, and it is difficult at best for the outgoing generation to contract successfully for such consideration from the one succeeding it.[85] The legal principles governing human relationships in these zones beyond contract are properly grounded in notions of equity, rather than the consent of the parties.[86]

In ordering the dependent relationship of children to those who raise them, the law ought to appeal to principles that the child can appropriate as he or she progresses towards autonomy and the capacity for consent. Basing parental rights on willingness and ability to pay is not such a principle. Allowing parental rights to flow from a de facto relationship of nurturance, however, is such a principle, as is permitting parental rights to flow from lineage.[87] Both nurturance and lineage represent forms of donation, the principle governing the laws of intestacy and inheritance and, therefore, relations between the generations. Further, both genetic endowment and nurturance of the child provide fundamentals of human identity underlying the child's emergent capacity for consent.[88]

Traditionally, the only natural endowment relationships an adult could enjoy with a child would be direct donation of the physical requisites of life: sperm, ovum, nurturance in gestation, or post-natal nurturance. The right to assume post-natal nurturance as a function of parental right belonged, in the past, to the gestational mother and the genetic father who tendered immediate post-natal nurturance.[89] Now, claimants also may include the donatrix of the ovum who has not provided gestational care, as long as she tenders immediate post-natal nurturance.[90] Arguably, procreative intent separated from a genetic or nurturance contribution might also be counted as a new source of claims in natural endowment. Its characterization as natural endowment rather than individual autonomy would focus upon the donation of life which the intention confers on the child.[91] However, this argument stretches the definition of natural endowment too far. The element of intention alone does not unite persons in a relationship. Even when donative, it is essentially an expression of individual autonomy. Only conferral of the requisites of life is sufficient to qualify as a basis for recognizing rights grounded in natural endowment.

In either its strong or moderate type, the natural endowment model of allocating parental rights rules out the acquisition of parental rights by contractual alienation. To resolve conflicts among the parties who may claim parental rights based on natural endowment, the law might give priority to gestational nurturance, as an established nurturing relationship with the child in being.[92] Other relevant principles might include recognizing that any other claim in natural endowment is contingent both on formal respect of marriage and the family as the preferred forum for child rearing generally[93] and, in a particular case, on the demonstrable best interests of the

141

child.[94] Under the natural endowment model, claims to parental relationship based on natural endowment would presumably be suppressed to no greater degree than deemed necessary for guaranteeing the best interests of children in general, and the best interest of the child in a particular case.[95]

The natural endowment model provides for the expression of individual autonomy in a wider array of procreative projects than the choice of marriage partner within the traditional regime of the marriage contract.[96] The model requires secondary state conferral of status to resolve foreseeable conflicts among mutually exclusive claims and, perhaps also, to support marriage and the family as the preferred forum for raising children, as well as state adjudication favouring the best interest of the child in concrete conflicts.[97] Yet the model receives normative validation within the American constitutional tradition precisely because it acknowledges that neither third-party contractual consent nor state conferral are reasons that justify the subjection of a new generation to the "parental" power of the generation raising it.

2. Enforcement of Promises to Reallocate Procreative Resources and Parental Rights

The reasons underlying the legal enforcement of promises have varied throughout the course of history and continue to do so. Normative evaluations of contract-based proposals for the new legal ordering of human reproduction sometimes begin by considering whether it is appropriate to enforce promises to reallocate procreative resources and parental rights, rather than seeking the abstract grounds for parental rights. When this occurs, the discussion shifts to an assessment of the reasons proposed for the enforcement of promises.

The most categorical reason supporting the legal enforcement of promises is the intrinsic moral force of promise itself. The idea of the intrinsic moral force of promise contributed to the emergence of the enforcement of purely executory contractual promises from the seventeenth to the nineteenth centuries.[98] Within Anglo-American case law, the idea crystallized in only one highly particularized version, the will theory.[99] In this form, it provides the pivotal justification of enforcement of obligation in classical contract theory.[100] According to the will theory, the state is justified in coercing the individual into performing the promise, based on the individual's own exercise of his autonomous will in choosing to be bound.[101] The state is required to coerce him, on the basis of his inducement of a similar exercise of will in another.[102]

Another ground for enforcement, related to morality, is the equitable conviction that one who induces another to rely on a promise should be held liable for detrimental harm that flows to the other from subsequent non-fulfilment of the promise.[103] This ground was used to justify some recoveries in assumpsit prior to the rise of the bargain theory of contract.[104] A second equitable conviction that has been used to support the enforcement of promises is the idea that one who is indebted to another for a performance received should be required to give compensation. This justification was used to support recoveries in common law debt actions.[105] A related principle is seen in the law of quasi-contract or unjust enrichment.[106] Both equitable principles are intelligible as applications of the traditional moral ideal of commutative justice.[107]

The enforcement of contractual promises has also been justified by reference to social policy or broader social goals.[108] In classical contract theory, the goal was to encourage private, future-oriented economic planning and the functioning of markets, both of which would generate wealth.[109] In particular, each would further the concrete tasks of implementing the technological discoveries of the industrial revolution and exploiting the natural resources that advances in transportation and communication made available to the mature colonial age.[110] A related justification is the legal organization of the private sphere around the self-interested bargain. Benefits flowing directly to the individual as a result of the availability of contract enforcement as well as benefits flowing indirectly from the aggregate enrichment of a society organized around the market were deemed to be a basis for obtaining common assent to the rule of law.[111]

In its contemporary form, the social policy justification has evolved to understand wealth in a more radically pluralist sense of satisfaction of individual preference. The furtherance of the market through the enforcement of contract is, in this form, deemed justified because it facilitates the greater aggregate satisfaction of all such preferences.[112] The current, related justification is the legal organization of the private sphere around maximizing individual satisfaction of discovered desires.[113]

In the legal system, as it has evolved since the height of classical contract theory, the role of contract is sharply limited, regardless of which rationale for enforcement is adopted.[114] The freedom to create contractual obligation does not structure the relationships that comprise the greater part of the so-called private sector. Complex corporate organizations largely dictate forms of cooperation and individual roles.[115] Individuals do not, in most cases, contract with each other for the productive generation of wealth. A relatively small number of corporations contract for this purpose.[116] Although individuals contract for the satisfaction of their preferences as consumers, many of their needs are satisfied under administrative law through the dispensation of governmental benefits.[117] Where they do contract for their needs, they generally do so under standardized form contracts that are heavily regulated by the state.[118] Patrick Atiyah argues that the judicial regulation of contract has become less a matter of enforcing expectations won in discrete bargains, and more a matter of adjusting conditions in ongoing relationships, with contract viewed as a channel for present exchanges.[119]

It is against this backdrop that the persuasiveness of arguments for the enforcement of promises to reallocate procreative and parental rights should be judged. Arguments based on the intrinsic moral force of promises and the autonomy of the will are now generally ignored. In nearly all sectors, the law shows a corresponding reluctance to enforce purely executory promises. "The somewhat mystical idea . . . that an obligation could be created by a communion of wills, an act of joint, if purely mental, procreation" has gone out of favour.[120] The historically conditioned character of the will theory is now apparent. Its credibility was dependent on the dominance of the small business in the economy such as occurred during the period of industrialization that spanned the century from 1770 to 1870.[121] Its emergence was related to a shift in the nature of property rights from a static, land-based system, under which rights were acquired to be retained, to one based on expectations for voluntary exchanges of rights of participation in corporate profits.[122] During its ascendancy, the will theory facilitated this transition by providing a formal notion of contractual obligation that could be applied neutrally to all particular circumstances, without regard to the disparate social roles of the parties.[123] It allowed the courts to overlook the harsh costs that the mercantile system imposed on particular classes.[124] And, it encouraged the market's ongoing levelling effect on status distinctions based on class or occupation.[125]

When it became apparent that "freedom of contract" led to monopolies and market failure, the will theory was shown to be inconsistent with its secondary economic rationale.[126] The resulting eclipse of the theory was hastened by a change in views on the relationship between law and ethics. Deep-rooted philosophical pluralism has led to hesitancy in applying moral imperatives directly to the justification of laws.[127] The will theory, in particular, suffers from a general shift in the law away from presupposing the existence or moral significance of free will.[128] Equitable rights and duties based on measurable benefits received and detriments suffered are another matter. But even the recognition of these has tended to shift from a commutative to a distributive model of justification.[129]

Curiously, arguments for legal enforceability based on the intrinsic moral force of promise have resurfaced in a surprisingly strong form in the case of reallocation of procreative resources and parental rights. One factor is explained by Patrick Atiyah:

> In one major area of life, there has been, it may be urged, a significant increase in the respect accorded to individual freedom of choice. In all matters concerned directly or indirectly with sexual morality, from homosexuality to abortion, from pornography to adultery, the trend both of social mores and of the law has been towards a greater recognition of the rights of consenting adults to lead their own private lives without interference from the State. It seems paradoxical if, while these developments have been taking place, there has been at the same time a decline in the values of individual freedom of choice in the economic or commercial sphere. But the paradox must be faced since there is no real doubt that both of these movements have been taking place over recent decades.[130]

In an increasingly structured, impersonal, and static society, the individualism cultivated by traditional market ideology finds expression in the private realm of sexuality and procreation. Within this realm, autonomy and choice are valued as supremely meaningful. Here the will theory of contractual obligation finds a new hold. Dimensions of life, which, in the classic model, remain the bastion of status because they are seen as the source of individual identity, become uniquely suited to appropriation and alienation by the individual. Thus, there is a plausible ring to arguments that promise to reallocate procreative resources and parental rights ought to be considered legally enforceable, because they represent an exercise of personal autonomy which has induced a reciprocal exercise of autonomy in another. Subliminal resonances from traditional ideas of the indissolubility of marriage, as well as from primitive notions of the irrevocability of sexual union, reinforce this argument for legal enforceability based on the moral force of promise in this context.[131] Such reasoning seems to underlie and inform Robertson's belief that the value of individual autonomy is uniquely implicated in procreation and his consequent insistence that contracts in the area should be enforced as consistently as commercial contracts were under the late nineteenth- century laissez faire approach.[132]

A second justification is drawn from the social policy favouring the generation of wealth. Once wealth is defined as the satisfaction of individual preferences, then societal wealth can be increased by encouraging exchanges that satisfy preferences.[133] Again, the paradigm of the individual exercise of preference has moved into the domain of sexuality and procreation.[134] Thus, some propose the enforcement of contracts reallocating procreative resources and parental rights on this basis. Under such a system of enforcement, however, market forces would rapidly effect social reorganization, and the state would respond with regulation. The satisfaction of individual preferences, then, would take place within a whole new framework of static constraints. In the Robertson approach, one can, in principle, imagine state intervention into the market process to uphold a favoured distribution of the requisites of sexual autonomy.[135] Opening up sexuality and procreation to contractual reallocation would gradually diminish the meaning and justification of autonomous choice. Procreative contracts would remain privileged just long enough to restructure the procreative dimension of social life.

The lessons learned from the role of the will theory in classical contract should be applied in this context as well. The theory itself has proved unpersuasive. It allows natural endowment to be appropriated, alienated, and commercially exploited. On the "other side" of the market waits a new static ordering. It would be ironic if the ideology of nineteenth-century laissez faire contract found one last instance of recognition, and, in so doing, undermined the very basis of belief in individual autonomy.

The argument that contractual reallocation of procreative resources and parental rights will make society richer in the aggregate satisfaction of individual preferences is also deficient. It aggregates satisfaction of preferences that can be fulfilled through individual exchanges but ignores satisfaction that emerges from inalienable identity and enduring personal relationships. More wealth in a market form means less "wealth" of another kind.[136] The trade-off is not one which market reasoning itself can properly resolve. Further, the normative force of the mandate that individual preferences should be satisfied depends on the moral dignity of the individual, a value which is undermined by commercializing human reproduction.

The equitable interest in charging an individual for the harm flowing from the reliance of another on his promise, or for a benefit which he receives in connection with his promise is, in other contexts, routinely made contingent on the societal judgement that individuals should be encouraged to rely on promises of the kind in question or to confer benefits in connection with them.[137] Admittedly, when reallocations of procreative resources take place, detrimental reliance or the conferral of benefits seem to be relevant to the equities of enforcement. However, these considerations are only relevant to the extent that the promisee has been led by society to consider reliance on the promise reasonable.[138] Even as between adult participants, they are not the only factors relevant to equity. There are no grounds that compel the enforcement of agreements to reallocate procreative resources or that justify the enforcement of transfers of parental rights by contract. Promises to reallocate procreative resources or to transfer parental rights would be appropriately enforced as binding only if such reallocations and transfers were found to be socially constructive for reasons independent of the promises themselves.[139]

3. Restrictions on the Alienation of Procreative Resources and Parental Rights

If the presumption of individual autonomy underlying liberalism, libertarianism, and the law and economics movement[140] is made the starting point of discussion, the evaluation of legislative responses to the new human reproduction turns on the validity of constraints on individual choice. A matter of peculiar appeal to liberalism and allied movements is the freedom to alienate rights and resources that an individual finds at his or her disposal.[141] Any constraints on alienation must be justified. When the normative discussion of contracts for the reallocation of procreative resources and parental rights is stated in these terms, the discussion turns to an examination of whether any ground is powerful enough to justify constraining alienation.

Judge Richard Posner makes the positive argument for the alienation of procreative resources, new born infants, and correlated parental rights.[142] Posner sets forth an individual right to maximize the satisfaction of one's preferences through exchanges with others.[143] Free exchanges, then, are self-validating in that both parties, by definition, prefer what they receive over what they sacrifice in the exchange.[144] Judge Posner also suggests that the parties have a right to government enforcement of promised performance because the expectation of enforcement increases the present value of the promise.[145] He applies this reasoning to demonstrate that contracts for the reallocation of procreative resources and parental rights should be permitted and enforced, since they enrich all adult parties to the exchange.[146]

Posner argues that constraints on enforceable contracts in this area create inefficiencies leading to social disruption.[147] One example, which Posner made famous in his 1979 article with Elizabeth Landes, is the shortage of babies now available for adoption which is simultaneously accompanied by an excessive number of abortions.[148] According to Posner, the net result of opening procreation and parental rights to reallocative exchanges would be an overall increase in efficiency, leading to higher quality babies obtained at reduced average cost.[149] By allowing individuals to freely exchange rights and resources, Posner believes that market forces are unleashed which further enrich society.[150]

In order to justify any constraint on the exchange or its enforcement, in Posner's view, one must show either that the prospect of mutual enrichment is illusory or that it is offset by external costs to others, so that its value for efficiently fulfilling aggregate preferences disappears.[151] For instance, information costs may render the prospect of mutual enrichment illusory. A case for prohibiting the sale of human blood, for example, was once made, based on the impossibility of discovering which blood offered for sale with the prospect of financial gain was contaminated. After reliable tests were developed, this argument lost its force, since the necessary information for a reliable bargain was available at reasonable cost.[152] A parallel argument, at least for the voidability of hired maternity contracts, is that a woman has no way of knowing how she will feel about relinquishing a child after encountering her humanly unique offspring following childbirth. Posner, however, argues that avoidance would occur so seldom that no provision should be made for it.[153]

In assessing the economic efficiency of a transaction, the costs and benefits imposed on all the parties to the transaction must be taken into account. In the adoption setting, the emotional welfare of the mother must be economically balanced against the welfare of the baby in assessing the net gain.[154] Tort and criminal law sanctions are intended to channel transactions to the market-place. If, for example, theft were not outlawed, economic actors would not be likely to look to the market-place to acquire goods. The law against rape, then, can be seen as designed to protect the marriage market.[155] The rationale for any inalienability of immunity under tort or criminal law would be based on efficiency and a breakdown in the possibility of rational choice.[156] Posner recognizes that the children traded would be forced to bear such externalities. However, he asserts that these costs could be adequately checked by licensing parents before they enter arrangements and regulating their parenting after they have taken custody of the child.[157] The requirement of licensing is the only restraint on alienation Posner is willing to recognize in bargains involving infants. The cost to the child in the bargain is a lack of immunity from overt child abuse. Posner's licensing requirement substitutes for the child's incapacity to contract to sell its immunity. In focusing on the palpable harms of overt child abuse, Posner accounts for the most superficial dimension of the external effect on the child of procreative contracts entered into by third parties precedent to conception or birth.[158] This approach ignores the disposition of the child's expectancy in life and relationship to others without its consent. The weight of the practical and moral costs strains the limits of Posner's notion of market failure.

If the exchanges in question are defined narrowly as the reallocation of procreative resources, leaving the ultimate allocation of parental rights to some alternative justification, then Posner's argument may, to some extent, be plausible. Once parental rights are declared alienable, however, the parties do not merely expose a third party, the child, to incidental harm that can be countered with suitable regulation. They also assign power over every aspect of the child's future. Appropriating and disposing of the child's future for their own gain cannot be justified under the rubric of the contracting party's right to free choice. Posner's failure to draw this distinction leads to a fundamental inconsistency in his attempt to justify the enforcement of contracts for the reallocation of parental rights based on the value of individual preference.

The child may not exist at the time the contract is entered but will exist when the buyer attempts to assert rights over the child based on the contract.[159] The child may have received the benefit of existence because of the parties' belief that the contractual provision assigning parental rights would be enforced. However, this simply signifies a donation by the intending parties to the child. If individual autonomy is made the basis for parental rights, donation does not justify the deprivation of the child's right to consent to a third-party assignment of his future.

The exchange of resources requires that the resources be subject to appropriation and disposal; they must be subject to "reification" or "commodification" sufficient to organize common understanding of the requisites of transfer and separate ownership.[160] Posner agrees that the baby subject to a procreative contract should not be delivered over to abuse.[161] He asserts that the standard of care required in relating to a person may be enforced in the case of the child, and that this guards against the evil which the expression "commodification" connotes. However, he misses the point. If the child is a person, then parental rights are essentially "bipolar", and cannot be alienated without at least the substituted consent of the child. Unilateral alienation by the parent implicitly amounts to treating the right as a right in rem. It is on this ground that personal services contracts are generally not subject to delegation.[162] By making parental rights subject to the unilateral alienation of the parent, Posner implicitly treats the child as a thing or commodity.[163] At the very least, the restrictions he admits as appropriate on the treatment of the child are indistinguishable from regulations prohibiting cruelty to animals.

149

An argument could be made that it is in the interest of children generally to be subject to a general rule that parental rights be extended over the child according to a contract between third parties contributing to the child's conception and gestation or their assigns. In that case reference to state conferral and not alienation by contract itself would account for the allocation of rights. Posner does not recognize or pursue the need for such a step in his argument. If he were to attempt it within the limited framework he has already developed, the argument would fail. At most, he can say that the rule generally leads to "better quality" children at "lower cost".[164] But quality is determined by the preferences of third parties. The benefit of reduced cost likewise accrues to third parties. In the individual case, only concrete circumstances and not the contract itself could possibly establish whether the enforcement of the contract would lead to the material best interests of the child.

Posner's framework is insufficiently nuanced to alert him to the error he makes here even within the terms of his own system. While Richard Epstein vigorously rejects most limits on alienability of rights and resources, he recognizes that consistency in his postulates requires that alienability be restricted by the negative norms of the criminal and tort law, since they provide the normative ground for upholding the enforcement of contract.[165] This normative consideration offers a reasoned basis to limit the alienation of parental rights, even within a perspective according maximum recognition to the market, while avoiding the problems associated with Posner's approach.

However, arguments for the inalienability of parental rights may also be traced to externalities falling elsewhere than on the children. Externalities of exchanges can not only fall on individuals, but can affect what are called "common pool" assets.[166] The management of common pool assets can be used to justify restrictions on alienation, without departing from the basic norm that individual exchanges should be permitted wherever they maximize the aggregate of individual preferences.[167] Susan Rose-Ackerman treats the management of the human population as a common pool problem, suggesting that the state limit forms of alienation of procreative resources that would lead to overpopulation.[168] While there may be a tendency to more readily credit common pool assets of a tangible nature, it would be arbitrary not to credit intangible common pool assets as well.[169] One example is social lineage. A parent cannot contract away his or her rights, without also contracting away the relationships of grandparents, aunts, uncles, and so forth.[170] On a greater level of abstraction, a parent cannot contract away his or her rights without undermining the currency and meanings of relationships based on lineage within society generally.

Others have attempted to go further and articulate grounds beyond efficiency and consistency which may justify inalienability, even if their goal at times may seem to be as much to restrict as to expand the range of grounds that merit recognition. One ground for limiting alienability is the redistribution of wealth.[171] It must be understood that inalienability, in the liberal view, is a redistribution of wealth, from those denied the opportunity of exchange to third parties who benefit from the prohibition on the exchange.[172] Some hold that any redistribution is wrongful and that any rule of inalienability must be accompanied by payment to those subject to its restriction to offset its redistributive effects.[173] Since the initial allocation of economic power is the premise from which Pareto optimality is assessed, even an efficient distribution is subject to criticism from the perspective of distributive justice.[174] Others, therefore, admit that redistribution achieved through inalienability may be acceptable, but request that the state establish that the redistribution is "just" under some secondary norm.[175]

Assuming that the redistributive effects of inalienability are, in principle, subject to justification, the normative consideration that justifies the denial of opportunities to undertake procreative projects to those who are only able to do so through reallocative exchanges must be identified. Similarly, a justification must be offered for denying opportunities to make money and to experience the subjective satisfactions of employment as a donor or vendor of procreative resources and parental rights in order to redistribute implicitly corresponding advantages to those who can reproduce without such reallocations. The corresponding advantages under this system of "inalienability" would be the "end-use" enjoyment of parental rights, since those who are able to reproduce without the reallocation of procreative resources would be equally prohibited from alienating their parental rights. Thus, this system works to the advantage of those who can procreate naturally and, at the same time, wish to retain the custody of their children.

On another level, those who derive psychic satisfaction from the continuing meaning of lineage as a basic term of social organization would also be deemed recipients of advantages.[176]

One normative justification which the proponents of alienability raise and reject as inappropriate is the superior worth of those endowed naturally with procreative resources.[177] Another is a natural superiority in the psychic preferences of some for the continuing meaning of lineage.[178] Both normative justifications are criticized as violations of the principles of equality and neutrality.[179] But these are not the norms that ought to be proposed to support the "redistribution" implicit in the inalienability of procreative resources. Rather, the relevant justification is that respect for

151

non-market, natural endowment distribution of opportunities for parenthood best serves the needs of children, and, perhaps, also produces the most desirable societal pattern of relationships related to procreation.[180]

Even if one concedes, for the sake of argument, that respecting natural endowment is "redistributive", this purpose is more than sufficient justification. All legislative activity within a society dominated by an activist state has redistributive effects.[181] The fact that the means of redistribution takes the form of an imposition of inalienability rather than a system of tax and subsidy or some other means is irrelevant, beyond the need to take into account the peculiar costs inalienability may have for society.[182] Under the existing activist welfare state, all that is generally required to justify such redistributions is a rational state purpose, except where costs fall on the exercise of a "fundamental" right or disproportionately on a "suspect class", in which case justification requires a compelling state interest. The freedom of contract is not viewed as a "fundamental" right.[183]

Calabresi and Melamed assert that some legitimate reasons for restricting alienability, while technically redistributive, are viewed more precisely as "other justice" concerns that are subject to their own descriptive labels. Generally, they refer to such special grounds for distribution as "moralisms".[184] One such ground is "paternalism".[185] Although the idea of paternalism is anathema to liberalism, some degree of paternalism is unavoidable in law, because some members of society are less than autonomous.[186] Paternalism, in fact, underlies all law dealing with the choices of infants and children, and it accounts for the law's restriction on the right of children below the age of capacity to contract.[187] In addition, the more substantial proposals to restrict the freedom to enter into contracts related to procreation are grounded in a concern for defending the equality and welfare of children from the incursions of others, namely self-interested adults.[188] This concern is entirely unrelated to the quintessential case of paternalism, the protection of the person from the consequences of his or her own choices.[189] The assertion that restrictions on procreative contracts are based on paternalism and, thus, are indefensible from the perspective of liberalism largely misses the point.

Secondary arguments against such contracts are adduced on the grounds that harm may flow to adult participants. This is particularly true with respect to the potential harm to the gestational mother as a result of forcible severance of the mother-child bond at birth, based on an earlier promise.[190] Calabresi and Melamed note that paternalism is always a societal option, although many would argue for a heavy presumption against it.[191] Paternalism would appear to be particularly offensive when directed against women, who have historically suffered from masculine "imperialism" in the guise of paternalism.[192]

However, it is not correct to identify most arguments against procreative contracts based on potential harm to adult participants as simply paternalistic. Instead, they are what Calabresi and Melamed term "self-paternalism".[193] Where the reasonable person would recognize that conditions may undermine valid assent, he or she may wish for rules of law which protect against the consequences of predictable weaknesses of judgement in those circumstances.[194] In the context of contracts concerning human reproduction, this reason would support policies making some promises voidable, especially in the case of hired maternity. Such a policy is not sexist because it is premised not on any perceived weakness peculiar to the feminine mind, but rather on the objective characteristics of gestation.[195]

Self-paternalism would avoid irrevocably binding a party to a hired maternity contract for the personal performance of a service which is against his or her bodily inclinations. This is one reason that personal service contracts are not specifically enforceable and one cannot alienate present certainty over future personal performance.[196] If the gestational mother is irrevocably bound in advance to deliver over the baby upon birth, she will find herself in the position of alienation from her own bodily inclination for the part of the pregnancy remaining after a change of mind. She may be forced to relinquish the newborn contrary to a deep physiological disinclination.[197]

A somewhat weaker argument, also based in self-paternalism, could be directed against the enforcement of irrevocable promises to alienate parental rights even where gestation is not concerned. Identity flows, even in an advanced culture, on at least one level from lineage and genetic relationship. One can psychologically overcome an irrevocable alienation of personal property. However, this may not be possible with a promise to desist from asserting a genetic relationship. The genetic relationship will always remain a horizon of basic meaning which the person is forever barred from exploring by such a promise, notwithstanding entirely unforeseen changes in life circumstances.[198] Self-paternalism could explain a rule making contractual alienation of parental rights provisional. The best interests of the child would not be served by this power of avoidance extending much beyond the time of birth. The reason is that the child has a right to establish an irrevocable bond of nurturance with particular parents. This right is itself a matter of natural endowment: it undermines the claim that parental rights ought to be subject to unilateral alienation by contract. It simultaneously limits the freedom to revoke a waiver of parental rights once the child's "right to nurturance" has concretely arisen.

Calabresi and Melamed propose one last "moralism" as a ground for restricting alienability; that is, the psychic injury that flows to observers who consider a given act morally offensive, where such injury does not lend itself to "collective measurement" permitting the sufferer to be compensated objectively for his or her suffering.[199] An example would be the widespread conviction, embodied in law, that human flesh ought not to be prepared and eaten as a victual or prepared and sold for this purpose.[200] This notion is destined to be the locus of much of the debate critical to whether society ultimately validates the contractual reallocation of procreative resources and parental rights. Some writers, like Judge Posner, tend to dismiss all arguments against the enforcement of procreative reallocations as "symbolic" and "psychic" emotivism.[201] They mean to reduce all these arguments to "moralisms" and to dismiss moralisms as non-probative.

As shown, the most substantial restriction on alienability proposed in this area flows from the bipolar nature of parental rights. Such an argument does not necessitate direct reference to the concept of moralism, but rather consistently applies the premises of individual autonomy and efficiency.[202] Discussion of the normative standing of moralisms should not detract from this fundamental limit on the alienability of parental rights. Still, this fundamental limit alone might not apply to reallocations of procreative resources that do not expressly transfer parental rights in the resulting child. In other words, the scope of enforceable exchanges might extend only to the physical disposal of gametes and gestational capacity within a procreative project. Contractual reallocations might enable the autonomous individual to plan and execute the procreation of the child, but not directly determine the allocation of parental and rearing rights.[203]

In this latter scenario, the state might intervene to allocate parental rights based either on natural endowment or state conferral, allowing a role for contract only before the child's conception. Contract would be available as an instrument for manipulating the physical preconditions of conception for the purpose of establishing eligibility for parental rights based on secondary grounds of natural endowment or state conferral. For instance, a party might contractually arrange to enjoy absolute priority under a scheme of natural endowment, by being the one to gestate the baby or to have extralegal possession of the baby at the moment of bonding. As such, contract might provide a point of entry into status, which in turn would provide the basis for subsequent legal ordering.

The normative status of moralisms is decisive in deciding whether contractual exchanges of procreative resources, which are distinct from parental rights, ought to be enforced. One question concerns the specific enforcement of promises to contribute gametes or gestational capacity. At this point, no one seriously proposes enforcement of either kind of promise. As to the vending of gametes, present performance by the vendor triggers a contractual obligation on the part of the purchaser to pay, not the other way around.[204] Future planning is facilitated by the long-term storage of gametes, once the gametes are obtained.[205] The purchaser has no incentive to seek to specifically enforce promises of future donations of gametes. The constitutional barriers to enforcing such promises would be difficult to overcome.[206]

The purchaser of gestational capacity has little or no incentive to obtain a binding promise for future performance. The number of women willing to serve this purpose and a rough equivalency in quality of the service, once the woman's health and nutrition are ensured, yield a well-supplied market. Once again, there are significant constitutional barriers to the specific enforcement of promised future performance.[207] The purchaser would only have a significant incentive to obtain the enforcement of promises to continue gestation once it had begun. But here the right to an abortion would seem to pose an insurmountable constitutional barrier to obtaining specific performance.[208]

Apart from the enforceability of contractual reallocations of procreative resources is the issue of whether a "moralism" justifies the restriction of even unenforceable monetary exchanges for procreative resources.[209] There are arguably several of these moralisms, the strongest being that these exchanges inescapably create the public impression that the essence of the transaction is nothing other than the transfer of parental rights by contract in violation of the dignity and emerging autonomy of the child. Of equal concern is the likelihood that the public will interpret the passage of money as the purchase of the child.[210]

Another relevant moralism is that the adult participants should not be treated as objects. Whether or not efficiency-based arguments are in concurrence, it is generally believed that it is not appropriate to enforce promises of self-enslavement or to waive the immunities of the criminal law.[211] Contractual promises to engage in sex acts are not only unenforceable, but are generally prohibited.[212] As these rules indicate, while the right to alienate labour freely was one instrument that allowed modern liberal society to supplant feudalism, there has been a concomitant trend to restrict alienation where necessary to protect fundamentals of personality and the political worth of the individual.[213]

One way to frame the issue is to ask whether the alienation of gametes or gestational capacity for money offends basic notions of human personality

155

and dignity. At this point, commentators such as Rose-Ackerman register concern that Calabresi and Melamed's concept of "moralism" is too broad, opening the door to a paternalism incompatible with respect for individual autonomy.[214] Rose-Ackerman proposes that this category of restriction on alienability should be limited to rights of citizenship, as for example in the sale of votes.[215] In such cases, she concedes alienability should be prohibited, but only because the transfer in question undermines a basic governmental function. If votes could be sold, governmental decisions would suffer from distortion in favour of the interests of the wealthy.[216] Rose-Ackerman thus does not ground the limitation on concern with controlling the distribution of votes, but rather bases it on concern with governmental function,[217] presumably because she believes distributive concerns would embrace anti-pluralist moral notions of merit or right.

The more extreme position, described earlier, validates restrictions on alienability only where necessary to correct market failure.[218] Rose-Ackerman's concern appears to be less with efficiency, however, than with preservation of conditions of fundamental moral pluralism required to uphold her vision of individual autonomy.[219] The enactment of any "moralism" does impose costs on those who come within its scope but disagree with its direction. To this degree, the enactment of moralisms conflicts with individual autonomy. That is not to say the enactment of moralisms is avoidable, even if individual autonomy is the ultimate goal.

The premise underlying respect for individual autonomy is itself a moralism.[220] Maximizing the scope accorded the market by limiting restrictions on alienability also imposes costs on individual autonomy. The protection of the market may be univocal with respect to the generation of material wealth, but the equation of the market with individual autonomy is not. The market ensures autonomous economic exchanges, but it is not as clear that it ensures the expression of individual autonomy by members of communitarian groups such as the Amish or Communists.[221] The choice of the market is itself driven by a powerful moralism, built on the assumption that the pursuit of individualist projects and material wealth is a common goal among all divergent personal and moral visions. Since free exchanges facilitate these pursuits, autonomy, as expressed in market exchanges, becomes normative.

Rose-Ackerman's restrictions on the use of moralism to constrain alienability actually enshrines the particular moralisms embodied in the market system. As such, it appears arbitrary and overly rigid. The functional value of government, which she upholds, requires reference to some goal. If this goal is truly political in nature, it requires reference to the political equality of the individual, a moralism implying manifold restrictions on alienability.

If mere market efficiency is the goal, then efficiency is the moralism underlying the market. This is a choice to honour the normative value of a particular conception of autonomy. Without this moralism, the preservation of the market would not be a normative value. To fulfil its ultimate political value, the market must take into account the preferences of all those capable of autonomous choice. The political realm must aim to uphold this structural inclusiveness, as well as to prevent market failure.[222]

Rose-Ackerman's limiting mechanism would be more plausible if it were broadened to require only that any enactment of a moralism be justified as essential to the expression of the political dignity and equality of all persons. At points, this would be a matter of preserving equal and inalienable access to the political process. At other points, it would be a matter of symbolic protections of human dignity, in a more abstract sense. The prohibition on the alienation of human flesh for consumption as food provides a symbolic zone of protection of human political dignity and equality. So, too, does the prohibition on the commercial alienation of sex. Countervailing factors include the dissatisfaction imposed by majority enactments on those communities that exercise autonomous choice according to alternative values.

Restrictions on even the present exchange of money for gametes and gestational services may be deemed a necessary symbolic protection, essential to society and the central political value of the emerging child's dignity and equality. The sale of the physical constituents of the child's procreation might be deemed to create the appearance that the child is put at the disposal of others in a manner incompatible with both political personhood and the value of individual autonomy which makes the market a normative goal. This would be particularly true if the sale of procreative resources could not be distinguished from the sale of parental rights or even the sale of the child.[223] The countervailing costs to both the efficient satisfaction of affected preferences and the psychic dissatisfaction of minority communities not convinced of the validity of the constraint would be substantial and politically relevant, but not dispositive of the normative issue.

Society may reasonably deem restrictions on the exchange of money for gametes and gestational capacity a necessary symbolic protection or "moralism" supporting the political dignity and equality of the contributor of gametes or gestational capacity. A restraint on alienability grounded in this symbolic concern would resemble existing restraints on the sale of organs, prostitution, and self-enslavement.[224] The features associated with the sale of gametes and gestational capacity that trigger this concern include both the relation of these procreative resources to the bodily and psychosexual identity of the contributor and their relation to the contributor's capacity for essential human relationships.[225] This restraint must be distinguished from one grounded in paternalism, since its purpose is not to save the person restrained from suffering harm, but rather to uphold the essential core meaning of the value of political dignity and equality, and, to a degree, the normative force of individual autonomy as the value underlying societal preference for the market. Paternalism does not explain the objection to alienability in this context. Therefore, the voluntary or consensual element of the proposed transaction does not stand in mitigation of this symbolic objection.

Even if society does not deem restraints on the exchange of money for gametes or gestational capacity a necessary symbolic protection for the political dignity and equality of either the child or the contributor of gamete or gestational capacity, it might, nonetheless, deem limitations on the enforceability of these exchanges necessary as symbolic protection, at least with respect to the contributor. By treating these exchanges as voidable, the law would avoid the objectification implied in coercing involuntary performance.[226]

In conclusion, arguments, such as those of the law and economics school, based on the liberal presumption of alienability fail to provide any conclusive arguments in favour of legally enforceable alienation of either parental rights or procreative resources as separate from parental rights. The essential bipolarity of parental rights prevents their exchange without violation of the fundamental postulates of individual autonomy and market efficiency, understood as normative goals. A rule of commercial inalienability prevents the market redistribution of procreative resources and results in a pattern of distribution according to natural endowment. This distributive choice is premised not on the merit of parents, but on the dignity and welfare of the children. Any element of paternalism at work in this redistribution is an essential aspect of the state's ordinary and appropriate desire to protect children. The principle of "self-paternalism" justifies, at a minimum, the voidability of any contractual obligation to provide gestational services. The idea of "moralism" explains the prohibition of exchanges of money for procreative resources, as well as the voidability of promises to transfer procreative resources. Symbolic limits indirectly maintain the values of individual autonomy and political dignity that sustain the market as a normative goal.

4. Balancing the Spheres: Politics, Privacy, and the Limits of the Market-place

Choices within each phase of normative discussion, so far addressed, have consequences for the balance of the political, private, and market spheres, which, at a basic level, constitutes the social order. The normative evaluation of proposals for the reallocation of procreative resources and parental rights by contract, intended here, will be complete when their implications for this fundamental balance have been explored. If it is to rest on a sound foundation, the exploration must begin with self-reflective clarification and validation of this final formulation of the normative question.[227] The ramifications of the contractual reallocation of procreative resources and parental rights for the balance of politics, privacy, and the market-place can then be meaningfully elaborated and normatively critiqued.

Judge Richard Posner contests that the balance of politics, privacy, and the market-place poses a meaningful moral or political question.[228] He assumes that human nature is biologically determined, and that there is little besides economic efficiency that politics should hope to achieve in attempting to shape human society.[229] History, nonetheless, reveals some startlingly diverse configurations of the market, in relation to both the family and politics.[230] Even if one attempts to explain these as adjustments aimed at maximum economic efficiency under circumstances of time and place, the measure of efficiency depends on three variables that economics itself cannot supply. Arguably, each requires separate resolution even where the market is assumed as a universal political ideal. These variables are: 1) who is an economic actor; that is, whose preferences count?[231] 2) what is the initial distribution of wealth?[232] and 3) what preferences do or should economic actors seek to fulfil through economic activity?[233]

While libertarians may argue that politics exceeds its proper scope when it concerns itself with the second or third questions, the first is, by any standard, a necessary concern of politics even within "the economics of justice".[234] The normative appeal of economic efficiency, as a modern political goal, presupposes respect within both economics and politics for the equality of all those capable of economic choices, that is, all citizens, more or less.[235] Perhaps most societies in history have, in fact, failed to respect this principle. Efficiency in these societies would have been measured by unequal regard for the preferences of their members, as, for example, has been the case in slaveholding societies. From the perspective of the most extreme market ideology, the recognition of the equality of all rational

159

decision makers remains a political goal alongside and underlying the goal of economic efficiency. Even from this extreme perspective, politics has something to be concerned about besides the proper functioning of the market. At a minimum, politics must balance its activities to foster political equality and, consequently, the market.

Classical nineteenth-century liberalism solved this problem by mandating a minimalist laissez faire state, which protected domestic order and political equality, as reflected in the bill of rights, and otherwise looked to the market to organize and fulfil social needs.[236] A primary function of the state was the furtherance of the market through enforcement of private contract.[237] In this dichotomous scheme, the activities of the state fell within a "public" or political sphere.[238] The activities of the market defined a "private" sector of public social life.[239] The family formed a third pole in the construct.[240] The family, like the market, was considered private, but, like the state, was organized around inalienable rights and duties and was clothed in a "public" interest.[241] The separation of family and market into mutually exclusive dimensions of privacy served critical functions. First, it anchored the political dignity and equality of the citizen in a kind of "natural", non-market source. Second, it created a sphere of organization for the personal relations of dependence and interdependence that are unavoidable in human society, but were thought to be inexplicable in market terms. As a sphere of interdependency, the family was the "womb" within which individual autonomy could ripen to the point of emancipation enabling the formation of market relationships.[242]

As an explanatory model, this construct was dealt a fatal blow by the entry of the state into the organization of private welfare during and after the New Deal.[243] Yet, like the classical theory of contract itself, it is a construct that continues to give a kind of gravitational orientation to a legal system no longer properly explained by it. Heirs of nineteenth-century market ideology, like Gary Becker, first suggested that economics could be helpful in explaining non-market "transactions" within the family by analogy to market phenomena.[244] Others, like Judge Posner, have taken the next step by proposing the enforcement of cash transactions in the formation of basic family relationships, thereby eliminating the political distinction between family and market.[245] While proponents of the "economics of the family" are the heirs of nineteenth-century liberalism, their bold moves prove the complete collapse of the legal and social vision of classical laissez faire principles.

Employing contract for ordering reallocations of procreative resources or parental rights bluntly contradicts the ordering of society according to classical laissez faire principles. Those advancing these proposals bear the

160

burden of explaining and justifying the societal balance of politics, private realm, and market-place, to which their proposals would contribute. Defining market behaviour as "natural" and asserting market efficiency as the legitimating ideal that drives lawmaking does not suffice to carry this burden.[246] Rather, proponents of contract must justify the market as a political ideal. They must also justify the dominant social structures created by the pursuit of the market.

The constructive effort called for cannot be accomplished in the language of economics or market ideology. What is needed is a language of political discourse adequate to describe economic efficiency as a political ideal and to assign its place in relation to other ideals.[247] It is, in fact, the breakdown in the language of meaningful political discourse that has encouraged the hardy weed of law and economics to clog and obscure the channels of political choice which would permit full and rational consideration of all relevant values on questions like the new reproductive technologies.[248] When the language of economics is substituted for the discourse of politics, the result is the undue conceptual restriction of "freedom" to mean the freedom to engage in economic exchanges, and the undue conceptual restriction of "the good to be achieved by political choice" to mean the maximization of utility attained through such exchanges.[249] As a "thought experiment", the use of economic categories to understand the moral or political meaning of freedom may be useful.[250] But, if the metaphorical or analogical character of the experiment is lost, society loses its capacity to perceive the value of the broader range of freedom at stake in a given issue. Judge Calabresi succinctly expressed the danger of overextending the scope of economic analysis in attempts to understand moral and political questions: "[t]raduttore, traditore" or, imperfectly translated, "to translate from one language to another is to betray".[251]

The minimal objectives of market-oriented politics include the preservation of the value of equality of all rational decision-makers, and some provision for allowing unemancipated minors to develop the individual autonomy required for meaningful rational decision. However, when a fully political viewpoint is adopted, even these goals must be subsumed into the larger range of issues related to safeguarding the political dignity and equality of persons and the pursuit of diverse societal ideals, only one of which is the generation of material wealth.[252] As a political matter, it is necessary to ask whether the social world, constituted by the balance of personal and familial privacy, the market-place, and politics resulting from the enforcement of contracts for the reallocation of procreative resources and parental rights, would be a good one. In order to answer this question, the first step is to describe the balance that the contractual ordering of human reproduction would create. The second is to pursue the normative evaluation of that balance.

Each model sketched in the taxonomy reached in the book's first chapter tends implicitly to represent one point of balance on the spectrum of possible forms of interplay among politics, privacy, and the market-place. By returning to those models employing contract, it is possible to draw out their respective ramifications for this final question of societal balance. For example, in the event that the individual autonomy model, in either its strong or its moderate type, was adopted, logic demands an expectation of major change in the relation of the market-place to the private sphere of family and personal social interaction. In some percentage of cases, the planning of children would be taken out of a context of personal and social bonding and expressly pursued according to modes of "production" and "acquisition" typifying the commercial market-place. In the cases remaining, the "natural" generation of children for retention and rearing would come to be understood, at least in part, as an alternative to market alienation and acquisition.[253] The basis of legal recognition of parental rights even in the latter cases would also necessarily shift towards the value of individual autonomy. In such cases, rights would, as a legal matter, almost certainly come to be recognized as based on the autonomous choice to produce a child for retention as an alternative to alienation.[254]

If reproduction comes to be understood as the project of autonomous individuals, pursued even in part through ordinary contract, the marital contract would lose further its raison d'être as a status relationship. The way would be paved for the further "contractualization" of marriage and other relationships of cohabitation, with the consequence that the marital and cohabitative partners could more fully decide participation in common property, as well as rights and duties related to reciprocal services.[255] The allocation of procreative resources and parental rights, whether within the relationship or *ad extra*, would become just one of a range of commodified exchanges available to the individual partners.

In all but one improbable scenario,[256] the recognition of parental rights under the individual autonomy model would be based on contractual alienation. The consequence is the commodification of children.[257] At the time custody is acquired, the child is disposed of as a res, not respected as a person. The justification of parental power over the child throughout its minority continues this in rem treatment. The transition to autonomy as a party capable, for example, of contract would take on an arbitrary and problematic character. The logic of the model tends towards expressly classifying not just procreative resources and unborn children, but also children below the age of consent as chattel. In this view, human maturation brings into play a transition "from property to personhood". In fact, considerable state regulation of the treatment of children is compatible with their status as chattel.[258] While reclassifying children as chattel would unquestionably serve the convenience of the present parental generation, it is not hard to see that it is vulnerable to a devastating political critique. First, insofar as individual autonomy is considered a political value, the psychological sciences show that personal respect must be shown to children as a condition of their development as autonomous adults. Children must be treated as persons before they can be expected to mature into autonomous citizens.[259] Second, when the intergenerational transition is considered as a primary political concern, the younger generation must be able to appropriate, as just, state acquiescence in the power of parents over children.[260] The in rem treatment of children is not subject to such personal appropriation.

Another effect of contractualizing procreation within the individual autonomy model would be a substantial realignment of the respective societal spheres of the "public" and the "private".[261] Under the traditional nineteenth-century market ideal of the minimalist state, the private sphere had two tiers. The first tier was the market, in which the government interfered only to enforce "private intentions". The second tier of the private sphere was the family. The government did not intervene even to enforce contracts, but limited its intervention to that susceptible of parens patriae justification. The market sphere has long since lost its status as purely "private" and has become quasi-public, or, in some views, public.[262] State regulation to one degree or another harnesses private contract for public purposes. Privacy is increasingly defined, in non-market terms, as immunity from state intrusion into personal space, individual consciousness, and autonomous self-determination, particularly with respect to the body and procreative choice.

Proposals to contractualize reproduction, according to the individual autonomy model, would essentially weld nineteenth-century notions of market privacy to the twentieth century notion of individual immunity from governmental intrusion. The result is a new domain of laissez faire enforcement of contracts within the sphere formerly occupied by marriage and the family. This development would bring with it a complete restructuring of this zone of more intimate privacy. In the revised structure, dyadic and triadic relationships grounded in lineage and nurturance would tend to give way to relationships grounded in individual autonomy. In some cases, this change would occur by direct operation of law. In the cases remaining, the availability of legal coercion as an instrument in furtherance of projects based on individual autonomy would bring change through a secondary reorientation of basic societal attitudes.[263]

The balance resulting from adopting contract to order procreation, on the ground of individual autonomy, would inject the family and other important, intimate dimensions of personal relationships into the market-place.[264] At the same time, the privacy traditionally acknowledged as part of this intimate sphere, if preserved at all, would be retranslated into heightened barriers to state regulation and more thorough enforcement of contractual obligation. Increased restrictions on freedom of contract in non-procreative exchanges, flowing from increasingly complex and exhaustive corporate organization of human enterprises, state regulation for public purposes, and common pool problems represented by escalating ecological crises would tend to further the identification of procreative exchanges as the illustration of market freedom par excellence. Market enthusiasts may envision a world in which state regulation disappears and is replaced by enforcement of contractual obligation both in business generally and in human procreation in particular. The likely outcome of the acceptance of the individual autonomy model, however, would be that publicization of the traditional market sphere would be left intact. The intimate privacy of the family sphere would yield to a marketization, which is itself a further retreat of privacy before state intrusion.[265] The locus of intimate privacy would shift away from dyadic and triadic relationships of lineage and nurturance and centre, more strictly, on the individual autonomy of eligible adults. The sphere protected from state intrusion would be defined by the scope of decision making about whether, how, and when to enter privileged reproductive contracts. Communications and interactions protected would centre on relationships between the individual and professionals and bureaucrats.[266]

To understand fully the balance of politics, privacy, and market-place which contractualizing procreation would bring about, it is important to focus on an intrinsic dynamic favouring an evolution from the individual autonomy model to the state conferral model, even where individual autonomy is adopted as the model of choice. Under the individual autonomy model children must, at some point, graduate from property to personhood. The recognition of personhood, under the individual autonomy model, would tend to coincide with legal majority, so that the child's status prior to that time would be discontinuous with what follows. If personhood is openly acknowledged substantially prior to the emergence of autonomy, the idea of transferring parental rights contractually is untenable. The obvious solution is to rely on state conferral as the basis of personhood or eligibility to claim rights based on individual autonomy.

164

By conferring personhood, state conferral achieves a priority over individual autonomy as a value. The state must then determine the reasons that it should be willing to accept individual autonomy based on its own conferral without also claiming to confer parental rights. In addition the state retains a strong interest in providing for the best interests of children, both at birth and in the course of rearing. These elements of state referral may inevitably lead to grounding parental rights in that model rather than individual autonomy. Ultimately, a choice of any form of the individual autonomy model in fact will lead to the adoption of the moderate form of the state conferral model. Within this model, contract would be used to organize the exchange of procreative resources. Individual autonomy would be allowed to the extent that it would yield desired state conferrals of parental rights.[267]

Within this evolutionary dynamic, the regulatory force of government would be brought to bear within the privileged contractual sphere of procreative projects. Market "privacy" would be allowed to operate only to the extent necessary to supersede natural endowment as the source of parental rights. Once contract serves the purpose of reorganizing human conduct and relationships in the area of procreation, state regulation would become even more pervasive under the banner of the best interests of the child than it already is in the general market-place. The government then would be functioning as parens patriae and not in loco parentis. As an incident to this evolution towards state conferral the Lockean idea of the social contract, in which legislative powers are constrained by natural rights,[268] will be fully displaced by the Hobbesian notion of social contract, in which governmental powers are constrained by whatever limits the government chooses to respect.[269] A dichotomous scheme comprised of dual sovereignties, the state and the individual, would replace a system drawn to three poles: state power, individual choice, and natural rights.

Because the value of individual autonomy, if adopted as the basis of parental rights, would almost certainly come to rely on state conferral for its validation, state power would receive priority in the duality of state and individual. Individual autonomy would tend to become just one among many state purposes.[270] The reasoning of the Ontario Law Reform Commission illustrates the implicit consequences of attempting to replace natural endowment with contractual transactions as a basis for parental rights. In the final analysis, the Commission saw only one category: state action. The question that remains is whether the moderate form of state conferral could be adopted as a stable option, or whether it would itself tend to gravitate towards the strong form of the model: the reproductive bureaucracy of Aldous Huxley's *Brave New World*.

The danger of applying contract to ordering human reproduction ultimately is that all rights and respect for individual autonomy will come to be viewed as conferred by the state. This is a result that is incompatible with the American political tradition. Within that tradition, the state has a twofold interest in procreation. The first is in the welfare of children. The second is the maintenance of the human population within society more generally. This latter interest, however, is misrepresented if it is characterized as the state's need for generating bureaucrats and soldiers. The interest is, rather, one exercised on behalf of society. Every individual within society needs the goods, services, and other contributions provided by diverse societal sectors. As the individual ages, these needs can be fulfilled only if there is a subsequent generation. The state has an interest in ensuring that such a generation comes into existence, for no other reason than that society has such a need. Until now, the state has pursued this twofold interest by facilitating, regulating, and encouraging certain dyadic and triadic relationships based on lineage and nurturance. In removing the normative value of these relationships, the individual autonomy model of contract opens the way for the state to claim a more direct interest in human reproduction, thereby undermining the implicit basis of democratic values.

In finding the correct balance between politics, privacy, and the marketplace, society must, on the one hand, seek to defend the political equality of all persons as a goal distinct from, if related to, that of defending the efficient functioning of markets. On the other hand, it must respect the basic human meaning of relationships grounded in lineage and nurturance as fundamental givens. Within this balance, individual autonomy, from most political perspectives, remains a key goal.

Increasingly, however, community, nurturance, and personal relationships are also acknowledged as goals to be valued and pursued with political resolve.[271] Proposals to apply contract to ordering human procreation fail to withstand normative evaluation because they effectively remove the meaning of relationships grounded in lineage and nurturance.[272] The consequence is a system of dual sovereignties, individual autonomy and state conferral. In such a bipolar system, it is predictable that the pull of state conferral will eventually extinguish individual autonomy.

Endnotes

1. The choice is a political one, but it is so basic in its implications that it comes close to establishing the society's basic vision of the moral meaning and value of political life.

2. Grobstein claims:

> [T]he present period may be viewed . . . as the beginning of a second great human transition. The first transition was from a biological to a cultural mode of human progression . . . .
>
>   . . . .
>
>   . . . This is the nature of the new great transition we are approaching. We are moving from unconscious cultural determination of human biological progression to a degree of conscious self-determination.

C. GROBSTEIN, *supra* note 2 Intro., at xi, xii. The magnitude of the challenge is a cause of the lack of consensus or even a general understanding of the challenge: "[I]n an era of technological, cultural, and legal transition, . . . the setting for developing a clear comprehensive policy . . . involve[s] fundamental personal and societal values about which there remains significant disagreement, resulting in a profound absence of consensus about what the legal resolution ought to be". Healey, *supra* note 5 Ch. 1, at 142. At issue is not just an objective change in the human situation, but also, perhaps, a shift in the categories within which problems are conceived. The latter shift can be termed a shift in paradigms. T. KUHN, *supra* note 10 Intro.; *see infra* note 247 Ch. 3.

3. "Any discussion of human nature must recognize a set of basic attributes that are strongly linked and that represent an important foundation of human culture". C. GROBSTEIN, *supra* note 2 Intro., at 60. The change in view is rooted in a move from internal to external conception and gestation. "[T]he sudden displacement of so primordial a process [cannot] be treated as a simple translocation in space from internal to external. The wrench is epic in human history . . . . [T]he translocation cannot fail eventually to generate profound emotional, cultural, and social reverberations", the very magnitude of the change serving to delay the full perception of its occurrence. *Id.* at 61. As Grobstein analogizes: "The victim merely blinks and then exclaims, 'Ha, you never touched me!' 'Wait,' says the executioner, 'until you turn your head!'" *Id.*

4. The fundamental issue is the nature and source of "humanness". *Id.* at 74. Grobstein suggests that science may make a critical contribution to the needed discernment. While science divides opinion in society, by adding "the latest in human experience", it can assist in resolving conflicts by creating verifiable objectivity as common basis. *Id.* at xv (emphasis omitted).

5. Extracorporeal fertilization creates the "window" allowing genetic manipulation. *Id.* at 50-57.

6. *See Id.* at 42-3, 125-32 (discussing existing technologies for combining genes from several sources, cloning, and parthogenesis).

7. *Id.* at 125.

8. *See id.* at 60-62 (arguing that internal gestation initiated via sexual intercourse is strongly bound up with the basic human experiences of masculinity, femininity, marriage, child-bearing, and parenting); L. KASS, *supra* note 12 Intro., at 110 (discussing the views of alienation of procreative resources from an ethical perspective).

9. *See* C. GROBSTEIN, *supra* note 2 Intro., at 130-32 (discussing potential forms of genetic manipulation and calling for consideration of the policy implications). IVF presents conditions conducive to cloning humans. The incentive to pursue asexual reproduction is that it permits absolute control of the offspring's genotype and avoids the tendency of offspring to revert towards the biological mean. One observer believes that human clonal reproduction can be expected within the next twenty to fifty years, perhaps sooner, if some nation promotes the venture. Watson, *supra* note 17 Intro., at 605.

10. In the future, the gestational "surrogacy" of human embryos will be possible in human males and in apes according to Dr. Lee Silver of Princeton University. *Embryo Biopsy*, *supra* note 169 Ch. 1. Already "in high relief against the tableau of history is the rapidity with which the roles of the sexes, the relations of the age groups, the marriage relation, and the structure of the family are being transformed". M. Glendon, *supra* note 189 Ch. 1, at 4. Attitudes towards children, "not to mention everyone's values about their individual uniqueness, could be changed beyond recognition if [asexually reproduced] children became a common occurrence". Watson, *supra* note 17 Intro., at 605.

11. *See* C. GROBSTEIN, *supra* note 2, Intro., at 60-62 (noting that the shift from internal to external gestation is "epic in human history"). Some commentators have been particularly cautionary:

> The ultimate difficulties of any arbitrary, artificial, moral, or rational reconstruction of society center around the problem of social continuity in a world where individuals are born naked, destitute, helpless, ignorant, and untrained, and must spend a third of their lives in acquiring the prerequisites of a free contractual existence. The distribution of control, of personal power, position, and opportunity, of the burden of labor and of uncertainty, and of the material produce of social industry cannot easily be radically altered, whatever we may think ideally ought to be done. The fundamental fact about society as a going concern is that it is made up of individuals who are born and die and give place to others; and the fundamental fact about modern civilization is that it is dependent upon the utilization of three great accumulating funds of inheritance from the past, material goods and appliances, knowledge and skill, and morale. Besides the torch of life itself, the material wealth of the world, a technological system of vast and increasing intricacy and the habituations which fit men for social life must in some manner be carried forward to new individuals born devoid of all these things as older individuals pass out. The existing order, with the institutions of the private family and private property (in self as well as goods), inheritance and bequest and paternal responsibility, affords one way for securing more or less tolerable results in grappling with this problem. They are not ideal, nor even good; but candid consideration of the difficulties of radical transformation, especially in view of our ignorance and disagreement as to what we want, suggests caution and humility in dealing with reconstruction proposals.

F. KNIGHT, RISK, UNCERTAINTY AND PROFIT 374-75 (1971).

12. Grobstein does not pursue this question. C. GROBSTEIN, *supra* note 2 Intro., at 131.

13. *Id.* at 132-35. The concern has been voiced most notably by Huxley: "[T]o use applied science, not as the end to which human beings are to be made the means, but as the means to producing a race of free individuals". A. HUXLEY, *supra* note 12 Intro., at xix.

14. According to Grobstein, "a unifying element of the tableau has suddenly been snatched away". C. GROBSTEIN, *supra* note 2 Intro., at 61. A similar description of the moral crisis facing modernity, of which the use of new reproductive technologies is a central concern, was provided by Kierkegaard:

> "It happened that a fire broke out backstage in a theater. The clown came out to inform the public. They thought it was a jest and applauded. He repeated his warning, they shouted even louder. So I think the world will come to an end amid general applause from all the wits, who believe that it is a joke". P. RAMSEY, ETHICS AT THE EDGES OF LIFE: MEDICAL AND

168

LEGAL INTERSECTIONS vii (1978) (quoting S. KIERKEGAARD, EITHER/OR).

15. C. GROBSTEIN, *supra* note 2 Intro., at 133-35.

16. *Id.* at xii-xiii. One philosophy, however crude, is eugenics. *See, e.g.*, Miller, *The Guidance of Human Evolution*, in EUGENICS: THEN AND NOW, *supra* note 154 Ch. 1, at 197. For a critique of eugenics, see P. RAMSEY, *supra* note 12 Intro., at 130-60 (criticizing dehumanization through technological control of procreation). For a sociobiological perspective, see J. BECKSTROM, SOCIOBIOLOGY AND THE LAW (1985) (examining interparental child custody disputes within the framework of empirical research guided by sociobiology); E.O. WILSON, SOCIOBIOLOGY: THE NEW SYNTHESIS (1975) (changing the gene structure advances the individual and aids the natural selection process).

17. *See* C. GROBSTEIN, *supra* note 2 Intro., at 13-58, 121-32.

18. "A number of these possibilities raise significant ethical, social, and political issues". *Id.* at 57. Nobel laureate ethicist, James Watson noted that society must act decisively in the matter or it may find that it has no free choice. Watson, *supra* note 17 Intro., at 605.

19. *Contra* C. GROBSTEIN, *supra* note 2 Intro., at 135 (analysis should "clearly unite purpose, implementation, and consequence"). For a literary caution about the implications of eugenics, see A. HUXLEY, *supra* note 12 Intro., at xviii.

20. The cultural reverberations to be expected are, according to more than one commentator, "epic". *See* C. GROBSTEIN, *supra* note 2 Intro., at 61; *see also* Healey, *supra* note 5 Intro., at 139 (examining the legal ramifications of artificial insemination).

21. Regarding a residual "shadow" role for contract under natural endowment, see *supra* text accompanying notes 190-92 Ch. 1.

22. *See* E. BODENHEIMER, *supra* note 6 Ch. 1 at 95-9 (1974) (examining John Austin's analytical position and the "separation of jurisprudence from ethics"); Brest, *supra* note 72 Ch. 1, at 1297 (discussing the Hobbesian view that "citizens entering into civil society relinquish all natural rights and possess only those rights granted by [civil institutions]").

23. In this view, law tends to be instrumental, and the secondary principle tends to be teleological. E. BODENHEIMER, *supra* note 6 Ch. 1, at 95-96.

24. *See id.* at 85-88 (examining the utilitarian philosophies of Bentham and Mill); R. DWORKIN, *supra* note 143 Ch. 2, at 432 n.6 (noting the popularity of utilitarian positivist theories in democracies).

25. Individual autonomy and natural endowment are, by definition, mutually exclusive. State conferral, on the other hand, may depend on individual autonomy or natural endowment for normative direction, unless it is specified that the command of the state has value as an end and not just as a means.

26. Conformity with recognized tradition is a basis of constitutional argument. *See* Snyder v. Massachusetts, 291 U.S. 97, 105 (1934) (recognizing as fundamental those rights "rooted in the traditions and conscience of our people"); *see also* Palko v. Connecticut, 302 U.S. 319, 325 (1937) (arguing that the Constitution lays out a "scheme of ordered liberty" analogous to traditional notions of justice); Hafen, *supra* note 103 Ch. 1, at 491 (viewing the Supreme Court's protection of the family as based on traditional values and not explicit constitutional provisions).

27. For example, the Supreme Court has repeatedly held that a state may not infringe on the parental right to decide how children will be educated. *See, e.g.*, Wisconsin v. Yoder, 406 U.S. 205 (1972); Pierce v. Society of Sisters, 268 U.S. 510 (1925); Meyer v. Nebraska, 262 U.S. 390 (1923).

28. One line of cases bases parental rights on the individual's right of privacy. *See, e.g.*, Roe v. Wade, 410 U.S. 113 (1973) (holding that a woman's right of privacy includes choosing not to become a parent by terminating pregnancy); Eisenstadt v. Baird, 405 U.S. 438 (1972) (holding that a person's right of privacy includes choosing not to become a parent

169

by using contraceptives). Another set of cases finds parental rights extending from the parent-child relationship. *See infra* note 46 Ch. 3.

29. The interest has to be compelling. A state's interest in prohibiting contraception has been held subordinate to the right of married couples to choose whether to have children. *Eisenstadt*, 405 U.S. at 453. Likewise, a state's desire to "improve the quality of its citizens" cannot usurp parents' decisions regarding the education of their children. *Meyer*, 262 U.S. at 401.

30. Proposals grounded in state conferral tend to focus on protection of the child, even at the expense of the mother's freedom. *See* Knoppers & Sloss, *supra* note 70 Ch. 1, at 667.

31. Hence, the Uniform Status Act explicitly applies to all rights derived from the parent-child relationship created through assisted conception. *See* UNIF. STATUS ACT, *supra* note 6 Intro., § 11.

32. *See supra* note 4 Intro. and accompanying text.

33. *See In re* Baby M, 109 N.J. 396, 537 A.2d 1227 (1988) (invalidating a hired maternity contract as violative of state family law principles).

34. *See, e.g.*, UNIF. STATUS ACT, *supra* note 6 Intro., at 11 (creating a state conferral-based legal framework).

35. *See* Surrogate Parenting Assocs., Inc. v. Commonwealth ex rel. Armstrong, 704 S.W.2d 209 (Ky. 1986) (urging the legislature to formulate a public policy on new reproductive technologies).

36. "People want their child to be . . . perfect . . . . [P]arents . . . go to extraordinary lengths through education and rearing to mold children to their image of perfection . . . ". Robertson, *supra* note 9 Intro., at 429-30. If their desires are recognized, they would have "the right to abort fetuses or to refuse to implant embryos with undesired gender or genetic traits . . . . [T]hey would have the freedom to pick egg, sperm, or gestational donors to maximize . . . desirable physical features" in their children. *Id.* at 431; *see also* Annas & Elias, *In Vitro Fertilization and Embryo Transfer: Medicolegal Aspects of a New Technique to Create a Family*, 17 FAM. L.Q. 199, 214-16 (1983) (if frozen gametes are commercially obtainable "[o]ne can envision catalogs of embryos, with pictures and personal histories of the sperm and oocyte vendors, from which prospective parents can choose their own 'dream child.'").

37. Aldous Huxley warns:
> "Eugenics . . . is capable of becoming the most sacred ideal of the human race, as a race; one of the supreme religious duties . . . . Once the full implications of evolutionary biology are grasped, eugenics will inevitably become part of the religion of the future, or of whatever complex of sentiments may in the future take the place of organized religion".

Huxley, *Eugenics and Society*, in EUGENICS: THEN AND NOW, *supra* note 154 Ch. 1, at 244, *reprinted from*, 28 EUGENICS REV. 11, 11 (1936).

38. "Without the surrogacy arrangement, that particular child would never have come into existence. Surely existence with some psychological risk is infinitely preferable to never having been born". Eaton, *supra* note 21 Intro., at 709. As an example of the belief that stressing status issues is in the best interests of children, see Krause, *supra* note 80 Ch. 2, at 193. *See generally* Hershkowitz, *supra* note 128 Ch. 2, at 249-52 (outlining the history and development of the parens patriae power).

39. Traditionally, the rationale for the best interests rule is that "[t]he integrated totality of family functions in a natural family appears somehow to be greater than the sum of the individual functions". Hafen, *supra* note 103 Ch. 1, at 474.

40. Posner, *supra* note 7 Intro., at 23 (positing that in the case of hired maternity, the "best interest" of the child is the opportunity to exist).

41. Current psychological research indicates that early bonding creates a foundation for individual development that is strongest if the parent-child relationship continues without interruption. *See* Sroufe, *The Coherence of Individual Development*, 34 AM. PSYCHOLOGIST 834 (1979). The principal goal for a more comprehensive regulatory approach is greater protection for children who might be born with the assistance of new technologies. The law currently governing adoption is the most obvious model for a legislative response. *See* Wadlington, *Artificial Conception, supra* note 29 Ch. 1, at 511. The adoption model functions within the natural endowment model. The transfer of parental rights is justified in terms of waiver and nurturance or a willingness to nurture, rather than state conferral. Recent trends favoring joint custody or custody with visitation rights to the remaining parent also falls within the natural endowment model with a stress on informal social cooperation.
42. Alexander Malahoff and Judy Stiver, the parties to a hired maternity contract, each refused to accept custody of the child born, purportedly pursuant to an agreement, because the infant suffered from microcephaly. Andrews, *supra* note 177 Ch. 1, at 56; *see also* NEW YORK, STATE TASK FORCE, *supra* note 192 Ch. 1, at 120 (noting that, in hired maternity arrangements, "[p]otentially, neither parent will have a bond with the child at birth").
43. It is important for the biological parents and the child to have some contact. Although only intermittent contact may have occurred, biological parents, even when inadequate, continue to be significant in a child's development. The biological family is the source of identity for a child. Children feel part of the biological family and its roots: they resemble their parents, possess some personality traits of their parents, and have the family health problems. What a child knows and imagines about the biological family helps to mold the child's self-perception. The child's self-respect derives from characteristics most likeable about the parents. Hopes for the future are also connected to failures and successes of the biological family. Finally the child's desire for parental love demonstrates the continuing connection to the biological family.
Beyer & Mlyniec, *supra* note 108 Ch. 1, at 237-38 (citation omitted).
44. Through the concept of "constructive donation", the gamete donor yields the parental relationship to the birth mother and her husband. NEW YORK STATE TASK FORCE, *supra* note 192 Ch. 1, at 133-34. Nurturing and generating life are two different aspects of the parental bond. McCormick, *Reproductive Technologies: Ethical Issues*, in 4 ENCYCLOPEDIA OF BIOETHICS 1439, 1456 (1978).
45. The disaster of National Socialism in Germany showed progressives the dangers of relying on the state to define public interest, and led them to adopt interest group pluralism as a counterweight to the state. Horwitz, *supra* note 272 Ch. 2, at 1427; *see infra* note 270 Ch. 3.
46. *See* Eisenstadt v. Baird, 405 U.S. 438 (1972) (extending the right of privacy to include the decision by single people whether to have children); Skinner v. Oklahoma, 316 U.S. 535 (1942) (prohibiting states from involuntarily sterilizing individuals); *see also* Shapiro, *supra* note 271 Ch. 2, at 541 (arguing that the expansion of substantive process is "an affirmation of the importance of personal autonomy").
47. *See* Robertson, *supra* note 148 Ch. 2; Robertson, *supra* note 8 Intro., at 954-57; Robertson, *supra* note 9 Intro.; Robertson, *supra* note 193 Ch. 1; Robertson, *Procreation Rights Ignored by Court*, N.J.L.J., Feb. 18, 1988, at 26-27, col. 3. ("Regulated paid, enforceable surrogacy could bring great good to surrogates, infertile couples and their offspring, without tearing the moral fabric of society", although he concedes that "[a]t the same time, a community concerned about the potential for exploitation and other risks of surrogacy might reasonably choose to deny infertile couples this avenue to rearing biologically related offspring".) Others express similar reasoning. *See, e.g.*, Note, *Redefining Mother, supra* note 21 Intro., at 199 (arguing that "[p]rocreation has anthropological and

sociological significance supporting its designation as a fundamental right. No other creative function ranks with the process of procreation in its importance to individuals and to society. . . . If the right to procreate is to be fully protected, it requires the assurance of certain derivative rights".).

48. Robertson, *supra* note 9 Intro., at 410, 430-31.

49. *Id.* at 429; Robertson, *supra* note 193 Ch. 1, at 32. Robertson suggests that Supreme Court precedents already support his contention that "the right" belongs to married people. *supra* note 8 Intro., at 962-64; *see also* Hafen, *supra* note 103 Ch. 1, at 944, 1189; Ikemoto, *supra* note 103 Ch. 2, at 1281-2.

50. Robertson, *supra* note 193 Ch. 1, at 32; Robertson, *supra* note 8 Intro., at 966-7. "This right will include the ability to contract with others for their sperm, ovum, uterus, or child and the ability to forge an agreement for assigning the entitlements and duties that affect the child". Robertson, *supra* note 9 Intro., at 429. Robertson concedes that the Supreme Court might require that the contract be coordinated by those in the status of a married couple. *Id.* at 432.

51. Robertson argues that contract should be given wide latitude:

> [A] constitutionally coherent concept of procreative liberty protects a
> wide range of decisions affecting human embryos and reproductive
> collaborators. Procreative liberty protects the freedom to contract for
> the provision, receipt, transfer, and storage of embryos and gametes, when
> necessary to achieve protected reproductive goals. It also protects
> collaborative reproductive transactions with donors and surrogates. In
> most instances, the interests of embryos, offspring, the family, and others
> do not justify interference with these choices.

Robertson, *supra* note 8 Intro., at 1040.

52. Robertson, *supra* note 47 Ch. 3, at 27, col. 3; Robertson has coined the term "collaborative reproduction" to describe the relationship between those buying reproductive resources and those selling them. Robertson, *supra* note 8 Intro., at 1001-3.

53. Robertson, *supra* note 8 Intro., at 1029-32. The specialized aspects of procreation include: child initiation, preparation, gestation, and rearing. Note, *Redefining Mother*, *supra* note 21 Intro., at 193.

> [T]he biological experience of bearing and giving birth is so important for
> women that it should be recognized as an independent exercise of procreative
> freedom . . . even if they never see or rear the child.
>
>   . . . .
>
> Each aspect of reproduction can thus be a separate source of fulfillment and
> significance . . . . Procreative freedom includes the right to separate the
> genetic, gestational, or social components of reproduction and to recombine
> them in collaboration with others.

Robertson, *supra* note 9 Intro., at 409-10 (footnotes omitted).

54. Robertson, *supra* note 9 Intro., at 405. *See generally* J. REED, THE BIRTH CONTROL MOVEMENT AND AMERICAN SOCIETY: FROM PRIVATE VICE TO PUBLIC VIRTUE (1978) (goals of this movement include promotion of autonomy for women and the reduction of differential fertility between social classes). Robertson is influenced by a vestige of the same nineteenth-century progressivism that inspired the Historical School of Jurisprudence and Sir Henry Maine. *See* E. BODENHEIMER, *supra* note 6 Ch. 1, at 74-75. The weight of informed opinion follows Anita Allen's opposing judgment that hired maternity arrangements, for example, are "a step backward from what could be seen as post-Civil War America's progress toward the decommercialization of human worth". Allen, *supra* note 15 Intro., at 1763.

55. Robertson, *supra* note 9 Intro., at 414-20.

56. "What then about the one in eight married couples who are coitally infertile? Surely their interest in having and rearing offspring is no less than that of the coitally fertile". Robertson, *Procreation Rights Ignored by Court, supra* note 47 Ch. 3, at 27, col. 1.

57. Sexual privacy is fundamental enough, according to Robertson, to render the prohibition of "tissue farming" of foetuses, at least for use by marriage partners, their offspring, and parents, unconstitutional. Robertson, *supra* note 170 Ch. 1, at 488. Reproductive projects are a particularly "powerful experience", with special "personal value and meaning". Such projects "satisf[y]" an individual's natural drive for sex and his or her continuity with nature and future generations. [They fulfil] cultural norms and individual goals about a good or fulfilled life, and many consider [them] the most important thing a person does with his or her life". Robertson, *supra* note 9 Intro., at 408.

58. Robertson repeats this often with no convincing explanation that the concept is an accepted component of constitutional jurisprudence; it is an incantation. *See* Robertson, *Procreation Rights Ignored by Court, supra* note 47 Ch. 3, at 27, col. 3 (conceding that procreation is not explicitly protected by the Constitution yet arguing for the application of strict scrutiny); Robertson, *supra* note 148 Ch. 2, at 8-11 (asserting strict scrutiny protection for reproductive decisions of coitally infertile couples). He refers to "the meaning of a right of autonomy in procreation". Robertson, *supra* note 9 Intro., at 414-20, 430.

59. Robertson, *supra* note 9 Intro., at 414.

60. *Id.*

61. *See generally* R. POSNER, ECONOMIC ANALYSIS OF LAW 139-43 (3d ed. 1986) (considering the possible effects of a free market in babies); Posner, *Wealth Maximization Revisited*, 2 NOTRE DAME J. L. ETHICS & PUB. POL'Y 85, 100-05 (1985) (favoring the use of "wealth maximization" as a legal principle in common law development).

62. *See infra* note 138 Ch. 3 and accompanying text.

63. The commodification of children yields other negative consequences. Posner admits that contractual reallocation of parental rights and procreative resources will have the effect of making it more difficult for "hard to adopt" children to find parents. Posner, *supra* note 7 Intro., at 24. It has been argued elsewhere that the failure to recognize nonmonetized variables in family relationships has helped determine what forms are socially or legally acceptable. Goode, *Comment: The Economics of Nonmonetary Variables*, in THE ECONOMICS OF THE FAMILY 345 (T. Schultz ed. 1974); *see also infra* note 244 Ch. 3.

64. Wealth would be increased in terms of more and better babies born. Prichard, *A Market for Babies?*, 34 U. TORONTO L.J. 341, 345 (1984). Even if it meant simply redistributing babies, law and economics would view the redistribution as an increase in wealth since it would lead to a greater overall satisfaction of preferences.

65. "[I]f . . . a market is allowed to operate" in an area, "resources will gravitate toward their most valuable uses". Kronman & Posner, *Introduction: Economic Theory and Contract Law*, in THE ECONOMICS OF CONTRACT LAW *supra* note 14 Ch. 1, at 1-2; *see also* Coase, *The Problem of Social Cost*, 3 J.L. & ECON. 1 (1960); Hollinger, *supra* note 6 Intro., at 886-88.

66. Robertson, *supra* note 9 Intro., at 428 (referring to "the natural lottery of physical equipment"); Westen, The Empty Idea of Equality, 95 HARV. L. REV. 537 (1982).

67. All contract law has been said to be distributive. *See* P. ATIYAH, ESSAYS ON CONTRACT 86 (1986); Dresser, *supra* note 9 Intro., at 159-74. For example, the trial court opinion in *Baby M* was arguably explained by class bias. Annas, *supra* note 192 Ch. 2, at 15.

68. J. RAWLS, *supra* note 148 Ch. 1.

69. Posner, *supra* note 171 Ch. 1, at 60.

70. *See* Robertson, *supra* note 9 Intro., at 414-20.

71. Posner and Kronman bring up the question, in general terms, of whether contract should be viewed as a tool which redistributes wealth, "whether to capitalists or to workers". Kronman & Posner, *supra* note 14 Ch. 1, at 267. But they assume an equilibrium and note that the question has been asked whether the law tends to redistribute to one or another class. *Id*.

72. *See* L. KASS, *supra* note 12 Intro., at 112 ("Clarity about your origins is crucial for self-identity, itself important for self-respect. . . ".); Krause, *Reflections on Child Support*, 17 FAM. L.Q. 109, 128 (1983) ("For now, knowledge of the identity of and financial access to *both* parents remains a necessary and fundamental human right of each child".); *See also* Hollinger, *supra* note 6 Intro., at 917 (identity formulation requires awareness of biological origin) (citing E. ERIKSON, LIFE HISTORY AND THE HISTORICAL MOMENT (1975); R. LIFTON, *supra* note 11 Intro.; Kass, *"Making Babies" Revisited*, 54 PUB. INTEREST 32 (1979)). While some discount the idea, *see, e.g.*, Robertson, *supra* note 148 Ch. 2, at 37, the international trend, even in the context of existing AID arrangements, is otherwise. *See* Knoppers & Sloss, *supra* note 70 Ch. 1, at 707; see also B. LIFTON, TWICE BORN: MEMOIRS OF AN ADOPTED DAUGHTER (1977).

73. *See* L. KASS, *supra* note 12 Intro., at 113-14 (discussing how hired maternity and adoption destroy the natural biological bonds between children and their parents).

74. On the incapacity of minors to contract, see E. FARNSWORTH, *supra* note 4 Ch. 1, §§ 4.2-4.4; DeMott, *Beyond Metaphor: An Analysis of Fiduciary Obligation*, 1988 DUKE L.J. 879, 903-05.

> If children are born or a relationship, whether marital or not, the model of
> contract leaves something to be desired. Children seem to be strangely
> untouched by benefits that equality may provide to their parents. Indeed,
> the privacy rights of their mothers may exclude them from being born or
> even conceived, and if they are born they may appear as intruders, since
> they are not parties to the contract or their parents.

Weyrauch, *supra* note 1 Ch. 1, at 433 (footnote omitted). *See generally* Comment, *The Rights of Children: A Trust Model*, 46 FORD. L. REV. 669 (1978) (discussing the rights of children as they relate to parents, trustees, the courts, and the schools).

75. *See* Rosenfeld, *supra* note 13 Intro., at 804-05 (contract has both "minimum conditions and maximum potential" and its goal is an "equilibrium between autonomy and welfare"). A similar argument of self-contradiction is employed by John Stuart Mill to justify prohibitions on self-enslavement. J.S. MILL, UTILITARIANISM, LIBERTY, AND REPRESEN-TATIVE GOVERNMENT 213 (A. Lindsay ed. 1951). It has also been noted that contracts increase the risk that biological parents will feel it is acceptable to abandon less-than-perfect infants after they have been born". Areen, *Handicapped Child Becomes "Damaged Goods"*, N.J.L.J., Feb. 18, 1988 at 25, col. 1.

76. *See* C. LASCH, HAVEN IN A HEARTLESS WORLD: THE FAMILY BESIEGED (1975); Hafen, *supra* note 103 Ch. 1, at 476-78 (culture and values of society are transmitted through the familial status relationships); Radin, *supra* note 28 Intro., at 1885-6 ("universal com-modification" reflects an "inferior conception of human flourishing"). John Locke argued that "natural freedom and subjection to parents may consist together, and are both founded on the same principle". J. LOCKE, THE SECOND TREATISE OF GOVERNMENT § 61 (J. Gough ed. 1956). Max Weber theorized that a purposive (commercial) contract presupposes an "unchanging core identity" independent from the contract, antedating and outlasting it relative to group status. 2 M. WEBER, ECONOMY AND SOCIETY: AN OUTLINE OF INTERPRETIVE SOCIOLOGY 671-73 (G. Roth & C. Wittich eds. & trans. 1968). *See generally* Rosenfeld, *supra* note 13 Intro., at 810-14 (discussing Weber's theories on status and contract and modern contract as an instrument of dissociation). Macneil sees essentially the same

distinction, but describes it in terms of "transactions" and "relations". He would trace relations into the commercial area. Macneil, *The Many Futures of Contract*, 47 S. CAL. L. REV. 691, 720-25 (1974).

The renewed importance of static relations in society is sometimes discussed in terms of "the new feudalism". E. FARNSWORTH, *supra* note 4 Ch. 1, § 1.7. By contrast, the continuing emphasis on "transactions" under capitalism is sometimes referred to as "commodity fetishism:"

> The transformation of the commodity relation into a thing of "ghostly objectivity" cannot therefore content itself with the reduction of all objects for the gratification of human needs to commodities. It stamps its imprint upon the whole consciousness of man; his qualities and abilities are no longer an organic part of his personality, they are things which he can "own" or "dispose of" like the various objects of the external world. And there is no natural form in which human relations can be cast, no way in which man can bring his physical and psychic "qualities" into play without their being subjected increasingly to this reifying process.

Radin, *supra* note 28 Intro., at 1874 n.91 (citing Lukács, *Reification and the Consciousness of the Proletariat*, in HISTORY AND CLASS CONSCIOUSNESS 100 (R. Livingstone trans. 1971)). For a discussion in the new reproductive technologies context, *see* Note, *supra* note 8 Intro.; *see also* note *infra* 210 Ch. 3.

77.   The movement of the progressive societies has been uniform in one respect. Through all its course it has been distinguished by the gradual dissolution of family dependency and the growth of individual obligation in its place. The Individual is steadily substituted for the Family, as the unit of which civil laws take account . . . .

. . . .

> Nor is it difficult to see what is the tie between man and man which replaces by degrees those forms of reciprocity in rights and duties which have their origin in the Family. It is Contract. Starting, as from one terminus of history, from a condition of society in which all the relations of Persons are summed up in the relations of Family, we seem to have steadily moved towards a phase of social order in which all these relations arise from the free agreement of Individuals . . . .

. . . .

> All the forms of Status taken notice of in the Law of Persons were derived from, and to some extent are still coloured by, the powers and privileges anciently residing in the Family . . . . [W]e may say that the movement of the progressive societies has hitherto been a movement *from Status to Contract*.

H. MAINE, ANCIENT LAW 168-70 (4th ed. 1870) (emphasis in the original).

78. J. LOCKE, *supra* note 76 Ch. 3, at 4: *see also* Allen, *Taking Liberties: Privacy, Private Choice, and Social Contract Theory*, 56 U. CIN. L. REV. 461, 480-90 (1987); Rosenfeld, *supra* note 13 Intro. (exploring the relationship between "freedom of contract" and the "social contract"). The value of individual autonomy vindicated under "freedom of contract", as received within the American legal tradition, finds its normative grounding in the idea of "social contract". The stress on autonomy in contemporary arguments is pushed beyond what the concept of social contract will bear. At a minimum, this approach to "freedom of contract" moreover, appears to shift from a Lockean to a Hobbesian conception of social contract, wherever discussions of utility assume that the state is responsible for the global distribution of benefits and burdens. either by action or by default. *See, e.g.*, Calabresi & Melamed, *Property Rules, Liability Rules. and Inalienability: One View of the Cathedral*, 85

HARV. L. REV. 1089, 1089-93 (1972) (discussing "entitlement" and state distribution of property).

At the same time, Rosenfeld notes that a fundamental postulate of liberalism is "an instrumental rationality of means" and corresponding scepticism about any "rationality of ends", so that liberal individualism is bound to reject as illegitimate any social organization seeking to impose a particular vision of the common good on society. Rosenfeld, *supra* note 13 Intro., at 779. Yet, if it is to avoid devouring itself, even a consistent liberalism must stop short of extending contract in such a way as to treat contracting parties as things contracted for. To remain coherent, the freedom of contract must be grounded in a social contract or some other mode of representing a shared vision of the value of the contracting individual. Since the inception of liberalism, the freedom of contract has tended to deconstruct the communitarian patterns that validate the dignity and value of the individual, but only to the extent that freedom of contract is burdened by the "myth of pure transactionism". The problem is that "[contractual relations] tend to merge past, present and future into a continuum in which the present, however sharply focused the consciousness, is part of both the past and the future, and they part of it". Macneil, *supra* note 76 Ch. 3, at 803. Notwithstanding the place of expectation interest in contract, the future must come, it cannot be made "here". *Id.*

Theoretically, the principle of individual autonomy also has a corresponding tendency to erode the Lockean natural justice foundation of individual dignity that is implicitly necessary to validate freedom of contract.

> Although nineteenth century courts and doctrinal writers did not succeed
> in entirely destroying the ancient connection between contracts and natural
> justice, they were able to elaborate a system that allowed judges to pick
> and choose among those groups in the population that would be its
> beneficiaries. And, above all, they succeeded in creating a great intellectual
> divide between a system of formal rules—which they managed to identify
> exclusively with the "rule of law"—and those ancient precepts of morality
> and equity, which they were able to render suspect as subversive of "the rule
> of law" itself.

Horwitz, *The Historical Foundations of Modern Contract Law*, 87 HARV. L. REV. 917, 955-56 (1974).

79. *See* M. WEBER, *supra* note 76 Ch. 3, at 668-81 (arguing that freedom of contract itself is the result of market forces); Weber, *Freedom and Coercion*, in THE ECONOMICS OF CONTRACT LAW, *supra* note 14 Ch. 1, at 230-33 (freedom of contract actually restricts the exercise of individual autonomy by those with few economic resources). One commentator notes:

> Thus the new technology of prenatal diagnosis and selective abortion does
> indeed offer new choices, but it also creates new structures and new
> limitations on choice. Because of the society in which we live, the
> choices are inevitably couched in terms of production and commodification,
> and thus do not move us to see new levels of genuine choice, or to provide
> us with genuine control.

Rothman, *The Products of Conception: The Social Context of Reproductive Choices*, 11 J. MED. ETHICS 188, 192-93 (1985).

80. P. BERGER & H. KELLNER, *supra* note 151 Ch. 1; *see supra* text accompanying notes 174-83 Ch 1.

81. *See supra* text accompanying notes 17-25 Ch. 1; *infra* text accompanying notes 114-19 Ch. 3.

82. *See* M. SANDEL, LIBERALISM AND THE LIMITS OF JUSTICE (1982).

83. *See supra* note 3 Ch. 3.

84. The concept of posthumous reproduction threatens to blur the concept of "generations". For example, in a French case, a widow won the right to inseminate herself with the preserved sperm of her late husband, who had been dead for two years. Judgement of August 1, 1984, Trib. gr. inst., Fr., 1984 G.P. II 560. Many proposals call for prohibiting posthumous retention of gametes.

85. "[T]he challenge confronting the law is to avoid the degradation of personhood and the debasement of birth by treating it as a matter of contract and technology rather than as a celebration of life and continuity". L. TRIBE, *supra* note 88 Ch. 2, at 1362 (footnote omitted). "[E]ven if a father is not in a position to make an immediate financial contribution, locating him, ascertaining his paternity and fixing his responsibility ultimately may turn into a valuable asset for his child". Krause, *supra* note 72 Ch. 3, at 129. This can also be viewed as a need to balance the values of individual autonomy with those of community and responsibility. *See* Ryder, Comment, in THE ECONOMICS OF THE FAMILY, *supra* note 63 Ch. 3, at 77 ("[T]he replacement of a continually aging citizenry by new recruits is much too important to the entire body politic to tolerate untrammelled individual choice to hold sway".).

86. AID laws have been criticized for not requiring permanent records. This practice impedes the application of equitable principles. Annas, *Fathers Anonymous: Beyond the Best Interests of the Sperm Donor*, in GENETICS AND THE LAW II 331, 338 (A. Milunsky & G. Annas eds. 1980). A preference for the birth mother in AID laws rests on the bond formed during the nine months of pregnancy rather than contractually expressed intention. L. KASS, *supra* note 12 Intro., at 114-15; J. TRISELIOTIS, *supra* note 135 Ch. 1; Bartlett, *supra* note 193 Ch. 1, at 30, col. 1.

87. In the words of Leon Kass:

> Our society is dangerously close to losing its grip on the meaning of some fundamental aspects of human existence . . . . [W]e noted a tendency . . . to reduce certain aspects of human being to mere body, a tendency opposed most decisively in the nearly universal prohibition of cannibalism. Here, in noticing our growing casualness about marriage, legitimacy, kinship, and lineage, we discover how our individualistic and willful projects lead us to ignore the truths defended by the equally widespread prohibition of incest (especially parent-child incest). Properly understood, the largely universal taboo against incest, and also the prohibitions against adultery, defend the integrity of marriage, kinship, and especially the lines of origin and descent. These time-honored restraint simplicitly teach that clarity about who your parents are, clarity in the lines of generation, clarity about who is whose, are the indispensable foundations of a sound family life, itself the sound foundation of civilized community. Clarity about your origins is crucial for self-identity, itself important for self-respect. It would be . . . deplorable public policy to erode further such fundamental beliefs, values, institutions, and practices.

L. KASS, *supra* note 12 Intro., at 113; *see also* P. RAMSEY *supra* note 12 Intro., (grounding the definition of human life in flesh and the nature of parenthood); Kass, *supra* note 72 Ch. 3, at 32-60.

88. L. KASS, *supra* note 12 Intro., at 254.

89. *See supra* text accompanying notes 136-37 Ch. 1.

90. *See supra* text accompanying notes 138-45 Ch. 1.

91. It has been suggested that this element of intentionality is meaningful to the child and may pre-empt lineage, if not nurturance. Note, *supra* note 103 Ch. 2, at 683.

92. Bartlett, *supra* note 193 Ch. 1. The exclusion of contract under the natural endowment model cannot be explained within typical law and economics formulas for moderating conflicts between persons who wish to procreate and others who wish that they do not. *See* Calabresi & Melamed, *supra* note 78 Ch. 3, at 1099 (hypothesizing a requirement that people buy the right to have children). Although the capacity for having children should be treated as inalienable, it does not fit clearly within the category of "merit good" which Calabresi and Melamed postulate as inalienable, because it may be required by every person attempting to fulfill an individual life plan. *Id.* at 1100. None of the law and economics formulas provides an adequate explanation of Pierce v. Society of Sisters, 268 U.S. 510 (1925) or Meyer v. Nebraska, 262 U.S. 390 (1923).

93. Hafen, *supra* note 103 Ch. 1., at 475-76.

94. Krause, *supra* note 80 Ch. 2, at 192.

95. *See supra* text accompanying notes 184-94 Ch. 1.

96. *Id.*

97. *Id.*

98. Contract as "moral obligation" or even "mere intention to make a present" evolved from Roman law in ecclesiastical courts. The concept remains in some civil law jurisdictions in forms like the French *cause*. However, the idea had limited influence in the development of the common law of contract because the English courts refused to use canon law to interpret agreements. W. HOLDSWORTH, *supra* note 24 Ch. 2, at 412-13. Nonetheless, some see modern contract as having roots in the enforcement of promises through actions for breach of faith (*laesio fidei*) in English ecclesiastical courts. *E.g.*, H. POTTER, *supra* note 13 Ch. 1, at 451.

The intrinsic moral enforceability of promises as a basis for legal enforcement, however, was lost in the wake of the doctrine of *nudum pactum* under common law. *Id.* at 452. One commentator has suggested that common law courts developed assumpsit as a basis for enforcing promises in order to compete with the equitable enforcement of promises available in ecclesiastical courts and the Chancery. *Id.* at 450. Moral enforceability resurfaced in the eighteenth and nineteenth centuries. P. ATIYAH, *supra* note 15 Ch. 1, at 40. However, public morality, social welfare, and considerations of enforceability, at some point, became reasons for limiting enforcement. *See generally* R. TAWNEY, RELIGION AND THE RISE OF CAPITALISM (1926) (tracing medieval through modern theological thought on social and economic issues).

The biblical story of Abraham begetting Ishmael of Hagar has been cited as a warrant for societal approval of hired maternity arrangements. *See, e.g.*, Hollinger, *supra* note 6 Intro., at 866; Ikemoto, *supra* note 103 Ch. 2, at 1273; Note, *Surrogate Motherhood and the Baby-Selling Laws, supra* note 20 Intro., at 1-2. However, exegesis of the biblical text does not support this use. In the narrative, the arrangement gives rise to serious discord, with the "intended" mother so abusing the "surrogate" that the latter is driven into the desert where she nearly dies. This presentation cannot be counted as a ringing endorsement by the biblical writer. The backdrop of the narrative is, moreover, an arrangement which would today be deemed slavery. The impregnation of the "surrogate", for instance, is presented as non-consensual. The text could as easily be used to support slavery as "surrogacy". *See Genesis* 16:1-16.

99. P. ATIYAH, *supra* note 15 Ch. 1. The will theory is said to be a product of formalism. *See* Barnett, *A Consent Theory of Contract*, 86 COLUM. L. REV. 269, 272-74 (1986) (wills are enforced as contractual obligations representing the testator's desire to be bound). *See*

generally Horwitz, *supra* note 78 Ch. 3 (discussing the development of will theory in the eighteenth and nineteenth centuries).

100. *See* P. ATIYAH, *supra* note 15 Ch. 1, at 41 ("[W]hat was new in contractual theory was not the idea of a relationship involving mutual rights and duties, but the idea that the relationship was created by, and depended on, the free choice of the individuals involved in it".). Calamari and Perillo identify five variations on this theme: "Sovereignty of the Human Will", "Sanctity of Promise", "Private Autonomy", "Reliance", and "Needs of Trade". J. CALAMARI & J. PERILLO, *supra* note 19 Ch. 1, § 1-4(f). "Five theories—the will, reliance, efficiency, fairness, and bargain theories—are most commonly offered to explain which commitments merit enforcement and which do not". Barnett, *supra* note 99 Ch. 3, at 271 (footnote omitted) (arguing for an updated theory based on "consent"). Formalism shifted the ground to the reasonable or "objective" interpretation of the individual's words. Nonetheless, choice, intention, and will still serve a normative role, with liability flowing from the appearance of choice. Linzer, *Uncontracts: Context, Contorts and the Relational Approach*, 1988 ANN. SURV. AM. L. 145-46.

101. P. ATIYAH, *supra* note 15 Ch. 1, at 71.

102. *Id.* Farnsworth calls this the "libertarian" justification. E. FARNSWORTH, *supra* note 4 Ch. 1, § 1.7; *see also* I. KANT, THE PHILOSOPHY OF LAW 134-44 (A. Albrecht trans. 1921) (defining the freedom of will as the source of law); Pound, *The Role of Will in Law*, 68 HARV. L. REV. 1 (1954) (describing the evolution of the extreme will theory of obligations to a foundation for the enforcement of reasonable expectations); Radin, *Contract Obligation and the Human Will*, 43 COLUM. L. REV. 575 (1943) (arguing that government should enforce all voluntary agreements) Ultimately, the shift away from the idea of a "just bargain", which had currency in the middle ages, to the enforcement of the intentions of the will, which formed the basis of classical contract theory, reflects the influence of Hobbes. *See* P. ATIYAH, *supra* note 15 Ch. 1, at 71 (noting that Hobbes' view of the individual as sovereign is the basis of property rights). The normative significance of will in classical contract is also seen in the doctrine of "wilful breach". Jacob & Youngs, Inc. v. Kent, 230 N.Y. 239, 244, 129 N.E. 889, 891 (1921). In classical doctrine, a broader notion of moral obligation is rejected as a ground of enforcement. *See* Mills v. Wyman, 20 Mass. (3 Pick. 207, 210) 225, 228 (1825) ("[I]f there was nothing paid or promised for it, the law, perhaps wisely, leaves the execution of [the agreement] to the conscience of him who makes it".). *See generally* 1 S. WILLISTON, *supra* note 9 Ch. 1, § 148 (moral obligations are unenforceable because the concept of morality is individual and thus too vague to serve as a test for enforceability) .

Arguments for avoidance of the contract reallocating parental rights need not rely on the impermissibility of the object. They may also be based on doctrines of unconscionability, fraud, illusory promise, or the inapplicability of specific performance. *See, e.g., In re* Baby M, 211 N.J. Super. 313, 376, 525 A.2d 1128, 1159 (1987), modified, 109 N.J. 396, 537 A.2d 1227 (1988).

103. J. CALAMARI & J. PERILLO, *supra* note 19 Ch. 1, §§ 1-4; Fuller & Perdue, *supra* note 26 Ch. 1, at 54.

104. *See* Fuller & Perdue, *supra* note 26 Ch. 1, at 68. *See generally* Feinman, *The Meaning of Reliance: A Historical Perspective*, 1984 WIS. L. REV. 1373 (discussing the rise of the reliance theory of contract).

105. P. ATIYAH, *supra* note 15 Ch. 1, at 189-93.

106. *Id.* at 181.

107. *Id.* at 71 ("Commutative justice . . . is receiving what you are contractually entitled to receive".); *see also* J.W. HURST, LAW AND THE CONDITIONS OF FREEDOM IN THE NINETEENTH CENTURY UNITED STATES 6 (1956); Rosenfeld, *supra* note 13 Intro., at 780.

108. P. ATIYAH, *supra* note 15 Ch. 1, at 36. A significant shift in the rationale underlying contract enforcement came with the eclipse of the subjective will theory in its pure form and its replacement by the "objective" theory of contract. "If . . . it were proved by twenty bishops that either party, when he used the words, intended something else than the usual meaning which the law imposes on them, he would still be held, unless there were some mutual mistake, or something else of the sort". Hotchkiss v. National City Bank, 200 F. 287, 293 (S.D.N.Y. 1911) (Hand, J.), *aff'd*, 201 F. 664 (2d Cir. 1912), *aff'd*, 231 U.S. 50 (1913).

109. Farnsworth calls this the "utilitarian" justification. E. FARNSWORTH, *supra* note 4 Ch. 1, § 1.7. "Only a contract that involves an actual meeting of minds satisfies the economist's definition of a value-maximizing exchange". Kronman & Posner, *supra* note 14 Ch. 1, at 5. *See generally* Williston, *Freedom of Contract*, 6 CORNELL L.Q. 365, 366 (1921) (discussing the development of contract). Enforceable promises have been described as a "unique social engine" and the greatest tool ever invented. D. FESSLER & P. LOISEAUX, *supra* note 28 Ch. 1, at 1. During the classical period, contracts were certainly valued as instruments to enforce autonomous market agreements. *See* L. FRIEDMAN, *supra* note 3 Ch. 1, at 83. For an explanation of "wealth maximization" as a normative ideal, see R. POSNER, THE ECONOMICS OF JUSTICE 88 (1983); Greenawalt, *Utilitarian Justifications for Observance of Legal Rights*, in NOMOS XXIV: ETHICS, ECONOMICS, AND THE LAW 139-47 (J. Pennock & J. Chapman eds. 1982) (explaining the benefits of utilitarianism to society through the operation of legal rights); Laycock, *The Ultimate Unity of Rights and Utilities*, 64 TEX. L. REV. 407 (1985) (explaining the optimal balance of individual rights and social utility). For a critique, see Dworkin, *Is Wealth a Value?*, 9 J. LEGAL STUD. 191 (1980).

110. This theory stands in contrast to the static social order of the middle ages. J. CALAMARI & J. PERILLO, *supra* note 19 Ch. 1, §§ 1-3.

111. "[Man] will be more likely to prevail if he can interest their self-love in his favour, and shew them that it is for their own advantage to do for him what he requires of them. . . . [N]ever talk to them of our own necessities but of their advantages". 1 A. SMITH, *supra* note 4 Ch. 1, at 26-7 (footnote omitted); *see also* P. ATIYAH, *supra* note 15 Ch. 1, at 81-3 (discussing Smith's proposition that individual interests and the common good benefit from the enforcement of promises); Rosenfeld, *supra* note 13 Intro., at 873-7.

112. See R. POSNER, *supra* note 61 Ch. 3, at 100-05 (discussing how wealth maximization reflects the preferences of those in society who produce the wealth); *see also* Coleman, *Efficiency, Utility, and Wealth Maximization*, 8 HOFSTRA L. REV. 509 (1980) (comparing wealth maximization theory to utilitarian theory).

113. The gestational mother in a hired maternity arrangement is said to receive not only economic gain, but also experience with positive social response, the opportunity to work out guilt over past abortions or children relinquished for adoption, and altruism. Robertson, *supra* note 193 Ch. 1, at 650.

114. *See* P. ATIYAH, *supra* note 15 Ch. 1, at 716-17; *see also* E. FARNSWORTH, *supra* note 4 Ch. 1, § 1.7 (tracing the evolution of contract theory). *But see* Epstein, *Unconscionability: A Critical Reappraisal*, 18 J.L. & ECON. 293 (1975) (arguing that increased public intervention in contract is inevitable).

115. *See* P. ATIYAH, *supra* note 15 Ch. 1, at 716-17, 734-5.

116. See *id.* at 716-17. Moreover, as business gets too complicated for courts to understand, the adjudication of contracts will not shape the conduct of business. L. FRIEDMAN, *supra* note 3 Ch. 1, at 200.

117. *See* E. FARNSWORTH, *supra* note 4 Ch. 1, § 1.7.

118. For discussions of the development of standardized contracts, see Siegelman v. Cunard White Star, 221 F.2d 189, 204-05 (2d Cir. 1955); O. PRAUSNITZ, THE STANDARDIZATION OF COMMERCIAL CONTRACTS IN ENGLISH AND CONTINENTAL LAW (1937); Kessler, *Contracts of Adhesion—Some Thoughts About Freedom of Contract*, 43 COLUM. L. REV. 629 (1943); Slawson, *Standard Form Contracts and Democratic Control of Law-making Power*, 84 HARV. L. REV. 529 (1971).

119. P. ATIYAH, *supra* note 15 Ch. 1, at 724-25. Lawrence Friedman sums up the development as follows: contract is "the system of rules applicable to marginal, novel, as yet unregulated, residual and peripheral business, and quasi-business transactions, transactions which might, in exceptional cases, call for problem-solving and dispute settling. 'Contract' stepped in where no other body of law and no agency of law other than the court was appropriate or available". L. FRIEDMAN, *supra* note 3 Ch. 1, at 198; *see also* Singer, *The Reliance Interest in Property*, 40 STAN. L. REV. 611, 647 (1988) (the consent basis of contract has been undermined by modern economic conditions).

120. P. ATIYAH, *supra* note 15 Ch. 1, at 407.

121. *Id.*

122. The alienability of land represents a societal "evolution from the feudal policy to the commercial policy". Alexander, *The Dead Hand and the Law of Trusts in the Nineteenth Century*, 37 STAN. L. REV. 1189, 1220 (1985).

123. *See* P. ATIYAH, *supra* note 15 Ch. 1, at 408.

124. *See, e.g.*, Monte v. Wausau Paper Mills Co., 132 Wis. 205, 111 N.W. 1114 (1907) (justifying failure to impose responsibility for death of worker upon employer). *See generally* Kronman & Posner, *supra* note 65 Ch. 3, at 267 (discussion of arguments that the application of the doctrine of constructive conditions to employment contracts was prejudicial to workers). Historically, the alienability of land has been said to have converted social relations into relations to things, obscuring the issue of owner state and owner non-owner relations. Alexander, *supra* note 122 Ch. 3, at 1220-21.

125. The generality with which the principles of classical contract are stated is to be contrasted with the particularity of earlier theory. In Blackstone's *Commentaries*, for instance, the law of contract is conceived of in terms of particular forms of relationships. Atiyah notes that in Blackstone's volume on the law of persons, chapters on Master and Servant, Corporations, Husband and Wife, and Parent and Child contain material that just forty years later, in a commentary written by Powell at the beginning of the classical period, would be contained in a treatment of the general law of contract. P. ATIYAH, *supra* note 15 Ch. 1, at 215-16.

126. The idea of efficient breach demonstrates that, at times, modern economics requires a departure from enforcing one's will. Where the marginal gain from breach exceeds the gain from completion to the other party, breach should be encouraged as "value-maximizing", notwithstanding the fact of bargain. R. POSNER, *supra* note 61 Ch. 3, at 90.

127. *But see* C. FRIED, CONTRACT AS PROMISE 16 (1981) (intentionally invoking a convention leading to enforcement justifies enforcement). According to Owen Fiss, "[t]he realists of the twenties and thirties were . . . intent on demystifying the law, and insisted that the law's claim to determinacy and objectivity was a sham . . . . Their critique was a prelude to having the law become an effective instrument of good 'public policy.'" Fiss, *The Death of Law?*, 72 CORNELL L. REV. 1, 9 (1988).

128. C. FRIED, *supra* note 127 Ch. 3.

129. "[T]o deny the remedy of restitution because a breach is wilful would create an ananomalous situation. . . ". Freedman v. Rector, Wardens & Vestrymen of St. Mathias Parish, 37 Cal.2d 16, 22, 230 P.2d 629, 632 (1951).

130. P. ATIYAH, *supra* note 15 Ch. 1, at 726-27. Such theories continue to be asserted but do not adequately describe what the law, in fact, does. *See* Goetz & Scott, *supra* note 27 Intro., at 1263-64 n.15.

131. *See* P. ATIYAH, *supra* note 15 Ch. 1, at 727.

132. Others urge a check on primitive, anti-social behavior.

> [Human beings] are . . . creatures among whose instinctual endowments
> is to be reckoned a powerful share of aggressiveness. As a result, their
> neighbour is for them not only a potential helper or sexual object, but
> also someone who tempts them to satisfy their aggressiveness on him,
> . . . to use him sexually without his consent . . . .
> . . . Civilization has to use its utmost efforts in order to set
> limits to man's aggressive instincts and to hold the manifestations of
> them in check by psychical reaction-formations.

S. FREUD, CIVILIZATION AND ITS DISCONTENTS 58-59 (J. Strachey trans. 1930); *see also* A. HUXLEY, *supra* note 12 Intro., at xix ("As political and economic freedom diminishes, sexual freedom tends compensatingly to increase".); L. KASS. *supra* note 12 Intro., at 114 ("For them the body is a mere tool, ideally an instrument of the conscious will, the sole repository of human dignity. Yet this blind assertion of will against our bodily nature [is] in contradiction of the meaning of the human generation it seeks to control . . . ".).

133. P. ATIYAH, *supra* note 15 Ch. 1, at 726-27. The business contract model of marriage would promote state neutrality regarding party intentions and preferences. L. WEITZMAN, *supra* note 3 Ch. 2, at 204, 245; *see also* Kronman, *Wealth Maximization as a Normative Principle*, 9 J. LEGAL STUD. 227, 242 (1980) (criticizing the use of wealth maximizing principle to intensify the effects of the natural lottery and proposing that these effects ought to be mitigated).

134. *See supra* note 132 Ch. 3.

135. Robertson, *supra* note 8 Intro., at 1040.

136. Dworkin, *supra* note 109 Ch. 3. The expectation of a binding marriage constitutes a non-market good. This expectation contributes to a distinctive type of societal wealth not subject to advancement through market transactions. Hafen, *supra* note 103 Ch. 1, at 486. Relational interests, such as sexual gratification, are distinct from interests in property and personalty. *Id*. at 534 n.348. "It may be said that the less the profit motive enters into any aspect of human reproduction, the more likely it is that having children will retain the qualities of love and dignity". DUNSTAN REP., *supra* note 33 Ch. 1, § 8.5.

With respect to legal restrictions on market exchanges, Owen Fiss argues that "[t]he issue is not quantity but quality: It is not that a larger role for law must be assumed, but rather that its role should be understood in qualitatively different terms . . . . [T]he duty of the judge is not to serve the market, but to determine whether it should prevail". Fiss, *supra* note 127 Ch. 3, at 7. Market rhetoric, if adopted by everyone and in all contexts, would change the social world. Radin, *supra* note 28 Intro., at 1884; *see also* Robertson, *supra* note 9 Intro., at 408 (arguing that it is not the market transaction per se that warrants protection, but the self-realization made possible by "procreative choice").

137. "A less than total commitment to the keeping of promises is reflected in countless ways in the legal system". Macneil, *supra* note 76 Ch. 3, at 730; *see also* Eisenberg, *supra* note 19 Ch. 1 (exploring the extent to which contractual promises should be enforced based on the bargain principle). Some have gone so far as to suggest that the present trend may favour dispensing with the enforcement of the expectation interest altogether in favour of compensating reliance. P. ATIYAH, *supra* note 67 Ch. 3, at 5-6. Even "will" theorists and objectivists concede that the scope of contract was set by the range of morally permissible or legal objects. It is the absence of such limits that makes the more unidimensional approach

of the new formalism such a potentially compelling force for social transformation. G. GILMORE, THE AGES OF AMERICAN LAW 108 146-7 n.11 (1977).

138. "[W]e have never had and never shall have unlimited liberty of contract, either in its phase of societal forbearance or in its phase of societal enforcement". A. CORBIN, *supra* note 3 Ch. 1, § 1376. Even if the promise is one that might be enforced, it can still be attacked as failing to meet the minimal meaningful conditions for valid assent. Carbone, *The Role of Contract Principles in Determining the Validity of Surrogacy Contracts*, 28 S. CLARA L. REV. 581, 597-600 (1988); *see infra* notes 194-98 Ch. 3 and accompanying text.

139. *See* J. STONE, SOCIAL DIMENSIONS OF LAW AND JUSTICE 253 (1966). As applied within the context of hired maternity, see Barnes, *Delusion by Analysis: The Surrogacy Motherhood Problem*, 34 S. DAK. L. REV. 1, 18-19 (1989) (courts should proceed from values rather than doctrine in choosing a child's parents).

140. *See* R. DWORKIN, A MATTER OF PRINCIPLE 181-204 (1985); C.B. MACPHERSON, THE POLITICAL THEORY OF POSSESSIVE INDIVIDUALISM (1962); R. POSNER, *supra* note 61 Ch. 3, at 113; Rosenfeld, *supra* note 13 Intro., at 777-79.

141. P. ATIYAH, *supra* note 15 Ch. 1, at 113. For a general treatment and critique, see Radin, *supra* note 28 Intro. From other perspectives, there is no such general presumption. Michael Walzer, for example, stipulates the enforceability of contract only within the sphere of goods appropriately treated as alienable. M WALZER, *supra* note 17 Intro., at 100-103. Under the Coase theorem, conferring entitlements furthers productivity and ultimately results in an efficient distribution, regardless of how and to whom these entitlements are initially granted, assuming that there are no transaction costs Coase, *supra* note 65 Ch. 3.

142. He has offered the proposal both in the adoption context, R. POSNER, *supra* note 61 Ch. 3, at 111, 139-43; Landes & Posner, *supra* note 166 Ch. 1, at 70; *Is Buying Babies Bad?*, The Economist, Jan. 12, 1985, at 14, and hired maternity context, Posner, *supra* note 7 Intro.; Landes & Posner, *supra* note 166 Ch. 1. The position is critically analyzed in Prichard, *supra* note 64 Ch. 3.

143. R POSNER, *supra* note 109 Ch. 3. Posner represents the head of this so-called "normative" branch of law and economics Harrison, *Trends and Traces: A Preliminary Evaluation of Economic Analysis in Contract Law*, 1988 ANN. SURV. AM. L. 73, 76 (1989).

144. Posner, *supra* note 7 Intro., at 22-23; Landes & Posner, *supra* note 166 Ch. 1, at 323. *But see*, Kennedy & Michelman, *Are Property and Contract Efficient?*, 8 HOFSTRA L. REV. 711, 760 (1980) ("For every legal entitlement there is an equal and opposite legal exposure".). On the separate question of monetary exchange or "market-alienability", ethical criticism is considerably sharper. It has been judged "inconsistent with human dignity that a woman should use her uterus for financial profit and treat it as an incubator for someone else's child". WARNOCK REP., *supra* note 21 Intro., §§ 8.10, 8.17. Based on similar reasoning, payment is considered, under existing law, to vitiate adoption consent. *See, e.g.*, Franklin v. Biggs, 14 Or. App. 450, 461, 513 P.2d 1216 (1973).

145. In the view of law and economics, contract's "basic function is to provide a sanction for reneging, which, in the absence of sanctions, is sometimes tempting where the parties' performance is not simultaneous . . . . [I]f such conduct were permitted, people would be reluctant to enter into contracts and the process of economic exchange would be retarded". As such, contract has been called "a standard set of risk-allocation terms". Even assuming that a predictable allocation of risks is socially useful, there are other ways of achieving predictive clarity than unwavering enforcement of contracted bargains. The value, seen in this particular allocation, is that it "discourages, *careless* behavior". Kronman & Posner, *supra* note 65 Ch. 3, at 4.

146. Enforcement would seem to include specific enforcement, wherever it is bargained and paid for. *See* Nerlove, *The New Home Economics*, in THE ECONOMICS OF THE FAMILY, *supra* note 63 Ch. 3, at 528, 532 ("the problem results from the condensation of a sequential, dynamic set of decisions into a theory of choice based on the maximization of a single, static, timeless utility function"); Posner, *supra* note 7 Intro., at 22-3; *see also* Schwartz, *The Case for Specific Performance*, 89 YALE L.J. 271 (1979) (arguing for greater availability of specific performance as a remedy). The law and economics approach has been criticized for assuming, without justification, the intertemporal consistency of desires. Kelman, *Misunderstanding Social Life: A Critique of The Core Premises of "Law and Economics"*, 33 J. LEGAL EDUC. 274, 277 (1983).

147. Landes & Posner, *supra* note 166 Ch. 1, at 324-27. According to these authors a commercial market already exists, but is not acknowledged. Posner, *supra* note 171 Ch. 1, at 59-60; *see also* Robertson, *supra* note 193 Ch. 1, at 28 ("long queues for distributing healthy white babies").

148. Landes & Posner, *supra* note 166 Ch. 1, at 343.

149. *Id.* at 341. Law and economics provides an efficiency argument even for instances of inalienability traditionally correlated with human dignity. For example: if it can be safely assumed that almost no one would have a reason for self-enslavement, self-enslavement contracts can be assumed almost always to be the result of fraud or duress, so that it is cheapest just to outlaw them, rather than determine on a case-by-case basis that most should be avoided. A. KRONMAN & R. POSNER, *supra* note 14 Ch. 1, at 259.

150. *Id.* at 334-39. For a discussion of the efficiency effects of allowing the market to operate in the production and distribution of human offspring, *see* Prichard, *supra* note 64 Ch. 3, at 345-47.

151. "[N]ot all limitations on an individual's freedom of contract are inconsistent" with a strong conception of individual autonomy which is a fundamental assumption of positive economic analysis of law. Kronman & Posner, Note on Paternalism, in THE ECONOMICS OF CONTRACT LAW, *supra* note 14 Ch. 1, at 253. An inalienability device which reduces the costs of contracting and thus facilitates rather than retards the voluntary transfer of entitlements would satisfy Posner's requirement. A limitation necessary to protect third-party interests would also suffice.

152. It has been proposed, on efficiency grounds, that there be no or only low payment for commercially exchanged sperm to avoid inducing non-disclosure of flaws in semen. Knoppers & Sloss, *supra* note 70 Ch. 1, at 684. Conversely, on efficiency grounds, it has been proposed that there be an open market in fetal tissues: "Persons who organize resources and invest capital to provide viable fetal tissue for transplant are performing a useful social activity . . . . [They should be given] the incentives necessary to organize and provide the services in question". Robertson, *supra* note 170 Ch. 1, at 477 (footnote omitted). On restricting markets in human tissues, *see* BLOOD POLICY: ISSUES AND ALTERNATIVES (D. Johnson ed. 1976); R. SCOTT, THE BODY AS PROPERTY (1981); R. TITMUSS, THE GIFT RELATIONSHIP: FROM HUMAN BLOOD TO SOCIAL POLICY (1971); Annas, *Life, Liberty & the Pursuit of Organ Sales*, HASTINGS CENTER REP., Feb. 1984, 22-23.

153. Posner makes an assessment of satisfaction similar to that employed by any other law and economics model. In making her decision, the gestational mother analyses the trade-off between giving away a baby and the utility derived from the contractual return. Posner asserts that the relatively low incidence of litigation over hired maternity arrangements indicates that women do not underestimate the personal cost of surrendering the child. Posner, *supra* note 7 Intro., at 24-6. *But see* Calabresi & Melamed, *supra* note 78 Ch. 3, at 1113 (the unusual circumstances of hired maternity contracts undermine the validity of assent and thus provide an efficiency rationale for denying the sale of entitlements).

154. *See* Posner, *supra* note 171 Ch. 1, at 60 (analysing an adoption transaction in terms of its economic efficiency).

155. R. POSNER, *supra* note 61 Ch. 3.

156. *Id*.

157. In Posner's view, the welfare of children cannot be harmed because by virtually any measure they are better off alive than not alive. Posner, *supra* note 7 Intro., at 23-24. However, where efficiency may be diminished due to child abuse, Posner suggests licensing participants as a condition to entering the contract. Landes & Posner, *supra* note 166 Ch. 1, at 343; Posner, *supra* note 171 Ch. 1, at 66.

158. There is no presumption that the satisfactions of the thing traded, in most
instances a meaningless concept, are also maximized. If we treat the child
as a member of the community whose aggregate welfare we are interested
in maximizing, there is no justification for ignoring how the child's
satisfactions may be affected by alternative methods of adoption . . . .
[The] willingness to pay money for a baby would seem on the whole a
reassuring factor from the standpoint of child welfare. Few people buy
a car or a television set in order to smash it. In general, the more
costly a purchase, the more care the purchaser will lavish on it.

Landes & Posner, *supra* note 166 Ch. 1, at 342-43. To the contrary, a rational economic actor buys a durable good like a car or a television to "junk it" when its useful economic life is over, or when a change in fashions or a change in the consumer's internal preferences prematurely negates its utility. "All children may be burdened by special fears and insecurities in a society where their parents may obtain money for family necessaries by giving away newborn siblings". Allen, *supra* note 15 Intro., at 1763.

159. Any attempt to regulate hired maternity without considering this fact would leave many problems unresolved. For example, there is the danger that the children "may be burdened with extraordinary feelings of indebtedness to their biological fathers and resentment toward their unknown natural mothers". Allen, *supra* note 15 Intro., at 1763.

160. Calabresi and Melamed view governmental acquiescence in "natural" patterns of parenting where no contract enforcement is involved as a recognition of an implicit form of property right or entitlement. Calabresi & Melamed, *supra* note 78 Ch. 3, at 1090-91. While these authors would stress that this property right is inalienable and does not amount to a right in the child as a thing, they severely tax the usage of the language in this regard. *Id*. at 1092-93. Even John Robertson makes this claim. Robertson, *supra* note 193 Ch. 1, at 653 (buying right to rear child is not to treat gestational mother or child as a commodity); *see infra* note 252 Ch. 3. An alternative to the economics approach is to characterize the natural patterns of parenthood in terms of given dyadic or bipolar relations, rather than individual rights and entitlements. Liability rules can be expressed in terms other than an entitlement to pursue individual preferences. They can be traced to both moral duties and a vision of the social good underling politics. Professor Fiss has argued that this moral dimension is an irreducible element in law, which law and economics can displace only by eliminating law. Fiss, *supra* note 127 Ch. 3, at 2-8.

161. Posner, *supra* note 171 Ch. 1, at 59.

162. *See* Wolf, *Enforcing Surrogate Motherhood Agreements: The Trouble with Specific Performance*, 4 N.Y.L. SC. HUM. RTS. ANN. 375, 403 (1987) (arguing that breach of a hired maternity, like any personal service contract, should be remedied by a damage award, not specific performance). The remedy of specific performance has been said to violate the 13th Amendment. Holder, *Surrogate Motherhood: Babies for Fun and Profit*, 12 LAW, MED. & HEALTH CARE 115, 117 (1984). Lawrence Tribe argues that "rights that are relational and systemic are *necessarily* inalienable: individuals cannot waive them because individuals are

185

not their sole focus". Tribe, *The Abortion Funding Conundrum, Inalienable Rights, Affirmative Duties, and the Dilemma of Dependence*, 99 HARV. L. REV. 330, 333 (1985).

163. "Children are potentially free, and life is the direct embodiment of this potential freedom. Hence they are not things, and cannot be said to belong to any one, their parents or others". HEGEL'S PHILOSOPHY OF RIGHT 177 (S.W. Dyde trans. 1896).

164. Efficiency in pursuing larger eugenics goals would clearly be more readily obtained through coordination by the state. Intermediate eugenics and commercial projects could be most efficiently pursued through corporate, rather than individual, activity. The conception of children to be reared in families hardly begins to touch on the commercial possibilities enabled by the new reproductive technologies, if pursued on a market basis. *See* A. HUXLEY, *supra* note 12 Intro., at 3-5. Restrictions based on conservation and supply management are efficiency-related. See Landes & Posner, *supra* note 166 Ch. 1, at 341.

165. As a libertarian, Epstein seems to acknowledge a consistent normative foundation bridging the market and other rights. This normative bridge allows him to justify the restriction of the market in the narrow cases of threatened aggression against third parties, overexploitation of common pool, exploitation of infants and insane persons, or breach of fiduciary duty, as well as to compensate for market failure. Epstein, *Why Restrain Alienation?*, 85 COLUM. L. REV. 970, 970, 983-90 (1985). According to Calabresi and Melamed, the legal system cannot afford to present its criminal penalties as a matter of what the scholastics called "a purely penal law", that is, one which citizens should feel free to ignore as long as they are willing to pay the penalties imposed by the authorities. To do so would impose economically quantifiable costs by undermining "rules and distinctions of significance beyond the specific case". Calabresi & Melamed, supra note 78 Ch. 3, at 1126.

166. See Epstein, *supra* note 165 Ch. 3, at 978 (A common pool exists where "one person is not the exclusive owner of a single resource, but shares it in indefinite proportions with other claimants".).

167. Rose-Ackerman, *Inalienability and the Theory of Property Rights*, 85 COLUM. L. REV. 931, 942 (1985).

168. *Id.*

169. For example, fish, pasture land, forests, oil pools, and deep sea minerals. *Id*. at 931-2.

170. In *Baby M*, for example, the grandparents sought visitation rights but were denied. *In re* Baby M, 217 N.J. 313, 401-08, 525 A.2d 1128, 1172-76 (1987); *see also* Foster & Freed, *Grandparent Visitation: Vagaries and Vicissitudes*, 23 ST. LOUIS U.L.J. 43 (1979). The status of the extended family underlies tribal rights to dictate child custody. *See* Indian Child Welfare Act of 1978, 25 U.S.C. § 1901 (1988).

171. G. CALABRESI, *supra*, note 102 Ch. 1, at 24-33; *see also* Calabresi & Melamed, *supra* note 78 Ch. 3, at 1093; Kronman, *Contract Law and Distributive Justice*, 89 YALE L.J. 472 (1980). In this view, wealth is broadly defined as maximal benefits relative to burdens on individual preferences. At some points, wealth, so defined, will be evenly affected by either outcome. Calabresi and Melamed stress that society must pursue some "distributional" goal external to efficiency in making its choice. They even concede that distributional goals may sometimes be appropriately pursued, even where doing so impedes the creation of wealth. What they wish to uncover and exclude, however, are cases in which private interests garner special wealth at a net overall loss to society, but do so by manipulating distributional goals to their advantage. Calabresi & Melamed, *supra* note 78 Ch. 3, at 1115. *See supra* note 64 Ch. 3.

172. As Posner puts it, "Are the infertile to be blamed for a glut of unwanted children? If not, should they be taxed disproportionately to alleviate the glut?" R. POSNER, *supra* note 109 Ch. 3, at 24. Assuming that there is no principled side-constraint on the market at this juncture, some would argue that it would be better to tax those disadvantaged by distributional goals and distribute the proceeds to those advantaged in the form of a direct subsidy. Epstein, *supra* note 165 Ch. 3, at 988-89. For a critique of the cost-benefit framework, see Kennedy, *Cost-Benefit Analysis of Entitlement Problems: A Critique*, 33 STAN. L. REV. 387, 388 (1981) ("[T]he program of generating a complete system of private law rules by application of the criterion of efficiency is incoherent".).

173. Within a scheme of universal commodification, any rule of inalienability is a taking. *See* Radin, *The Liberal Conception of Property: Cross Currents in the Jurisprudence of Takings*, 88 COLUM. L. REV. 1667, 1685 (1988) (discussing the role of "total individual control" of property as "the underpinning of the market society"). For a discussion of the dangers of attempting to achieve distributional goals through restraints on alienation, see Calabresi, & Melamed, *supra* note 78 Ch. 3, at 1114.

174. A distributive equilibrium is considered "Pareto-optimal" if no redistribution would serve to make everyone better off. *See* P. SAMUELSON, ECONOMICS 435 n.12 (11th ed. 1980); *see also* Calabresi & Melamed, *supra* note 78 Ch. 3, at 1093-94 (arguing for economic efficiency in determining entitlements).

175. *See* Posner, *supra* note 171 Ch. 1, at 64-68.

176. *Id.* at 68.

177. Some "other justice" arguments can be exposed as subterfuge providing "a hidden way of accruing distributional benefits for a group whom we would not otherwise wish to benefit". Calabresi & Melamed, *supra* note 78 Ch. 3, at 1115.

178. "The world is changing, and practices that seem weird and unnatural to members of the current adult generation will seem much less so, I predict, to the next generation". Posner, *supra* note 7 Intro., at 24.

179. *See supra* notes 177-8 Ch. 3.

180. In some areas, implicated deontological norms related to human dignity may be so basic that it is inappropriate to treat market equilibrium as the base line from which to identify redistributions. Relationships grounded in human procreative and rearing capacity constitute one such norm.

181. G. CALABRESI, *supra* note 7 Ch. 1; Calabresi & Melamed, *supra* note 78 Ch. 3, at 1098 ("All societies have wealth distribution preferences".). In the extreme view, equality would be the only goal acknowledged outside of efficiency, validating governmental redistribution of benefits and burdens. Equality might be defined as equal access by adults to the possibility of pursuing procreative projects. Contract, if seen as a "delegated public power", could be understood as furthering this distributional goal.

182. *Cf.* Williamson v. Lee Optical, 348 U.S. 483, 487 (1955) ("[I]t is for the legislature, not the courts, to balance the advantages and disadvantages".). *But cf.* First English Evangelical Lutheran Church v. County of Los Angeles, 482 U.S. 304, 328 (1987) (Stevens, J. dissenting) (despite the temporary cost to the individual, redistributive policies are not always a "taking" in the constitutional sense).

183. J. FEINBERG, HARM TO SELF 71-87, 91 (1986); Feinberg, *Autonomy, Sovereignty, and Privacy: Moral Ideals in the Constitution?*, 58 NOTRE DAME L. REV. 445, 467-83, 488 (1983). Moreover, a deontological norm rules out governmental redistribution of some elements of natural endowment, such as intelligence or kidneys. At the same time, most would agree that beneficiaries of this "initial" distribution have at least a supererogatory moral obligation to share their personal gifts with others, or to use them in serving others.

184. Calabresi and Melamed classify these concerns as aspects of distribution, the only categorical alternative to efficiency. However, within their economic framework, it is more precise to term them "other justice" concerns, as they themselves do on occasion:

> To the extent that one wishes to delve either into reasons which, though possibly originally linked to efficiency, have now a life of their own, or into reasons which, though distributional, cannot be described in terms of broad principles like equality, then a locution which allows for "other justice reasons" seems more useful.

Calabresi and Melamed, *supra* note 78 Ch. 3, at 1105 (footnote omitted).

185. Brock, *Paternalism and Autonomy*, 98 ETHICS 550, 551 (1988). This right is somehow kept distinct from "the right to decide the life or death of the child". Robertson, *supra* note 9 Intro., at 462. The child's psychic distress over its "weird" origins is acknowledged as an externality, but dismissed on the ground that this distress will diminish if such arrangements become customary. Posner, *supra* note 7 Intro., at 24. The reasoning Robertson proposes to support this point merits closer examination. He claims that the contract right is fundamental since two moral values are implicated, individual autonomy and the opportunity to pursue procreative experimentation. Because it has been granted a special status as "fundamental", contract excludes other moral values, including respect for relationships grounded in lineage and nurturance, and for the dignity of the person. Other than his two privileged values, all normal values are deemed by Robertson to be "interests" claimed by adoption agencies and "pro-lifers" or other moralists. The crucial move privileging his chosen values is attributing to them a fundamental status, which he never justifies morally, and which is unsupported in the jurisprudence of the Supreme Court of the United States. Robertson, *supra* note 9 Intro., at 426-29. Notwithstanding the lack of principled justification, Robertson holds that where the welfare of children and the unrestricted pursuit of his chosen values conflict, the burden of proof is on children's welfare. *Id.* at 434.

186. *See* Kronman & Posner, *supra* note 151 Ch. 3; Kronman, *Paternalism and the Law of Contracts* 92 YALE L.J. 763 (1983). For a moderate and well-argued view that some form of paternalism in lawmaking is unavoidable, but that it belongs more to legislatures than courts, see Shapiro, *supra* note 271 Ch. 2.

187. This "presents a challenge to libertarians". Kronman & Posner, *supra* note 151 Ch. 3, at 254-6; *see also* Calabresi & Melamed, *supra* note 78 Ch. 3, at 1113 (paternalism is sometimes based on the notion that adults know better than minors what is good for minors).

188. *See* Annas & Elias, *supra* note 12 Intro. at 157.

189. Paternalism, in its proper meaning, is present if the "sole justification for imposing it is to promote or protect the individual's own welfare (or happiness or good)". Kronman & Posner, *supra* note 151 Ch. 3. Moreover, "the only purpose for which power can be rightfully exercised over any member of a civilized community, against his will, is to prevent harm to others". J.S. MILL, *supra* note 147 Ch. 1, at 10-11.

190. Even advocates of an autonomy approach engage in paternalistic weighing of advantages and disadvantages to the gestational mother, if only for the sake of argument. *See, e.g.,* Robertson, *supra* 193 Ch. 1, at 34.

191. Calabresi & Melamed, *supra* note 78 Ch. 48, at 1113; *see also* Shapiro, *supra* note 271 Ch. 2, at 521 (arguing courts should only act on paternalistic grounds if legislature so directs).

192. A. JAGGAR, FEMINIST POLITICS AND HUMAN NATURE (1983); B. ROTHMAN, IN LABOR: WOMEN AND POWER IN THE BIRTHPLACE (1982); Rubin, *supra* note 194 Ch. 1, at 157; *see also* J.S. MILL, *The Subjection of Women*, in ESSAYS ON SEX EQUALITY 427 (A. Rossi, ed. 1970).

193. Consent theorists limit such grounds to those relating freedom maximation. See J. KLEINIG, PATERNALISM 55 (1984) (discussing the justifications of consent-based paternalism); Calabresi & Melamed, supra note 78 Ch. 3, at 1113.

194. Calabresi and Melamed offer the example of Ulysses tying himself to the mast. Calabresi & Melamed, *supra* note 78 Ch. 3, at 1113.

195. This is one version of inalienability, albeit weak, that can be applied to hired maternity. *See In re* Baby M, 109 N.J. 396, 537 A.2d 1227 (1988) (finding a hired maternity contract void after gestational mother wished to disaffirm the contract); Allen, *supra* note 15 Intro., at 1780 (suggesting that "the commercial character of the surrogate mother's aims and motives necessarily takes her outside the realm of constitutionally protected privacy"). It is widely acknowledged that "the nine-month gestational period creates a unique and powerful bond for both donor and offspring that seems to justify a claim in its own right". Robertson, *supra* note 193 Ch. 1, at 34. The restriction in question is a trade of short-term restriction of choice for longer-term, more meaningful freedom of choice. Calabresi and Melamed, *supra* note 78 Ch. 3, at 1113.

196. For example:

> [T]he vital question remains whether a court of equity will, under any circumstances, by injunction, prevent one individual from quitting the personal service of another? An affirmative answer to this question, is not, we think, justified by any authority to which our attention has been called or of which we are aware. It would be an invasion of one's natural liberty to compel him to work for or to remain in the personal service of another.

Arthur v. Oakes, 63 F. 310, 317-18 (7th Cir. 1894). Even where a contract would otherwise be specifically enforceable, enforcement will be denied where there is special reason to question the obligor's original assent, even where there is no contractual incapacity, or where public policy is offended, even where it is not so offended as to allow an award of money damages. *See* E. FARNSWORTH, *supra* note 4 Ch. 1, § 12.7 (discussing specific performance and injunctions generally); 11 S. WILLISTON, *supra* note 9 Ch. 1, §§ 1423, 1427, 1429 (discussing specific performance as it relates to employment contracts and mistake, and public policy reasons precluding such recovery).

The construct of classical contract law presupposes that money damages are the appropriate remedy. *Id.* § 1338. One measure of the scope of contract is to ask what kinds of transactions involve expectations which are properly monetizable, paralleling, on the one hand, the border of legality, and, on the other, that of equitable rights not subject to money damages. *See generally* Kronman, *supra* note 186 Ch. 3 (mistakes must be depersonalized through money damages).

197. *Cf.* Means, *supra* note 16 Intro., at 459-62 (noting the reluctance of American courts to specifically enforce personal service contracts). The idea that the assertion of money damages against the mother in lieu of specific performance would save the arrangement is not tenable. Such a rule would harm the child if the mother chose to retain custody and pay damages, and the choice itself would pose a cruel and solomonic dilemma for the mother. For an analogous proposal, see Robertson, *supra* note 193 Ch. 1, at 30 (noting that children of "surrogate" parents, like many adopted children, may have problems with self-esteem or try to discover the identity of the missing parent). The literature shows that the management of hired maternity, regardless of the particulars of the arrangement, tends towards a depersonalizing control over the gestational mother's personal autonomy.

> A major source of uncertainty and stress is likely to be the surrogate her-
> self. In most cases she will be a stranger, and may never even meet the [intend-
> ing] couple. The lack of preexisting relation between the couple and surrogate and

the possibility that they live far apart enhance the possibility of mistrust. Is the surrogate taking care of herself? Is she having sex with others during her fertile period? Will she contact the child afterwards? What if she demands more money to relinquish the child? To allay these anxieties, the couple could try to establish a relationship of trust with the surrogate, yet such a relationship creates reciprocal rights and duties, and might create demands for an undesired relationship after the birth. Even good lawyering that specifies every contingency in the contract is unlikely to allay uncertainty and anxiety about the surrogate's trustworthiness.

Id. at 29-30.

198. It has been alleged that adoption is an act of violence and that women miss their children years later. J. SHAWYER, DEATH BY ADOPTION 91-120 (1979).

199. The authors define moralism, in this sense, as a "nonmonetizable external cost". Calabresi & Melamed, *supra* note 78 Ch. 3, at 1111-12. They concede that, at some point, ethics has a place in public discussion: "Indeed when we approach bodily integrity we are getting close to areas where we do not let the entitlement be sold at all and where economic efficiency enters in, if at all, in a more complex way". *Id*. at 1125-6. They justify this observation by noting that psychic perceptions of the cost of moral violations of bodily and personal integrity are too subjective to allow a public aggregation of costs".[W]e would not presume collectively and objectively to value the cost of a rape to the victim against the benefit to the rapist". *Id*. at 1125. Another example they give is the moral affront of future generations threatened by a "despoiled, hazardous environmental condition which they are powerless to reverse". *Id*. at 1124. *Cf*. D. MEYERS, INALIENABLE RIGHTS 53 (1985) ("A moral system would fail . . . if it could require right-holders to relinquish the goods to which inalienable rights entitle them or could prescribe abridgments of inalienable rights".).

200. Another typical example is self-enslavement. *See* Kronman & Posner, *supra* note 151 Ch. 3, at 256-60.

201. Kronman and Posner treat "moralisms" as no more than the psychic anguish experienced by an offended majority. They characterize the concept as an essentially unpersuasive attempt to avoid the "embarrassment of paternalism". Further, they argue that before the concept can be shown to be relevant, it must be established that it draws on "a conception of liberty and personal dignity which is embodied in the central provisions of our Constitution and to which we are committed as a people", and, further that it is so basic that "no person in his right mind would abandon the moral ideal". *Id*. at 258-9. These authors question whether it makes sense to credit feelings that one person's self-respect is undermined by the self-enslavement of another. *Id*. at 258. A contrasting position can be seen in the work of Anita Allen who sees a distinction between "mere moralism and paternalism" and "degradation, exploitation, slavery, baby selling, or racism", fundamentally compromising the dignity of the person. Allen, *supra* note 15 Intro., at 1763. Posner's response is that the breakdown in a commonly affirmed moral fabric means that what once could pass as objective assaults on human dignity now must be interpreted as subjective, psychic moralistic injuries. *See* Landes & Posner, *supra* note 166 Ch. 1, at 344-46 (discussing moral objections to baby selling and the social costs of alternatives); *see also* Posner, *supra* note 171 Ch. 1, at 70-71 (arguing that the question is how to regulate baby selling, not whether it should exist).

202. *See supra* text accompanying notes 61-8 & 140-58 Ch. 3.

203. *See* Jansen, *Sperm and Ova as Property*, 11 J. MED. ETHICS 123 (1985) (discussing conflicting views of ownership of donated gametes in light of these cells' ability to carry readily usable genetic information).

204. *See supra* text accompanying notes 172-88 Ch. 2.

205. *See* Knoppers & Sloss, *supra* note 70 Ch. 1, at 671-2 (discussing state regulation of commercial human gamete banks of employees in Canada).

206. The right to decide not to bear a child would be infringed. *See* Eisenstadt v. Baird, 405 U.S. 438 (1972). Not even Judge Sorkow, who was otherwise enthusiastic about enforcing hired maternity arrangements, would restrict the gestational mother's freedom to abort the fetus in contravention of the contract. *In re* Baby M, 217 N.J. Super. 313, 375, 525 A.2d 1128, 1159 (Ch. Div. 1987), *aff'd in part and rev'd in part,* 109 N.J. 396, 537 A.2d 1227 (1988).

207. *See supra* note 206 Ch. 3. Ironically, in some interpretations, it is permissible to curtail autonomy through governmental restrictions on maternal behaviour during pregnancy, but not by allowing the avoidance of promised transfers of maternal rights. OFFICE OF TECHNOLOGY ASSESSMENT, *supra* note 21 Intro., at 277-78.

208. *See* Roe. v. Wade, 410 U.S. 113 (1973) (recognizing a woman's fundamental right to decide whether to terminate a pregnancy during the first trimester).

209. *See* Radin, *supra* note 28 Ch. 1, at 1930-36 (discussing the more subtle problems raised by hired maternity); *see also supra* text accompanying notes 185 Ch. 1 & 350-55 Ch. 2.

210. Prichard points out that "the pricing of babies" could contradict two closely held beliefs: "that life is infinitely valuable—'pearl beyond price'" and "that all lives are equally valuable". He notes that "[w]ith higher prices for white than non-white children, and higher prices for healthy than sick children, and other similar forms of price differentials, the reality and the ideal would again clash". Prichard, *supra* note 64 Ch. 3, at 351. The New York State Task Force on Life amplifies these concerns, noting that hired maternity may be "indistinguishable from the sale of children", and that it may undermine "basic premises about the nature and meaning of being human and the moral dictates of our shared humanity". NEW YORK STATE TASK FORCE, *supra* note 192 Ch. 1, at 118. Furthermore, it may carry "severe long term negative implications for the way society thinks about and values children". *Id.* at 119. Finally, as more immediate risks, it causes irrevocably and deliberately fractured genetic, gestational, and social relationships as well as the depersonalization of women, and human reproduction. *Id.* at 119-21. The Task Force concludes that:

> the assignment of market values should not be celebrated as an exaltation
> of "rights", but rejected as a derogation of the values and meanings
> associated with human reproduction [and] derived from the relationship
> between the mother and father of a child and the child's creation as an
> expression of their mutual love.

Id. at 121.

211. Michael Walzer holds that "blocked exchanges", those occurring outside the monetary system, are necessary to define equality in a whole range of contexts, one of which is "procreation and marriage". M. WALZER, *supra* note 17 Intro., at 100-103; *see also* D. MEYERS, *supra* note 199 Ch. 3. Commentators have implicitly adopted Walzer's approach in dealing with hired maternity: "Judicial enforcement, that is, would constitute an official imprimatur for the woman's depersonalized marketplace attitude toward her child and toward herself as a 'producer of children.' The Court [in *Baby M*] was correct to fear the social effects of this attitude and to withhold its approval from it". Burt, *supra* note 357 Ch. 2, at 27, col 1.

212. Even where prostitution is legal, it is generally illegal to induce women to become prostitutes, advertising is prohibited, minors are excluded, and prostitution is restricted to brothels. *See* J. DECKER, *supra* note 63 Ch. 2, at 55 (discussing regulation of prostitution in Western Europe and certain states such as Nevada).

213. R. SCOTT, *supra* note 152 Ch. 3. Posner dismisses this as a hypocritical token, since there is no persuasive evidence that parties to a hired maternity contract are not well informed of the consequences of their acts. Posner, *supra* note 7 Intro., at 25-26.

214. Rose-Ackerman, *supra* note 167 Ch. 3, at 931.

215. *Id.* at 961-69.

216. *Id.* at 963

217. *Id.* at 962-65

218. *See supra* text accompanying note 151 Ch. 3.

219. Rose-Ackerman believes this "is a way to rescue the concept of inalienability from its simplistic rejection by market-oriented economists or its overly enthusiastic embrace by paternalistic moralists". Rose-Ackerman, *supra* note 167 Ch. 3, at 969.

220. R. POSNER, *supra* note 109 Ch. 3, at 88-113; Posner, *The Ethical and Political Basis of the Efficiency Norm in Common Law Adjudication*, 8 HOFSTRA L. REV. 487 (1980). For a critique, see R. DWORKIN, *supra* note 109 Ch. 3, at 237 (arguing that social value is a form of wealth that traditional economic analysis fails to consider); Kelman, *supra* note 146 Ch. 3 (asserting that traditional economic analysis fails to consider that a person has continuous identity which distorts utility-maximizing behaviour.)

John Noonan finds connections between the inalienability that protects the element of fidelity in the marital and sexual relationship and that which protects the impartiality of justice in the political sphere. He notes the moral and legal decline in the ideal of marital fidelity, and asks whether this may not give rise to a parallel decline in the belief that justice should be considered inalienable. J. NOONAN, BRIBES 701-3 (1984). What Noonan does not pursue, but fits well with his hypothesis, is the idea that the decline in belief in the meaning of marital fealty should be followed by market alienability of sex and procreation.

Michael Walzer examines the connection on a functional level, and not in terms of etiology as does Noonan. Walzer sees inalienability as necessary to protect equal participation in various aspects of the political process: political power and influence, criminal justice, civil rights, emigration, exemptions from government service, and political offices. M. WALZER, *supra* note 17 Intro., at 100; *see also supra* note 74 Ch. 3 and *infra* note 247 Ch. 3.

221. Feminist writing is concerned that women should have the freedom to resist attempts to objectify that which their sexual desirability and procreative role make natural. They also stress that women have a more relational mode of reasoning. C. GILLIGAN, IN A DIFFERENT VOICE (1982). The operation of the free market threatens this freedom.

222. This is more generally true of liberalism. For example, one author has argued that the legitimacy of the criminal law is based in a public morality, but that the recognition of such a morality is kept at a minimum in respect for liberalism's guiding value, autonomy. The author argued further that such an approach represents a conscious departure on the part of the founders of the American republic from "classical republicanism's" commitment to overarching notions of public virtue. Richards, *Liberalism, Public Morality, and Constitutional Law: Prolegomenon to a Theory of the Constitutional Right to Privacy*, 51 LAW & CONTEMP. PROBS. 123, 123-24 (1988); *cf.* Epstein, *supra* note 165 Ch. 3, at 987 (discussing the rationale for the prohibition against the sale of votes in public elections).

223. The public would have to accept the assertion made by some commentators that "[t]he payments are not to purchase a child, but to compensate for personal services". Hollinger, *supra* note 6 Intro., at 893.

224. *See* National Organ Transplant Act, 42 U.S.C. § 274e (1988) (prohibiting the sale of human organs for use in transplantation): Note, *supra* note 170 Ch. 1 (discussing how a market in organs could be created); *see also* U.S. CONST. amend. XIII; Peonage Act, 42 U.S.C. § 1994 (1988); Robertson, *supra* note 8 Intro., at 986 (noting that symbolic harm

from using embryos for tissue farming might justify banning the activity). *See generally* R. SCOTT, *supra* note 152 Ch. 3 (discussing the social, moral, and legal implications associated with tissue and organ transplants); Barnett, *Contract Remedies and Inalienable Rights*. 4 SOC. PHIL. & POL'Y 179 (1986) (arguing that money damages are an insufficient remedy for breach of a contract involving inalienable rights).

225. One commentator has noted that the practice in hired maternity has evolved to prevent such relationships from forming.

> To avoid the risk of a recalcitrant surrogate, contemporary surrogacy practice now customarily uses donor eggs instead of the surrogate's egg. Thus practice seems to have moved ahead of the 'Baby M' Case, insofar as the invalid is explicitly based on the fact that "[T]he surrogacy contract guarantees permanent separation of the child from one of its natural parents".

S. GREEN & J. LONG, *supra* note 55 Ch. 1, at 67. Some literature stresses the depersonalization of such arrangements. *See* Radin *Property and Personhood*, 34 STAN. L. REV. 957 (1982). *But see* D'Aversa, *The Right of Abortion in Surrogate Motherhood Arrangements*, 7 N. ILL. U.L. REV. 1 (1986) (favoring development of methods to circumvent the constitutional prohibition of contractually alienating the right to terminate a pregnancy); Note, *supra* note 8 Intro. (arguing in favor of enforcement of hired maternity contracts).

226. *See* Wolf, *supra* note 162 Ch. 3, at 394-99, 404-06 (proposing a dual standard in evaluating hired maternity arrangements, including the "best interests of the child" test and a "competing parental claims" balancing test); *see also* Position of the National Organization for Women, Resolution on Surrogate Motherhood (May 1987) (urging rules that would retain the biological mother's rights until sometime after the birth of the child).

227. *See* M. WALZER *supra* note 17 Intro., at 279.

228. Posner, *supra* note 171 Ch. 1, at 70.

229. "People are what they are, and what they are is the result of millions of years of evolution rather than of such minor cultural details as the precise scope of the market principle in a particular society". Posner, *supra* note 7 Intro., at 26-27.

230. *See supra* text accompanying note 189 Ch. 1.

231. *See* R. NOZICK, *supra* note 150 Ch. 1, at 150-51, 153, 155-64 (discussing the entitlement theory of distributive justice); Baker, *The Ideology of the Economic Analysis of Law*, 1 PHIL. & PUB. AFF. 3, 32-41 (1975) (discussing Posner's consumer sovereignty concept of the market); Calabresi & Melamed, *supra* note at 78 Ch. 3, at 1090 ("[T]he fundamental thing that law does is to decide which of the conflicting parties will be entitled to prevail".).

232. *See* Calabresi & Melamed, *supra* note 78 Ch. 3, at 1096 (noting that market efficiency depends of the distribution of wealth in the economy).

233. *See* V. ZELIZER, PRICING THE PRICELESS CHILD: THE CHANGING SOCIAL VALUE OF CHILDREN 19 (1985) (discussing how the tension between the economy and personal values can obstruct the expansion of the market).

234. *See* R. NOZICK, *supra* note 150 Ch. 3; EPSTEIN, supra note 165 Ch. 3, at 970 (arguing that the law is designed to protect economic actors defined as property owners).

235. Equality itself presupposes that the individual does not exist for the good of society but may act on occasion for the good of society, whether intentionally or not. R. NOZICK, *supra* note 150 Ch. 1, at 32-33.

236. Soifer, *The Paradox of Paternalism and Laissez-Faire, Constitutionalism: United States Supreme Court, 1888-1921*, 5 L. & HIST. REV. 249, 252-53 (1987) (noting the concern among American jurists of the 1880s-1920s for "combating paternalism").

237. McCurdy, *Justice Field and the Jurisprudence of Government-Business Relations: Some Parameters of Laissez-Faire Constitutionalism*, 1863-1897, 61 J. AM. HIST. 970 (1975).

238. "[O]nly the nineteenth century produced a fundamental conceptual and architectural division [public/private] in the way we understand the law". Horwitz, *supra* note 272 Ch. 2, at 1424.

239. Contract serves to make such use of state coercion "private". *See* P. ATIYAH, *supra* note 15 Ch. 1, at 713 (discussing how government tempers and modified the risk/reward system of contract as an instrument of private planning). The public/private distinction is still spoken of this way. *See* D. FESSLER & P. LOISEAUX, *supra* note 28 Ch. 1, at 174 ("[i]t is not the function of government—of the courts—to make contracts for individuals, but to construe and enforce them"). Some authors do not find this view tenable within the picture of the modern legal system as a whole. *See e.g.*, Kennedy, *supra* note 2 Ch. 1, at 1349-57 (1982) (arguing that the public/private distinction no longer has analytical meaning); Pound, *Liberty of Contract*, 18 YALE L.J. 454 (1909) (arguing that the public/private distinction has blurred, making freedom of contract less distinctly private). The origin of the distinction goes back to John Locke's social contract theory. *See* J. LOCKE, *supra* note 76 Ch. 3.

240. Olsen, *supra* note 29 Intro., at 1501 (noting the place of the family as a world apart from the market or government).

241. The zone of illegality limiting contract did not include marriage and family relationships. *See* C. ASHLEY, *supra* note 9 Ch. 1, § 51(b)("The theory of modern civilization bases the welfare of the State upon the safety and happiness of the home. Hence the law favors marriage as an advantage to the community, and the Courts frown upon any arrangement which tends to interfere with the freedom of individuals to contract for or continue this status, or which has a tendency to taint the relationship with pecuniary motives.") J. LAWSON, *supra* note 8 Ch. 1, §§ 319-22 (noting that contracts impinging on marriage and family stability were unenforceable). *But see* Kennedy *supra* note 2 Ch. 1, at 1356 (arguing that the separation of family and state was artificial and never clear).

242. *See* Poe v. Ullman, 367 U.S. 497, 551-52 (1961) (Harlan, J., dissenting)(the home is "the seat of family life" and is fundamental to the formation of societal relationships).

243. *See* Hand, *Due Process of Law and the Eight-Hour Day*, 21 HARV. L. REV. 495 (1908) (noting how due process concerns have permitted the encroachment of government into private activities); Paul, *Searching for the Status Quo*, 7 CARDOZO U.L. REV. 743, 746-74 (1986) (arguing that public law has been "submerged" by public law in the courts and legislatures).

244. Becker, *The Economics of the Family* in THE ECONOMICS OF THE FAMILY *supra* note 63 Ch. 3, at 299; *cf.* V. ZELIZER, MORALS AND MARKETS, THE DEVELOPMENT OF LIFE INSURANCE IN THE UNITED STATES (1979) (discussing life insurance as creating a need for the evaluation of life, death, human organs, and children in monetary equivalents).

245. Landes & Posner, *supra* note 166 Ch. 1.

246. Posner, *supra* note 7 Intro. Within the sphere of commercial agreements, the imposition of fiduciary obligations is easier to justify under contract law than under a theory of self-interested bargain. *See* Demott, *supra* note 74 Ch. 3, at 892-3.

247. *See* R. DWORKIN, *supra* note 140 Ch. 3, at 205. More than the political value of the person is at stake, so too is some minimal vision of the social good adequate to sustain political life. *See* Bartlett, *supra* note 103 Ch. 2, at 313 (making reference to "the central political question of what kinds of families our society is prepared to allow or encourage"). The solution is not, however, to turn law and economics for normative political direction, which it cannot legitimately give. *See* Dworkin, *supra* note 109 Ch. 3, at 191. *See generally* Cass, *Coping with Life, Law and Markets: A Comment on Posner and the Law-*

and-Economics Debate, 67 B.U.L. REV. 73 (1987) (discussing four objections to the economic analysis of law); Michelman, *A Comment on Some Uses and Abuses of Economics in Law*, 46 U. CHI. L. REV. 307 (1979) (qualifying and clarifying Posner's theory of economic analysis); *see also* Calabresi & Melamed, *supra* note 78 Ch. 3, at 1090 n.2 (noting that a model such as law and economics is not to be mistaken for the total view of the phenomenon, but rather should be seen as resembling just "one of Monet's paintings of the Cathedral at Rouen").

Some commitment to seeking a common notion of authentic human flourishing is a necessary basis of pluralist political life. Radin, *supra* note 28 Intro., at 1877-86. A renewed structural understanding of the relationship between the political ideals of the dignity and equality of the human person and the deeper structures of the legal system is equally necessary. One solution would be to rethink and affirm some variant on the Lockean social contract. *See* Rosenfeld, *supra* note 13 Intro., at 847-73.

248. *See* Harrison, *Egoism, Altruism, and Market Illusions: The Limits of Law and Economics*, 33 UCLA L. REV. 1309 (1986) (economic analysis of law should be admired for its descriptive value, but not for its conclusions); Kelman *supra* note 146 Ch. 3 (law-and-economics approach has obscured legal study as much as it has enlightened it); Michelman, *Reflections on Professional Education, Legal Scholarship, and the Law-and-Economics Movement*, 33 J. LEGAL EDUC. 197, 209 (1983) (arguing "[n]ot that law-and-economics scholarship is evil, stupid, useless, trivial; just that it is partial and limited; that there are important tasks of inquiry to which it is ill suited and to which it does not pretend").

249. Posner, *supra* note 171 Ch. 1 at 61-62.

250. Calabresi & Melamed, *supra* note 78 Ch. 3, at 1127-8.

251. Calabresi, *Thoughts on the Future of Economics in Legal Education*, 33 J. LEGAL EDUC. 359, 364 (1983). Max Weber noted that expanding formal freedom may coexist with coercion in practice. M. WEBER, *supra* note 76 Ch. 3, at 230-33; *see also* Fiss, *supra* note 127 Ch. 3, at 8 ("The normative claim of law and economics can be defeated only by challenging its first premise, namely, the one that relativizes all values . . . . [A]ll values are [not] reducible to preferences and [not] . . . all have an equal claim to satisfaction. Values are values".); Singer, *supra* note 119 Ch. 3, at 645 (footnote omitted) (criticizing "the attempt to legitimate the mass of our social, economic, and institutional practices by reference to the myth of the free market. The ultimate effect of this project is to make the great bulk of market transactions appear to be the result of free consent".); West, *Authority, Autonomy, and Choice. The Role of Consent in the Moral and Political Visions of Franz Kafka and Richard Posner*, 99 HARV. L. REV. 384, 424 (1985) (footnote omitted) (arguing that Posner's ideas rest "on an inadequate picture of human nature").

252. *See* Sager *Pareto Superiority, Consent, and Justice*, 8 HOFSTRA L. REV. 913 (1980). Alienability in a matter so intimately connected with common human patterns of identity and relationships of personal intimacy must be subject to some restrictions if the idea of the citizen as a political and moral agent is to be preserved. *See* Meyers, *The Rationale for Inalienable Rights in Moral Systems*, 7 SOC. THEORY & PRAC. 127, 140 (1981).

253. Engaging in a reproductive project without desiring the offspring fundamentally changes the way society views children. Instead of seeing them as unique individual personalities to be desired in their own right, they may come to be perceived as commodities or items of manufacture to be desired because of their utility. *See* Krimmel, *supra* note 128 Ch. 1.

254. *See* Radin, *supra* note 28 Intro., at 1925-34.

255. *Contra* Robertson, *supra* note 193 Ch. 1, at 31 ("Surrogate mothering is another method of assisting people to undertake child rearing, and thus serves the purposes of the marital union".).

256. The exception would be based on the idea of notice filing and state-conferred status. *See supra* note 179 Ch. 1 and accompanying text.

257. For a current case that explores the issue of whether to treat embryos as persons or property, see Davis v. Davis, *supra* note 95 Ch. 2. There may be hazards associated with the depersonalization of children and potential children in contractual relationships.

> Where the market is allowed to follow its own autonomous tendencies,
> its participants do not look toward the persons of each other but only
> toward the commodity; there are no obligations of brotherliness or
> reverence, and none of those spontaneous human relations that are
> sustained by personal unions. They all would just obstruct the free
> development of the bare market relationship, and its specific interests
> serve, in their turn, to weaken the sentiments on which these obstructions
> rest.

A. KRONMAN & R. POSNER, *supra* note 14 Ch. 1, at 262 (quoting 2 M. WEBER, LAW IN ECONOMY AND SOCIETY) (G. Roth & C. Wittich eds. & Fischoff trans. 1968)). Further, "[i]n a market transaction, what is bought or sold must be an object, a commodity. The buyer or seller (the subject) relates only to an object: all orientations are subject-object, never subject-subject". Baker, *supra* note 231 Ch. 3, at 35.

The Warnock Report attempts to find a middle ground between acknowledging the difficulties in treating potential persons as property, while recognizing parental rights to embryos:

> We recommend that legislation be enacted to ensure there is no right of
> ownership in a human embryo. Nevertheless, the couple who have stored
> an embryo for their use should be recognized as having rights to the use
> and disposal of the embryo, although these rights ought to be subject to
> limitation. The precise nature of that limitation will obviously require
> careful consideration. We hope the couple will recognize that they
> have a responsibility to make a firm decision as to the disposal and use
> of the embryo.

WARNOCK REP. *supra* note 21 Intro. § 10.11 (emphasis omitted). In an attempt to define the parameters of donor rights, the committee states that the sale or purchase of human gametes is "undesirable", while allowing reimbursement of expenses to a licensed semen bank. The report suggests that commercial transactions should be permitted if the vendor is licensed. Unlicensed transactions, by contrast, would be criminalized. *Id*. § 13.13. Knoppers and Sloss suggest that committee reports, such as the Warnock Report, tend to take "a hybrid person-property approach to the question of the legal status of the embryo . . . . Even while the 'potential human person' approach advocates that the life of such a potential person be respected, the degree of control to be given to donors closely resembles ownership". Knoppers & Sloss, *supra* note 70 Ch. 1, at 699. The authors note that "even in the absence of declared real property rights, donors would generally maintain full control over the uses to which their material is put". *Id*. One leading treatise concludes that the trend is to treat children as assets and commodities, and that the "[p]roprietary conceptions of the parent-child relationship" may be "here to stay". Weyrauch & Katz, *supra* note 189 Ch. 1, at 498.

It has been argued that the most appropriate response to the new reproductive technologies is one based on a "body of jurisprudence conceptualizing the legal base for children's rights". *Wadlington, Artificial Conception, supra* note 29 Ch. 1, at 511. The implication that potential children have individual rights would seemingly rule out the contractual allocation of parental rights, whether grounded in individual autonomy or state conferral. The issue of the potential person's individual rights also surfaces in the contemporary "fetal abuse" controversy. *See, e.g. Pregnant? Go Directly to Jail,* A.B.A. J., Nov. 1988, at 20.

258. The Supreme Court has repeatedly considered the relative constitutional rights of the state, parents, and children, *See e.g.,* Carey v. Population Servs. Int'l 431 U.S. 678 (1977) (right of minors to contraceptives); Tinker v. Des Moines School District, 393 U.S. 503 (1969) (right of minors to free speech); *In re* Gault, 387 U.S. 1 (1967) (right of minors to due process); Prince v. Massachusetts, 321 U.S. 158 (1944) (right of minors to protection from parental control). *See generally,* Wald, *Children's Rights: A Framework for Analysis,* 12 U.C. DAVIS L. REV. 255 (1979) (proposing a framework for analyzing children's rights); Foster & Freed, *A Bill of Rights for Children,* 6 Fam. L.Q. 343 (1972) (proposing "Bill of Rights" which considers children as persons rather than property).

259. *See* BEYOND THE BEST INTERESTS, *supra* note 139 Ch. 1, at 6; Annas & Elias, *supra* note Intro. 12, at 157 ("To protect the interests of the resulting children and the integrity of noncoital reproduction, primary consideration should always be given to the welfare and the 'best interests' of the potential child, rather than to the donors, the infertile couple, or the physician or clinic".) (footnotes omitted); Bartlett, *supra* note 103 Ch. 2, at 303; Frankel & Miller, *The Inapplicability of Market Theory to Adoptions,* 67 B.U.L. REV. 99, 101-103 (1987) (outlining the dangers inherent in returning to the classification of children as property); Minow, *Beyond State Intervention in the Family: For Baby Jane Doe,* 18 U. MICH. J.L. REF. 933, 989-1009 (1985) (emphasizing that the rules governing family relations are based on trust).

260. This action is not equivalent to the social construction of the economically-useless child. *See* V. ZELIZER, *supra,* note 233 Ch. 3, at 11.

261. Prejudging the issue by saying that any attempt to order noncoital reproductive techniques according to public values must be based on "personal moral views" effectively blocks reasoned discourse, and invites subterfuge. *See* Robertson, *supra* note 148 Ch. 2, at 8-9. Insofar as the normative discussion revolves around the structure of societal spheres, liberal theorists have "cast doubts on the 'essential dichotomy'" of public and private, leaving an "ambivalent, if not contradictory, relationship of citizen and state that plagues modern liberal theory". Private realm constitutional protections do not prevent the state from acquiescing in private property seizures, parallel with the enforcement of contract in Shelley v. Kraemer, 334 U.S. 1 (1948). All that seems to remain of the social sphere is individualism. Brest, *supra* note 72 Ch. 1, at 1302. The solution must be something better than a superficial harmonization. Kennedy, *supra* note 2 Ch. 1, at 1352-7 (discussing the issues and difficulties in attempting to deal with the public and private spheres in one set of legal principles).

262. Horwitz, *supra* note 272 Ch. 2, at 1428.

263. Legal enforcement has traditionally been left out of the marital relationship for this reason: "One spouse could scarcely be expected to entertain a tender, affectionate regard for the other spouse who brings him or her under restraint". Kilgrow v. Kilgrow, 268 Ala. 475, 480, 107 So. 2d 885, 889 (1958). Weber stated that the "market community" constitutes "the most impersonal relation of practical life into which humans can enter with one another". KRONMAN & POSNER, *supra* note 14 Ch. 1, at 261-62 (quoting M. WEBER, ECONOMY AND SOCIETY (G. Roth & C. Wittich eds. & E. Fischoff trans. 1968)). The choice by the state to put coercive power behind private agreements raises questions of societal responsibility. *See* J. STONE, *supra* note 139 Ch. 3, at 253. The explication of racism that would accompany pricing people in this society is a general concern. *See* Allen, *supra* note 15 Intro., at 1763 ("The pouring of private resources into surrogacy so that couples may adopt healthy white babies sends a message of rejection and despair to non-whites and the handicapped"); Landes & Posner, *supra* note 166 Ch. 1, at 345 ("[P]rices for

babies are racially stratified as a result of different supply and demand conditions in the different racial groups, but perhaps bringing this fact out in the open would exacerbate racial tensions in our society".).

264. *See* L. WEITZMAN, *supra* note 3 Ch. 2, at 239-46 (discussing the various effects and criticisms of placing intimate relationships on the colder business plane).

265. Weitzman cites this as the ideal. *Id.* at 244 (noting that the bargaining process is a forum for sharing goals and desires, thereby increasing trust and intimacy).

266. P. BERGER & R. NEUHAUS, TO EMPOWER PEOPLE: THE ROLE OF MEDIATING STRUCTURES IN PUBLIC POLICY 20-21 (1977) (arguing that the parent-child relationship should be the next important consideration); Frug, *The Idealogy of Bureaucracy in American Law*, 97 HARV. L. REV. 1276, 1288-89 (1984) (noting the mutual interdependence of law and society); Singer, *supra* note 119 Ch. 3, at 652-55 (arguing that the market model distracts from basic human relationships).

267. State conferred individual autonomy liberates the child and the adult "from the shackles of such intermediate groups as the family . . . . " L. TRIBE, *supra* note 88 Ch. 2, at 1418. In this view, respect for human relationships grounded in lineage and nurturance is interpreted as an attempt to suppress the individual. Knoppers & Sloss *supra* note 70 Ch. 1, at 667 ("[I]n the name of protecting the 'unconceived' or conceived-but-not-yet-implanted, State control of the person . . . is expanding".).

268. J. LOCKE, *supra* note 76 Ch. 3.

269. T. HOBBES, LEVIATHAN 89-90 (L. Macpherson ed. 1968); *see also* M. GLENDON, *supra* note 1 Intro., at 119-25 (noting that Hobbes' state and its enforcement of its laws is based in power, not consent); Radin, *supra* note 173 Ch. 3, at 1685 n. 92 ("There is an interesting problem here lying in wait for those who think the body is property: can the government condemn kidneys at fair market value?").

Paul Ramsey develops the point in the following terms:

> Perhaps it is the fate of all the industrialized, urbanized, secular societies to *complete* the movement from status to contract in *every* human relation. Only not quite complete that movement, since where only contractual relations are the web of life there is anarchy, no society. There will remain the naked power of government over an aggregation of individuals, and the accoutrements of power.

P. RAMSEY, *supra* note 14 Ch. 3, at 12, n. 8 (emphasis in original).

270. One such purpose might be eugenics. The history of the introduction of technology to reproduction reveals an early connection to eugenics. However, proponents of the individual autonomy model, such as Robertson, typically fail to examine the provenance of the "rights" they assert. *See* Robertson, *supra* note 9 Intro., at 405. In fact, the birth control movement was thoroughly enmeshed at its origin in the eugenics movement, and linked with theories of racial superiority and proposed programmes of forced sterilization for the unfit. M. HALLER, *supra* note 154 Ch. 1, at 88-138. The understanding of enforcement of contract as an instrument for a state purpose in eugenics would be in keeping with an existing understanding of contract. *See* J. CALAMARI & J. PERILLO, *supra* note 19 Ch. 1, § 1.4(c)("[T]he foundation of contract law" is seen "as a sort of delegation of power by the State to its inhabitants".)

271. *See* M. GLENDON, *supra* note 1 Intro., at 139-42 (discussing the role of law in promoting social interaction); M. GLENDON, *supra* note 46 Ch. 2, at 459-60 (urging a view of law reflecting the interdependence within families and society); C. LASCH, *supra* note 76 Ch. 3 (the only way to preserve the family as a sanctuary in the face of an increasingly harsh world is to change the conditions of public life); *see also* R. DWORKIN, *supra* note 143 Ch. 2, at 195-97 (arguing that all relationships evolve, rather than being "formed in one act of deliberate contractual commitment"); Bartlett, *supra* note 103 Ch. 2, at 294 (notion of

parenthood based on benevolence and responsibility "intended to reinforce parental dispositions toward generosity and other-directedness" preferable to those grounded in "exchange and individual rights"). Paul Ramsey has commented:

> [T]he notion that an individual human life is absolutely unique, inviolable, irreplaceable, noninterchangeable, not substitutable, and not meldable with other lives . . . is so fundamental in the edifice of Western law and morals that it cannot be removed without bringing the whole house down.

P. RAMSEY, *supra* note 14 Ch. 3, at xiv; *cf.* Robertson, *supra* note 9 Intro., at 460 (mere "[m]oral concerns about the nature of the family or how the rearing role should be entered would not justify state interference" in the private sphere).

272. R. LIFTON, *supra* note 11 Intro. Respect for such relationships is essential to authentic human community.

CONCLUSION

Resort to contract proposals for ordering human procreation, whether in keeping with the state conferral or with the individual autonomy model described at the outset of this book, risks the structural breakdown of the American political tradition of respect for the dignity and equality of persons. Within the limits of this tradition, the choice raised by the new reproductive technologies is whether society wishes to adopt the strong or the moderate type of the natural endowment model. This is the same choice implicitly addressed by traditional family law,[1] and which underlies the changes in family law over the past thirty years.[2] In both the recent and distant past, the primary tension within the law of the family has been between rights and duties arising from genetic and gestational relationships, on the one hand, and a perceived need to ground rights and duties in the external social form of the family, only imperfectly mirroring the realities of genetic and gestational relationships, on the other.

While this book has used the term "liberal" in its classical sense, the popularly employed, contemporary liberal-conservative distinction, though ungainly, has some descriptive value in mapping the spectrum of alternative approaches. Liberal discourse is divided: some liberals, notably John Robertson, argue in favour of the contractual reallocation of parental rights and procreative resources because it advances individual autonomy. Other liberals, such as Ronald Dworkin and Anita Allen, would disfavour such reallocation because reliance on contract will allow those in possession of market power to extend their control and thus subvert individual autonomy. From a conservative perspective, Judge Posner advocates the enforcement of contractual reallocation in this context as a means of achieving market efficiency. This book has developed an argument against the enforcement of the contractual reallocation of parental rights and procreative resources which also might be considered conservative in a sense. It is conservative in that it preserves a continuity with the ideal that has animated the traditional legal approach to the family. This argument is based on the value of natural endowment. The natural endowment approach assumes that the fundamental relationships that give rise to meaningful individual autonomy and authentic forms of community, rather than the will of the individual or the state, justify the imposition of the force of law. Natural endowment emphasizes genetic, gestational, and nurturance bonds as the basis of parental rights.

The natural endowment approach is open to both traditional and progressive social arrangements. In its strong, traditional form, this approach resolves disputes between claims based on genetic or gestational rights in ways that give priority to the family as an external social form tending to revolve around marriage. The progressive, moderate form allows resolution of such disputes in a way that gives priority to honouring diverse interests based on genetic or gestational contribution, even though the results are unpredictable and polymorphous. It is along this spectrum that valid differences about the appropriate legal response to the new reproductive technologies can and should be proposed, debated, and resolved.

Endnotes

1. H. CLARK, *supra* note 23 Intro. Within the natural endowment model, there remains room for debate as to the place of marriage and the traditional family. Glendon, *supra* note 52 Ch. 2, at 715-17.

2. Some argue that framing the issue in these terms is misleading since this question is too complex and divisive to permit clear and definite resolution, at least within the short term. *See* Healey, *supra* note 5 Intro., at 144. One concrete legal reform this is required is clarification of the basis on which AID provisions operate as natural endowment, and not state conferral or individual autonomy. *See* Annas & Elias, *supra* note 12 Intro., at 149-50 ("It is an unfortunate paradigm, however, because it places the private contractual agreement among the participants regarding parental rights and responsibilities above the 'best interests' of the child.").